W9-CDM-813

The Correspondence of
Flannery O'Connor
and the Brainard Cheneys

The Correspondence of Flannery O'Connor and the Brainard Cheneys

Edited by
C. Ralph Stephens

University Press of Mississippi JACKSON AND LONDON

Manufactured in the United States of America
89 87 86 85 4 3 2 1
The paper in this book meets the guidelines for permanence and durability of the Committee on Production Guidelines for Book Longevity of the Council on Library Resources.

Library of Congress Cataloging-in-Publication Data

O'Connor, Flannery.
The correspondence of Flannery O'Connor and the Brainard Cheneys.

Includes index.
1. O'Connor, Flannery—Correspondence. 2. Cheney, Brainard, 1900– —Correspondence. 3. Cheney, Frances Neel, 1906– —Correspondence. 4. Authors, American—20th century—Correspondence. I. Cheney, Brainard, 1900– . II. Cheney, Frances Neel, 1906– . III. Stephens, Charles Ralph. IV. Title.
PS3565.C57Z483 1986 813'.54 [B] 85-26512
ISBN 0-87805-292-5 (alk. paper)

Contents

Acknowledgments

I wish to express particular thanks to the following people for their help with this project: Lon and Fannie Cheney, for their unfailing and peerless courtesy, hospitality, patience—and Christian charity; Professor Jackson R. Bryer, for convincing me that I could do this job and showing me how; William P. Ellis, Essex Community College, for clearing the way and urging me on; Martha Payne Schuberth, for her love, encouragement, and hard work; Professors Edwin S. Gleaves, Vanderbilt University, and Earl J. Wilcox, Winthrop College, my long-time friends, for their counsel and confidence; Sally Fitzgerald, for her kindness and forbearance in answering my questions; Professors David Farmer, University of Houston, Martha Cook, Longwood College, and Ashley Brown, University of South Carolina, for discussing problems and helping me find solutions; Nancy Davis, Special Collections, Ina Dillard Russell Library, Georgia College, for her help; the Special Collections staff, especially Cheryl Paterson, the Jean and Alexander Heard Library, Vanderbilt University; and Mary Sullivan, typist par excellence.

I would also like to thank my mother and my children Chuck, Matt, and Kate for their support.

Foreword

Soon after Flannery O'Connor died in 1964, *The Sewanee Review* published my obituary, titled "Flannery O'Connor's Campaign For Her Country," in which I sought to make some assessment of her significance as a writer.

My assessment was in no small degree informed by my correspondence with her over the years. There was—certainly in the early appearance of her work, considerable popular uncertainty of the meaning of her stories.

Our correspondence began with my letter to her in appreciation of her first novel, *Wise Blood.* At the time, mine was one of the first understanding appreciations she had received, she said.

And her writing continued to be the main theme of our correspondence over the years.

The letters Ralph Stephens has collected here bear on Flannery's literary concerns, as well as personal matters, and I recommend both his selection and comment.

Brainard Cheney
October 1985

Introduction

To the August 1952 issue of Washington and Lee University's *Shenandoah,* Brainard Cheney contributed a five-page appreciative review of Flannery O'Connor's first novel, *Wise Blood.*[1] Begun in 1948 and published in the spring of 1952, *Wise Blood* was widely reviewed but almost universally misunderstood, even by those who recognized O'Connor's talent and the novel's power. When Tom Carter, the young editor of *Shenandoah,* sent O'Connor a copy of Cheney's review, she was understandably pleased. She wrote to her friend and mentor Caroline Gordon to ask who Cheney was. Then, on 8 February 1953, she wrote an enthusiastic letter to Cheney, thanking him for "reading my book and writing about it so carefully and with so much understanding."[2]

Caroline Gordon was pleased too. She had read the manuscript of *Wise Blood* and helped O'Connor with it. And Caroline Gordon certainly knew Brainard Cheney.[3]

1. See Appendix A.

2. Curiously, Cheney's review has been overlooked by O'Connor bibliographers. It is not included in either of the two most comprehensive listings of O'Connor criticism: Lewis A. Lawson's bibliography in *The Added Dimension: The Art and Mind of Flannery O'Connor,* Melvin J. Friedman and Lewis A. Lawson, eds. (New York: Fordham University Press, 1966) or Robert E. Golden's *Flannery O'Connor: A Reference Guide* (Boston: G. K. Hall, 1977). This oversight is particularly striking when one considers that Cheney's interpretation of the novel is essentially the one which has come to be regarded as "standard," and that those who best knew O'Connor's intentions in the novel had warmly embraced Cheney's reading. Robert Fitzgerald, O'Connor's good friend and advisor and one of the first readers of the final form of *Wise Blood,* wrote to Cheney about his review: "I thought your review of *Wise Blood* in the *Shenandoah* was by far the best, and one of the best of any book I've seen lately" (unpublished letter from Robert Fitzgerald to Brainard Cheney, July 3, 1953, in Vanderbilt University Special Collections).

3. When she read Cheney's review, Caroline Gordon wrote him: "I can't wait to tell you how good I think your review of Flannery's novel is. Allen thinks it's fine, too. It's a long time since I've seen so much acute perception united with

She and her husband, Allen Tate, had been friends of Cheney and his wife, Frances Neel Cheney, the distinguished librarian and teacher at George Peabody College for Teachers in Nashville, Tennessee, for more than twenty years. Gordon had, in fact, long been Cheney's literary advisor and had read and commented on in meticulous detail the four novels Cheney wrote during the thirties and forties. She immediately encouraged a meeting of her two "students":

> I hope you and Fannie will run into Flannery O'Connor some time. I think you'd both like her. Cal [Robert] Lowell says she is a saint, but then he is given to extravagance. She may be, though, at that. She is a cradle Catholic, raised in Milledgeville [Georgia] where there are so few other Catholics that the priests would come to the house and make the piano an altar, but she sure is a powerful Catholic. No nonsense about her! She has some dire disease—some form of arthritis—and is kept going only by huge doses of something called ACTH. We are expected to adore all of the Lord's doings, but it does give you some pause when you reflect that this gifted girl will probably not be with us long whereas Truman Capote will live to a ripe old age, laden down with honours.[4]

On 22 March, Cheney replied to O'Connor's letter, introducing himself and noting their common interests and background: he and his wife had recently converted to Catholicism; he had written and seen produced a few months earlier a locally successful play, "Strangers in This World," "out of the same sort of material and on the same subject, by way of a somewhat similar argument" as *Wise Blood;* and, though he lived in Tennessee, he was a native of Georgia. He suggested "acquaintance" on the strength of their "common bent." O'Connor promptly issued an invitation to the Cheneys to visit her at her mother's farm, Andalusia, four miles from Milledgeville.

Acquaintance quickly blossomed into friendship, which

common sense in a review. . . . Your remarks are all telling, we both thought, and were made tellingly. I don't blame Flannery for being pleased. I don't know of any other reviewer who did half as well" (unpublished letter from Caroline Gordon to Brainard Cheney, February 10, 1953, in Vanderbilt University Special Collections).

4. Unpublished letter from Caroline Gordon to Brainard Cheney, February 4, 1953, in Vanderbilt University Special Collections.

spanned eleven years, from late spring 1953, until O'Connor's death in August 1964. On 6 June 1953, the Cheneys paid the first of many calls on O'Connor and her mother, Regina; by midsummer, O'Connor flew to Nashville to spend a weekend at Cold Chimneys, the Cheneys' antebellum home in Smyrna. The friendship was from the outset a warmly reciprocated one, punctuated by a frequent exchange of visits and letters. The record of that friendship, 188 surviving letters and carbons (117 from O'Connor, 71 from Cheney), is preserved in the Special Collections archives at the Vanderbilt University Library.[5]

By the time he met Flannery O'Connor, Brainard Bartwell Cheney's life had already been an interesting and varied one. He was born in Fitzgerald, Georgia, on 3 June 1900; in 1906, his family moved to Lumber City, a small sawmill town on the Ocmulgee River in southeast Georgia. His father, for whom Cheney was named, was a lawyer and part-time farmer who had grown up on his family's Georgia plantation and had been, at sixteen, a soldier in the Confederacy. His mother, Mattie Lucy (Mood) Cheney, was the daughter of a Charleston, South Carolina, physician. A remote and imposing figure to his small son, Cheney's father died in 1908, leaving his wife with three young children and a 2,100-acre farm to manage alone and with no knowledge of business affairs. Her intelligence, determination, and religious faith saw the family through difficult years and made lasting impressions on Cheney.

When he graduated from high school in Lumber City in 1917, the United States was at war with Germany, and Cheney, counseled by his mother, enrolled at The Citadel, in Charleston; he left, an undistinguished corporal, in the spring of 1919. In 1920, he spent a semester at Vanderbilt University and, in 1924, a summer term at the University of Georgia. Between 1919 and 1924, he worked at a variety

5. Only one other piece of correspondence between the Cheneys and O'Connor is known to survive: an Italian postcard, postmarked June 30, 1958, from O'Connor to the Cheneys, in the Flannery O'Connor Collection at the Ina Dillard Russell Library, Georgia College, Milledgeville. The front of the card consists of a photograph of "Roma—Piazza di Spagna con le azalee"; the reverse bears the message, "Have endured," and is signed "Cheers Flannery."

of jobs: bank clerk (Lavonia, Georgia), timber dealer (Lumber City), crosstie and timber camp operator (Wheeler County, Georgia), school teacher and principal (Jonesville, Scotland, and Bostwick, Georgia). In 1924, he returned to Vanderbilt, but dropped out at the end of the school year when his mother died. While at Vanderbilt, Cheney took courses under John Crowe Ransom, Edwin Mims, and Walter Clyde Curry and met members of the Fugitive poets group—Donald Davidson, Merrill Moore, and Andrew Lytle.

In 1925, he became a reporter and, later, a member of the editorial staff for the *Nashville Banner.* In 1928, Cheney married Frances (Fannie) Neel, of Newberry, South Carolina, who had just completed her B.A. in sociology at Vanderbilt and who had also taken a course with John Crowe Ransom—and with Donald Davidson, who was by then teaching at Vanderbilt. Like her husband, Frances was caught up in the exciting creative and intellectual atmosphere at Vanderbilt in the twenties and early thirties.

Cheney's friend, roommate, and fellow reporter at the *Banner,* Ralph McGill (later editor and publisher of the *Atlanta Constitution*) was best man at the Cheneys' wedding. McGill encouraged Cheney in his interest in writing poetry and short stories, as did Stanley Johnson, a member of the Fugitives before he became an instructor at Vanderbilt and then a reporter for the *Banner.* Cheney soon developed another important and lifelong friendship, with Robert Penn Warren. Warren was appointed to the Vanderbilt faculty in 1931, after three years as a Rhodes Scholar at Oxford University, and was returning to Nashville at about the same time that Allen Tate and Caroline Gordon were returning from Paris, where Tate had made use of a Guggenheim Scholarship to complete his biography of Jefferson Davis.

Through Warren, the Cheneys came to know the Tates, who were living not far from Nashville on the Tate estate, Benfolly, in Clarksville, Tennessee. The previous year (1930) Warren and Tate, along with Davidson, Lytle, and Ransom, had been among the Agrarians, the now famous group of "Twelve Southerners" who published *I'll Take My Stand: The South and the Agrarian Tradition* (New York: Harper and Brothers, 1930), a symposium advocating that the South return to its preindustrial values and traditions. The Cheneys, Warrens, and Tates fast became good friends, visiting often and sharing common interests in politics, literature, and social issues; and, quite naturally, it was a relationship which progressively included other members of the South's intellectual and literary community.

Throughout the thirties, Cheney became increasingly interested in writing longer fiction; and, though a number of the Vanderbilt-connected writers influenced and helped him (especially Warren, Johnson, and Lytle, who read and commented on many of his efforts), it was Caroline Gordon who became Cheney's chief literary counsel. When they met, Gordon had been writing for several years and had published several short stories and one novel. Not only did she understand the craft of writing fiction, she was exceptionally articulate on the subject and took infinite pains with those who asked her advice about their writing. She became, as Cheney was to say many times over the years, his "literary godmother."

By the end of the thirties, Cheney had written two novels. The first, "World Beyond Words," he was unable to publish. The second, *Lightwood,* which dramatizes the struggles of post–Civil War farmers in the pinewoods of southeast Georgia against a northern-owned lumber company, was published in 1939 by Houghton Mifflin. The novel was widely reviewed and, with some qualifications, very well received in major publications.

Although Cheney had distinguished himself as an unusually respected and effective political reporter and editor, he decided, in 1940, largely on the strength of his success with *Lightwood,* to resign from the *Banner* and devote himself full-time to writing fiction. With Donald Davidson's help, Cheney received a fellowship to Middlebury College's Bread Loaf Writers Conference, which he attended in the company of Wallace Stegner, Eudora Welty, Carson McCullers, Robert Frost, and John Ciardi. In

1941, he was awarded a Guggenheim Fellowship to complete his next novel, *River Rogue,* also set in Cheney's southeast Georgia, this one about raftsmen on the Oconee and Altahama rivers. *River Rogue* was published by Houghton Mifflin in 1942 and was chosen as a Book-of-the-Month Club selection. MGM took an option on it and began preliminary casting, but eventually passed up the project because of wartime budgetary considerations.

In 1943, eager to serve his country in the war effort but frustrated because of his age in his efforts to enlist in military service, Cheney accepted a position as advisor and executive secretary to U.S. Senator Tom Stewart of Tennessee, and the Cheneys moved to Washington, D.C. Frances Cheney had, since graduation, pursued her own career, completing B.S. (George Peabody College) and M.A. (Columbia University) degrees in library science, and serving, from 1930 to 1943, as head of the reference department at Vanderbilt University Library and at the newly incorporated Joint University Libraries. In September 1943, when Allen Tate received a one-year appointment to the Chair of Poetry at the Library of Congress, he asked Frances Cheney to be his assistant. Together they compiled the landmark bibliography *Sixty American Poets, 1896–1944,* published by the Library of Congress in 1945. While the Tates were in Washington, they shared a house with the Cheneys, and the two couples continued their long-established habit of entertaining writer friends with whom they shared advice and ideas.

When the Cheneys returned to Nashville in 1945, Mrs. Cheney joined the faculty of the George Peabody College Library School and Cheney retired, a second time, to reflect on what he had learned and to write. The realities of politics, learned first at the local and state levels during his years as a reporter and more recently in the national arena, had crushed his political idealism and caused him to question many of his fundamental assumptions and values. In addition to extensive reading in religion, political science, and philosophy and discussion with his conservative friends, Cheney sought to work through what he had learned by dramatizing his political experiences in a novel, "The Image and the Cry," which he wrote five times before abandoning. He also began a series of articles and book reviews which reflect his changed political views and his developing religious orientation.[6]

Cheney was at a critical juncture in his life when he met Flannery O'Connor. After several years of contemplation and struggle, in 1953 he and his wife had made the decision to become Roman Catholics. They were influenced particularly by the Tates, who had converted to Catholicism about 1947, but the decision was very much their own: for the Cheneys the Church offered the only alternative to values they had come increasingly to find hollow and cruelly disappointing—political and scientific meliorism, liberalism, and materialism. Although he had failed to bring off his political novel, in 1950 Cheney used a portion of the material from "The Image and the Cry" to write a play, "Strangers in This World," a folk drama with music and dance, about a rural Tennessee religious cult of snake handlers. Produced at both Vanderbilt (1952) and the University of Louisville (1956), it clearly reflected Cheney's preoccupation with both the attraction and problems of religious faith.

Another transition was that in 1952, after a seven-year retirement, Cheney returned to politics, to become a speech writer and public relations officer for Tennessee Governor Frank Clement. Cheney's disillusionment with politics had by no means destroyed his interest; in Frank Clement, Cheney found a politician whose blend of integrity and effectiveness he admired, and with whose philosophies of politics and religion he was sympathetic.

Flannery O'Connor was not far beyond the threshold of

6. "The Leader Follows—Where?" *Georgia Review*, 2 (Spring, 1948), 3–9; "Too Late, Too Soon" [review of V. O. Key, Jr.'s *Southern Politics*], *Sewanee Review*, 58 (Spring, 1950), 374–78; "The Conservative Course by Celestial Navigation," *Sewanee Review*, 62 (Winter, 1952), 151–59; *A New "Crown of Thorns" for the Democratic Party* [under the by-line "a Life-Long Democrat"], privately published by Cheney in 1956; "The Crocodile or the Crucifix: The Politics of Syncretism, Toynbeeism, and Revelation," *Sewanee Review*, 66 (Summer, 1958), 507–18; "What Endures in the South?" [review of *The Lasting South*, James J. Kilpatrick and Louis Rubin, Jr., eds.], *Modern Age*, 2 (Fall, 1958), 408–10; "Christianity and the Tragic Vision—Utopianism USA," *Sewanee Review*, 69 (Autumn, 1961), 515–33.

her short but productive career when the Cheneys first visited Andalusia. She had worked five years on *Wise Blood,* publishing four parts of it, in 1948, 1949, and 1952, in the *Sewanee Review,* the *Partisan Review,* and *New World Writing;*[7] outside of *The Corinthian,* the creative writing journal at Georgia State College for Women, she had published only four other stories.[8] She was at work on the remainder of the stories which would comprise the collection *A Good Man Is Hard to Find and Other Stories* (New York: Harcourt, Brace and World, 1955), three more of which would be published by the end of 1953.[9]

The facts of her early biography are quickly summarized and well known. She was born in Savannah, Georgia, on 25 March 1925, the only child of Regina L. Cline and Edward F. O'Connor, Jr., who was in the real estate business. Both families were Roman Catholic, and O'Connor attended parochial schools. The Clines were a prosperous family, and when Edward O'Connor became fatally ill with disseminated lupus in 1939, the O'Connors moved to Milledgeville to live in the Cline family's antebellum home.

O'Connor graduated from Peabody High School the year after her father died, and enrolled in the Georgia State College for Women in Milledgeville. She majored in sociology and took an active interest in creative writing and cartooning. When she completed her B.A. in 1945, she left Milledgeville for the Writer's Workshop at the University

7. "The Train," *Sewanee Review,* 56 (April–June, 1948), 261–71 [revised and expanded as Chapter 1 of *Wise Blood*]; "The Heart of the Park," *Partisan Review,* 16 (February, 1949), 138–51 [revised as Chapter 5 of *Wise Blood*]; "The Peeler," *Partisan Review,* 16 (December, 1949), 1189–1206 [revised as Chapter 3 of *Wise Blood*]; and "Enoch and the Gorilla," *New World Writing, First Mentor Selection,* No. 1 (April, 1952), 67–74 [rewritten as Chapter 11 of *Wise Blood*]. See David Farmer, *Flannery O'Connor: A Descriptive Bibliography* (New York: Garland Publishing, 1981), pp. 67–68.

8. "The Geranium," *Accent,* 4 (Summer, 1946), 245–53; "The Capture," *Mademoiselle,* 28 (November, 1948), 148–49, 195–96, 198–201; "The Woman on the Stairs," *Tomorrow,* 8 (August, 1949), 40–44; and "The Life You Save May Be Your Own," *Kenyon Review,* 15 (Spring, 1953), 195–207. See Farmer, pp. 67–68.

9. "The River," *Sewanee Review,* 61 (Summer, 1953), 455–75; "A Late Encounter with the Enemy," *Harper's Bazaar,* 87 (September, 1953), 234, 247, 249, 252; and "A Good Man is Hard to Find," *The Avon Book of Modern Writing,* William Phillips and Philip Rahv, eds. (New York: Avon Publications, 1953), pp. 186–99. See Farmer, pp. 12, 68.

of Iowa, where she won a Rinehart Fellowship for her fiction. She sold her first short story, "The Geranium," to *Accent,* in 1946, and completed her M.F.A. in Literature in 1947. After another year at the University of Iowa, O'Connor was recommended, in part on the strength of work she had already done on *Wise Blood,* to attend Yaddo, a writers retreat in Saratoga Springs, New York. After a few months there, she left, in the spring of 1949, for New York City. She had, in February of that year, become acquainted with Robert and Sally Fitzgerald, with whom she later lived as a friend and boarder when they moved from New York City to a country house in Ridgefield, Connecticut. Late in 1950, as she was finishing the first draft of *Wise Blood,* she was stricken with the disease that had killed her father. She underwent months of hospital treatment in Atlanta, her life saved and prolonged by an experimental cortisone derivative, ACTH. In the spring of 1951, recovering but too weak to climb the stairs of the house in Milledgeville, she moved with her mother to a nearby family dairy farm, Andalusia, where they lived, Mrs. O'Connor managing the farm and O'Connor writing, until her death on 3 August 1964.

Cheney had for years traveled from Nashville to coastal Georgia, where he had relatives and friends and where he could find time and solitude to write. Not long before he became acquainted with Flannery O'Connor, he had purchased a piece of property on St. Simons Island, with the somewhat vague notion of making it a permanent retreat. After their first meeting, stopping by Milledgeville on route soon became routine; and Cheney, and his wife, when she could get away from her duties at Peabody College, visited Andalusia often throughout the fifties and early sixties. And, O'Connor became a frequent weekend guest at Cold Chimneys, along with other academic and literary people, a number of whom O'Connor met there for the first time.[10]

10. Two such people, mentioned a number of times in the Cheney-O'Connor letters, are Russell Kirk and Ashley Brown. Invoking the familiar comparison between the literary renaissances in Ireland and in the southern United States, Ashley Brown recently wrote, "In retrospect it seems to me that Cold Chimneys

In interests and temperament, the Cheneys and O'Connor found they had much in common, and their letters make clear that they thoroughly enjoyed each other's company. When they were together, they talked of literature, sociology, politics, and religion; read aloud and swapped manuscripts; exchanged news and gossip; told stories and revived anecdotes. The Cheneys toured Andalusia and Milledgeville, eating with the O'Connors at home and at the Sanford House tearoom and getting to know the people and places of O'Connor's fiction. O'Connor met the Cheneys' friends in Nashville and enjoyed Mrs. Cheney's celebrated meals.

In their letters, they solicited and looked forward to visits, and delighted in recounting details of them. After one weekend in the summer of 1956, O'Connor wrote the Cheneys: "I am planning to paint, draw, or somehow perpetrate, a memorial of my visit. It will depict the buff orpington hen dining with the goose and the wren. . . . I certainly had a good time as I always do and I'll get back to my novel with renewed vigor" (Letter 34). A remark in another of O'Connor's letters is not only typical of her attitude but might well have been made by either of the Cheneys: "I don't want my coming to see you to interfere with your coming to see me. We are expecting you just the same" (Letter 21). When the Cheneys decided to take a trip to Rome in 1955, they couldn't imagine a more delightful companion than O'Connor; Cheney wrote her an impassioned plea to join them:

> We have had what seems to us a WONDERFUL idea. It could be called innocents in Rome, or the true story of the three wisemen—two of whom were women. . . .With the three of us I think it would be a real lark, or maybe it would be more pious to liken it unto a pilgrimhawk. Anyhow, we would get culture no end, and maybe, even a little religion, out of it. (Letter 25)

was something like Coole Park in County Galway, Lady Gregory's house, where for thirty years William Butler Yeats and his friends gathered" ("Flannery O'Connor: A Literary Memoir," unpublished seminar speech delivered in Denmark, Summer, 1984). In the mid-seventies, another visitor at the Cheneys' home called it "as close to Gertrude Stein's 1920s salon as we're likely to have anywhere in this part of the country" (Grace Zibart, "Fannie and Lon Cheney: Their Home Is a Writers' Haven," *Vanderbilt Alumnus*, 62 [Autumn, 1976], 20.

In her last letter to Cheney, written from her bed on 16 July 1964, less than three weeks before she died, O'Connor's mind is on visiting: "I hope you all get to see Robt. [Fitzgerald]. If I were on foot, I'd just come up there and join you" (Letter 188).

As his *Shenandoah* review makes clear, Cheney's attraction to *Wise Blood* had deep roots in his recognition in it of a kindred point of view; and as he came to know its author, he found himself increasingly in awe of her commitment and skill in the service of her profound religious vision. He is, he tells her in his first letter, a "set-up" for her, a reader fully sympathetic and receptive to her themes. Their correspondence reflects the broadening and deepening of that sympathy to include the conviction, as he was to say years later, that "she understood my aspirations and limitations as no one else did, [and] shared my spiritual concerns."[11]

His letters often show Cheney to be very much the self-conscious, anxious convert, who looks to O'Connor, the "cradle Catholic," the "born variety," whose faith seems so unstudied and steady, for guidance and affirmation. Not infrequently, Cheney adopts a wry, self-recriminating tone: "I am a sodden sinner—this isn't a confession, it's a chronic state I only half work at" (Letter 42). "Look not upon the wine when it is red, nor upon the whiskey at any time—I think that Scripture should read. . . . It was truly scandalous of me, here on Passion Sunday" (Letter 113). He berates himself for his laziness and his weak theology. He apologizes for visiting Andalusia during Lent.

O'Connor takes little direct notice in her letters of Cheney's confessions of spiritual inadequacy, and she gives little in the way of religious instruction. However, in her comments on the manuscripts of his novels, she is quick to tell Cheney not to let his religion call attention to itself. She writes to him about two of his characters in "The Tiger Returns":

> The worst thing you do is to say that they both discovered their *preference* was for the Catholic Church. This kills me. The

11. Unpublished notes for a talk given by Brainard Cheney at George Peabody College for Teachers, Fall, 1964, Vanderbilt University Library Special Collections.

> word *preference* just will not do. For those who come into it, the Catholic Church is not a preference but a necessity; but you still don't have to say Catholic Church. You need just say the Church. (Letter 144)

She goes on to tell him to let "the reader get the point without thinking that what he's been reading is a piece of Catholic propaganda. When ever you deal with the Catholic Church, you have to cover your tracks, iffen you are a member" (Letter 144). On another occasion, she cautions him: "I would leave out that stuff about the rosary beads. Catholic writers must always avoid plugs for the Church" (Letter 94).

Later letters, beginning in 1962, reflect their common interest in Pierre Teilhard de Chardin, the French Jesuit priest and paleontologist-philosopher whose controversial works attempted to reconcile science and religion. Cheney's enthusiasm for Teilhard is effusive, his tone apologetic:

> Perhaps I get over excited about any book that reforms or extends my viewpoint. But [Teilhard's] TPOM [*The Phenomenon of Man*] is the book I have been waiting for, looking for, for fifteen years! Coming to it tardily, as I have, I realize that my exhibition of enthusiasm may seem naive to you, if not wearying. Yet, I suspect your being a cradle Catholic and, so to speak, well adjusted to the idea of mysticism from birth, you may not sense altogether what an iconoclast de Chardin is for the idolatry of Modernism. (Letter 152)

O'Connor's reply is measured: "I'm glad you have discovered Teilhard. I think he's great. The science is over my head, but I think he's also a great visionary" (Letter 153). Then, after a year of correspondence about Teilhard, she writes: "We may see Teilhard canonized yet. I don't know about his theories, but I don't doubt his sanctity" (Letter 173). And she is complimentary about an article Cheney was writing on Teilhard for the *Sewanee Review*.[12] She writes him from her hospital bed in Milledgeville: "I was much taken with the paper on Teilhard, not that I understand any of the scientific stuff but the work you've done

12. "Has Teilhard de Chardin *Really* Joined the Within and the Without of Things?" *Sewanee Review*, 73 (Spring, 1965), 217–36.

on it is sure impressive & what I do understand makes sense" (Letter 182).

Finding themselves philosophically and religiously aliens in a strange land (ironically, in their own land, the South), their common purpose as writers created a kind of foxhole camaraderie, in which they respected, praised, and encouraged each other's efforts. From the beginning, Cheney and O'Connor exchanged manuscripts, as well as published copies of their works, asking each other for reaction and advice. O'Connor sent the Cheneys several of the *A Good Man Is Hard to Find* stories in manuscript and solicited their response. Cheney was very enthusiastic about "A Late Encounter with the Enemy," calling it "a corker!" and "a truly powerful anecdote!" (Letter 5). When he suggested fuller development of her protagonist in "The Displaced Person," in order to create more emotional impact with his death, O'Connor agreed: "You were certainly right about the story and I have operated on it and improved it to some extent" (Letter 12). On a visit to Andalusia, he advised an alteration in "A View of the Woods," which O'Connor adopted; she later wrote him, "Your visit was not only enjoyable for both of us (me & Regina) but profitable for me as I have made a new ending onto my story—that I think is better—giving the old man time to realize that he's not getting anywhere fast" (Letter 45). When the collection was published in 1955, Mrs. Cheney reviewed it for the *Nashville Banner* (see Appendix B), where Cheney later reviewed *The Violent Bear It Away* (New York: Farrar, Straus and Cudahy, 1960) (see Appendix C), which the Cheneys had also read in manuscript.

O'Connor read nearly all of the articles and reviews Cheney wrote during the period of their friendship. She read his second play, "I Choose to Die" (which was produced at Vanderbilt in 1960), about Sam Davis, boy hero of the Confederacy. And she read and sent him detailed written comments on three of his novels, one of which, *This Is Adam* (New York: McDowell-Obolensky, 1958), was published during her lifetime. (Its post-publication history is also the subject of considerable discussion in their letters.) The second novel, "Quest for the Pelican," which Cheney worked on from 1959 to 1961, was never published; the third, which O'Connor knew as "The Tiger Returns," was published as *Devil's Elbow* in 1969 (New York: Crown). When she read the first three chapters of *This Is Adam*, O'Connor wrote to Cheney, "I certainly think you ought to be pleased with what you have done. The 2nd and 3rd chapters are wonderful. The farther you get into this, the more your writing seems to relax and become natural sounding" (Letter 49).

Cheney frequently sought O'Connor's interest and involvement in other projects, political as well as literary. In 1956, when he published a political essay in pamphlet form, *A New "Crown of Thorns" for the Democratic Party*, he asked O'Connor to let her name be used as one of its sponsors, and she readily agreed to become a member of the Committee for Renewing the Democratic Party, without first reading the essay and far more out of implicit regard for Cheney's integrity and philosophical positions than out of interest in national politics. She was a willing participant, too, when he asked her to join a group of writers interested in raising national foundation money to create a Tennessee Provincial Theatre, a dramatic workshop that would encourage and support the writing of plays.

Cheney sent O'Connor a draft, and they discussed at length the article he was writing for the *Sewanee Review*, "Miss O'Connor Creates Unusual Humor Out of Ordinary Sin" (see Appendix D), in which Cheney took issue with an article by John Hawkes, "Miss O'Connor's Devil" (*Sewanee Review*, 70 [Summer, 1962], 395–407). As usual, O'Connor was pleased with Cheney's understanding of her work: "I really like this. . . . I got some ideas from it myself that I may work into that paper for Sweet Briar to kind of pull it together" (Letter 161). "I think that piece is going to do a lot of good as far as giving people a second thought about my stuff" (Letter 173).

O'Connor's comments on Cheney's fiction are an interesting and valuable part of the correspondence, particularly for what they demonstrate about O'Connor's own fictional strategies—and because none of the published

O'Connor correspondence includes such detailed examples of O'Connor's critical principles being applied. Echoing their old friend and writing teacher Caroline Gordon, O'Connor reminds Cheney repeatedly that the fiction writer must dramatize, not report: "[In "The Tiger Returns"] there ought to be a lot less reported and more dramatized through out. For instance, when they cut Dunk down from the tree, you then report what he says. I think we ought to hear him say it. You could at least break up long stretches of reporting with some scenes. Caroline would blow a fuse over this" (Letter 144). She calls him to order for clumsy diction and awkward, ill-considered imagery: "Don't have [one of Cheney's characters in "Quest for the Pelican"] use a bogus word like *boohoo* when she means cry. You want pathos here and you ain't going to get it out of a word like that" (Letter 94). "Take out such words as *chilily, intoxicatedly,* such colloquialisms and slang as *on their pins, dried up* (for stopped talking), *'em* when you mean them, *'im* when you mean him (except in direct discourse)" (Letter 144). In response to a draft of *This Is Adam* she comments:

> Occasionally there is an image that sticks out and becomes too noticeable. Such as those freckles standing out as if on stems. Maybe my literal imagination but I keep seeing the stems. It's too much. Also the one about his mouth being as tight as the door of a dutch oven or something. I don't know what the door of a dutch oven looks like but no matter that image don't work. This is not the kind of book that will depend on such things so anything like that that sticks out, I'd just remove it. When in doubt, operate, according to Dr. O'Connor. Which may be why she can't accumulate more words on her own behalf. (Letter 55)

And she points out his failures to establish and control appropriate tone and perspective.

> Occasionally [in *This Is Adam*] you seem to let the omniscient narrator talk like Adam (He was filled with wonderment etc) or at least it seems to be the omniscient narrator; anyway there's some confusion about who it is. Caroline is always telling me that when the om. nar. talks like anyone of the characters or uses colloquialisms that you lower the tone. (Letter 55)

> You need to be able to stand back and get some distance on [the narrator] from time to time. You need to establish the narration objectively, see [the narrator] from the outside sometime as well as seeing the events from his eyes. (Letter 144)

O'Connor's own control of tone—and her ability to "get some distance" on the world around her—is of course a quality readers of her fiction, Cheney early among them, have much valued. And it is one of the chief delights of her letters to the Cheneys. More often than not, the object in focus from O'Connor's "distance" is herself. When *Nashville Tennessean* editor Ralph Morrissey took pictures of O'Connor while she was a guest at the Cheneys' one weekend in 1955, Mrs. Cheney sent O'Connor copies, to which she responded: "That decidedly ain't me except in the picture which looks like an ad for acid indigestion. . . . [Morrissey] sure missed his calling. He ought to work for Photoplay or Snappy Story—to make a divebomb out of the old oaken bucket!!" (Letter 18). And she wrote of other photographs: "The grim pictures arrived. That face over the 'fiery Flannery' caption looked like an old potato the mice had been at" (Letter 15).

When she began to walk on crutches, she wrote the Cheneys that she'd love to visit, "If you are willing to stash me away downstairs and to remove any low altitude vases you have set about" (Letter 21). She wrote them about a talk on "the Wholesome Novel" she was supposed to give to the ladies of the Catholic Parish Council in Macon: "Unfortunately I don't know what a wholesome novel is . . . I am never informed on the subjects I discuss" (Letter 43). "I am now back from being the woman of the hour," she wrote after participating in the 1959 Vanderbilt literary symposium, "to being the woman of the barnyard" (Letter 87). Ten days before she was to give a talk in Savannah, she broke out with hives: "This was perfect timing. The doctor said I could not go. This is what you call anticipatory illness and illustrates psychosomatic disease at its best. I hope that my carcus will bring off another triumph like this the next time it is necessary" (Letter 115). She wrote of another series of speaking engagements: "I am weary of riding upon airyplanes and being The Honored Guest. I think the reason I like chickens is that they don't go to college" (Letter 121).

Such ironic self-deprecation is charming, but one hears in her remarks, too, O'Connor's earnest struggle with her own limitations—chief among them her physical vulnerability. From the first, Cheney was aware of O'Connor's precarious health (her "deadly malady," he called it later), but her "saltiness," her ironic detachment from her limitations and her pain, and her absolute dedication to her work and her vision were often effective distractions even for those closest to her. "As well as I do know," he wrote her in the spring of 1964, "I sometimes can't realize the degree of hazard in which you live" (Letter 183).

Shortly after her death, Cheney spoke informally of his friend to a group of faculty and students at George Peabody College, attempting to sum up what were for him the qualities of her "greatness": "her judgment, absence of partisan blindness, her clear eye and charity for human foibles; her wariness of her own limitations—her ability to measure her effort and herself 'AGAINST TRUTH.' "[13] He was saying again, more succinctly, things he had said many times in his reviews and his letters to O'Connor—and he was revealing as much about himself as about his friend. His list of her qualities is a list of his own ambitions, the aims of his own struggle as a man and a writer.

It is finally the sense of movement and energy, rather than detachment, that perhaps most informs the correspondence. "The eleven years of my friendship with Flannery," Cheney said, "now seem like a stirrup cup, a gay-grim passage in which greeting and goodbye were the sides of a spinning gold coin."[14] It is a note Cheney had struck years earlier, when he wrote her, "Your image has been much in my mind's eye, somewhat as if you were in another revolving door being moved in the opposite direction" (Letter 27). Their letters are testimony to lives in motion, to writers striving according to their own best lights but with common purpose to show and say what they saw, and to be understood.

13. GPC notes.
14. GPC notes.

Editor's Note

This edition represents all known surviving correspondence between Flannery O'Connor and Brainard and Frances Neel Cheney, beginning 8 February 1953, and ending 16 July 1964. The correspondence consists of 188 items: 117 are from O'Connor (55 to Cheney, 23 to Mrs. Cheney, 39 to both), 71 from Cheney. All letters are a part of the Brainard Cheney materials housed in the Special Collections archives of the Jean and Alexander Heard Library, Vanderbilt University in Nashville, Tennessee.

Without exception, the Cheney letters in this collection are carbon copies of letters written by Mr. Cheney; Mrs. Cheney retained no copies of her letters to O'Connor. While Mr. Cheney was conscientious in his habit of making carbon copies of his correspondence, some of his letters are obviously missing in the exchange; there are gaps, too, created by the missing letters Mrs. Cheney wrote. The Cheney carbons are, fortunately, for the most part legible and complete (even to the point of bearing signatures), suggesting that the original letters were not likely altered to any great extent, though it must be assumed some handwritten changes and postscripts were made. All letters have been transcribed whole and uncut, with the exception of deletions made (and editorially noted) at the request of Flannery O'Connor's literary executor in letters 6, 84, 87, 90, and 151.

The follow abbreviations describing the physical form of the letters have been used in the headings: TLS, typed letter, signed by author; TL, typed letter unsigned; ALS, autograph letter signed by author; AL, autograph letter unsigned; TL(cc), typed letter, carbon copy; TLS(cc), typed letter, carbon copy signed by author in carbon; PCS, postal card signed. Numbers in the headings indicate the total number of pages of the original letters.

The letter headings, closings, and signatures have been regularized to appear flush to the right margin. Where the date or a part of the date does not appear in the original, it has been supplied in square brackets. Variations in the typed presentation of the bodies of the letters (paragraph indentation, single or double spacing, etc.) have also been standardized. Obvious inadvertent spelling, punctuation, and typographical errors have been silently corrected, although every effort has been made to retain the idiosyncratic spelling and punctuation of the writers. Square brackets have been used for minor editorial interpolations to promote clarity or provide factual information. Footnotes have been used to provide additional information.

The Correspondence of Flannery O'Connor and the Brainard Cheneys

1. *To Brainard Cheney from Flannery O'Connor. TLS 1p.*

Milledgeville, Georgia, February 8, 1953

Dear Mr. Cheney:

A few weeks ago Mr. Thomas Carter[1] sent me a copy of your review[2] of my book, "Wise Blood."[3] I wrote Caroline Tate[4] and asked her if she knew you because she appears to know everybody who ever wrote anything in Tennessee and yesterday I had a letter from her in which she sent me your address. I only want to tell you that I liked the review.

There have not been many good ones. I've been surprised again and again to learn what a tough character I must be to have produced a work so lacking in what one lady called "love." The love of God doesn't count or else I didn't make it recognizable. So many reviewers too thought this was just another dirty book and enjoyed it for that reason.

I must confess that I didn't see the patrolman as the tempter on the mountain top. The Lord's dispatchers are mighty equivocal these days anyhow. I only knew I had to get rid of that automobile some way and having the patrolman push it over and then say the things he did seemed right to me; I didn't think why. Perhaps you are right and he became the tempter, but when he pushed that car over, he was an angel of light, I am sure. However, as the word "myth" occurs in that paragraph, too, I am afraid to give it much study. That is one word I stay away from. I used to encounter it in the graduate school I attended and I always give it a wide berth now. I don't yet know what it means.

I thank you again for reading my book and writing about it so carefully and with so much understanding. I bought three copies of the review to show to some of my connections who think it would be nicer if I wrote about nice people.

Sincerely yours,
Flannery O'Connor

1. Editor of *Shenandoah*, a journal published by Washington and Lee University, Lexington, Virginia.

2. Untitled review of *Wise Blood*, in *Shenandoah*, 3 (Autumn, 1952), 55–60. See Appendix A.

3. Flannery O'Connor's first published novel. New York: Harcourt, Brace and World, 1952.

4. Caroline Gordon (Mrs. Allen Tate) (1895–1981), novelist, literary critic, and creative writing teacher, had read the manuscript of *Wise Blood* and offered extensive comment and praise. Gordon had read and commented on all of Cheney's fiction, as she was subsequently to do for most of O'Connor's work.

2. *To Flannery O'Connor from Brainard Cheney. TL(cc) 1p.*

Smyrna, Tennessee, Sunday Night, March 22 [1953]

Dear Miss O'Connor,

It is gratifying to a reviewer to know that an author thinks well of his interpretation. It is also interesting to know how far the author will go with him in his say about it.

I am not surprised that your novel did not find popular acceptance, or very many understanding reviewers—after some 15 years experience with them myself.[1]

I'll have to confess that I was a set-up for your story: an ex-Protestant, ex-agnostic, who had just found his way back (after 10 or 12 generations) to The Church.

Moreover, I had been trying to bring off a play out of the same sort of material and on the same subject, by way of a somewhat similar argument—though not so directly or cogently employed, I may say.

My effort, a musical play with dancing,[2] was about Dolley Pond Church of God, in Grasshopper Valley (Tennessee hillbillies) fumbling for a substitute for the mass—about which they had never, of course, heard. Vanderbilt Theater produced it for me last year and everybody said he liked it but nobody understood it—and with good cause—

I had, to be sure, heard of you—through the Tates

[Caroline Gordon and Allen Tate]. They are old friends. I consider Caroline my literary godmother—and now she is my godmother in The Church.

And I will volunteer for the pleasure of it: My wife and I were baptized into The Church here Saturday evening a week ago. (The Tates were not here of course—Allen being at large on a lecture tour and Caroline on her way to the Great Northwest—only by proxie.) We are very happy over our change of life.

I will confide further that I am not a Tennessean at all, but a Georgian—from a little-known but priceless community called Lumber City and did a couple of novels about that vicinity and way of life some 10 to 12 years ago.[3]

Moreover I should like to pursue this introduction into acquaintance, with your permission. There are not so many of us that we should set the common bent at naught. We usually manage a trip to Georgia every once and a while. We would like to detour by way of Milledgeville (on our way to St. Simons)[4] to see you sometime?

Incidentally, I feel properly put in my place about my glib use of the word *myth*. I won't defend it, but I can't now get along very well without it—having been so much exposed to the "social sciences" as an undergraduate.[5]

Sincerely yours,

1. Cheney had published two novels: *Lightwood* (Boston: Houghton Mifflin Co., 1939) and *River Rogue* (Boston: Houghton Mifflin Co., 1942).

2. "Strangers in this World: A Folk Musical." Music, Charles N. Bryant; Choreography, Joy Zibart; Direction, Joseph E. Wright. Produced, Nashville: Vanderbilt University Theatre, February 6–9, 1952. "Strangers" was a very popular production, breaking all attendance records at Vanderbilt.

3. *Lightwood* and *River Rogue* are novels set in post-Civil War southeast Georgia.

4. St. Simons Island, southeast Georgia, is a resort area visited over the years by the Cheneys; they owned property there for several years.

5. Cheney attended The Citadel, Charleston, S.C., 1917–19; University of Georgia, Summer, 1924; and Vanderbilt University, 1920, 1924–25.

3. *To Brainard Cheney from Flannery O'Connor. TLS 1p.*

Milledgeville, Ga., March 29, 1953

Dear Mr. Cheney,

My mother [Regina Cline O'Connor] and I hope very much that you and Mrs. Cheney will stop by to see us on your way to St. Simons. We are not staying in town right now but are four miles out of Milledgeville on the road to Eatonton, on my mother's dairy farm, a place called Andalusia, and if you would drop us a card when you might be through, we would arrange to be at home. I'm usually here anyway myself.[1]

Finding the Church after ten or twelve generations must be equal in good fortune to hanging onto it for that many or rather to having it hung onto you, for I have the sense that my ten or twelve have been trying to get rid of it for that long and only by the grace of God haven't succeeded. You find the Catholic sides of your family sluffing off through the children's marryings outside the Church and whatnot and wonder what keeps the main line standing. I suspect a combination of Charity and the scruples but I don't know.

I'd like to have seen your play ["Strangers in this World"] to find out how you did what you were trying to in it. I can't see any way to write as a Catholic unless you make what you write brutal, since now there aren't any mutually understood words above a certain level. I don't believe in theorizing about it though. In the end you do just what you're able to and don't know what that has been.

Yours sincerely,
Flannery O'Connor

1. The Cheneys made their first visit to Andalusia June 6, 1953. On June 28, 1953, Cheney wrote to Robert Fitzgerald: "Incidentally I dropped by to see Flannery O'Connor the other day on my way down to the Georgia coast—I had never met her—and was delighted with her. I think she is a very talented girl" (unpublished letter in Vanderbilt University Library, Special Collections). In a June 7, 1953, letter to Sally and Robert Fitzgerald (published in *The Habit of Being,* ed. by Sally Fitzgerald [New York: Farrar, Straus and Giroux, 1979], p. 58), O'Connor wrote:

> The Cheneys stopped by yesterday on their way to South Ga. and we liked them very much. They wanted to know what *Conversations at New-*

burgh were but I couldn't enlighten them. Is it some more philosophers and bums and priests conversing at a retreat at one of those farms or what? They had a Japanese Fulbright student with them whose gold teeth fascinated Regina. Mrs. C. is a liberry science teacher at Peabody, but she is very nice inspite of that. In fact you would never know it.

No O'Connor/Cheney letters survive from April through September 13, 1953, but O'Connor visited the Cheneys in late July or early August, 1953. She wrote to Sally and Robert Fitzgerald in August, 1953: "Last weekend I flew to Nashville to see the Cheneys and Ashley Brown (a friend of theirs and correspondent of mine) and had a most agreeable time" (*The Habit of Being*, p. 62). On October 13, 1953, O'Connor wrote her friend Robie Macauley: "Also this summer I went to Nashville to see the Cheneys who had stopped by previously to see me on their way to St. Simons. They had Ashley [Brown] at the same time. I heard a lot of Tennessee politics and more literary talk, most of it over my head, than since I left [the School for Writers at the State University of] Iowa" (*The Habit of Being*, p. 64).

---

4. *To Brainard and Frances Neel Cheney from Flannery O'Connor. ALS 1p.*

Milledgeville, Sept. 14, [19]53

Dear Lon[1] & Fanny,

The enclosed is in one of those magazines[2] that people with good sense don't read so I send it to you. I hope you all have enjoyed your vacation as much as I did mine—both of them, the one to Nashville and the one to Ridgefield.[3]

I've had notes from Ashley [Brown] which indicate he is surviving the Irish.[4]

Yours,
Flannery

1. Cheney acquired the nickname "Lon" when he was a student at Vanderbilt: Lon Chaney's movies, especially "The Hunchback of Notre Dame" (1923) and "The Phantom of the Opera" (1925), were popular at the time.

2. *Harper's Bazaar*, 87 (September, 1953), which contained O'Connor's story, "A Late Encounter with the Enemy," 234, 247, 249, 252.

3. In August, O'Connor had visited the Fitzgeralds (almost three weeks in Ridgefield, Connecticut) and the Cheneys. Cheney wrote to Robert Penn Warren, August 24, 1953: "Flannery O'Connor was up to see us for a week-end last month and we enjoyed her so much—she seems a very solid sort and salty. She appeared almost simultaneously with her story, THE RIVER, in the Sewanee Review,

and she read it for us in her good Georgia drawl: the exact tone of voice for the story, which I believe is her finest, perhaps" (unpublished letter in Vanderbilt University Library, Special Collections).

4. Ashley Brown, an instructor at Washington and Lee University, was a friend of the Cheneys and a correspondent of O'Connor's; he was traveling in Ireland at the time. It was Brown who suggested to Tom Carter, editor of *Shenandoah*, that Cheney be asked to write the review of *Wise Blood.*

5. *To Flannery O'Connor from Brainard Cheney. TLS(cc) 1p.*

Cold Chimneys,[1] Smyrna, Tennessee—October 10th [1953]

Dear Flannery,

The LATE ENCOUNTER ["A Late Encounter with the Enemy"] was a corker!

You did it with the flick of the wrist, so to speak: gave him (your old man) a good death—gave it almost before I recognized what was happening—right in the midst of his macabre mummery. Your skeletal picture stood up—it achieved sharp reality. A truly powerful anecdote!

We so much appreciate your sending it to us—for we don't see the BAZAAR [*Harper's Bazaar*].

We are now back a couple of weeks from our summer's interlude of quiet—we went to Vermont, Bread Loaf Mountain and holed in a mountain shanty a mile from the nearest store, etc—about four miles from the Middlebury College campus atop the mountain. I got in about three weeks work on my novel[2] and Fanny, to pass away the time, did a couple of articles on Japan.[3]

On our way back, we went by to see the [Robert] Fitzgeralds—arriving just behind a prospective renter for their house, the renting of which was holding up their departure for Italy. He was the first prospect who had shown any real interest and we were very happy when he decided that he would take it, but, since our time was short, we didn't see much of them. I had never seen Sally before, nor the children—all of whom I found most attractive.[4]

They told us that you had been there only recently—we wished that we might have overtaken you there. You furnished us a topic, let me say, of enthusiastic conversation.

Now we are back—Fannie out lecturing to librarians, as far away as Memphis today—and me, up to my eyes in politics.

Though I am about to take a brief break—I have been doing the "paper work" for the Governor's huddle with the President [Eisenhower] in behalf of TVA—it occurred Thursday and so successfully that I am giving myself a vacation from politics for a week—in which I hope to get as far away as trying to write fiction.[5]

By the way, we hope we can find or contrive sufficient excuse to get you up here again sometime this fall—we will go into town after Christmas to spend the winter[6]—really October is Tennessee's most attractive month—how about it?

F. joins me in warm regards.

Yrs.
Lon

1. "Cold Chimneys" was the name the Cheneys gave the house in Smyrna, Tennessee, Mrs. Cheney inherited in 1946; the homeplace of Mrs. Cheney's Middle Tennessee ancestors; its original name, "Idler's Retreat," was restored in the late 1950s or early 1960s.

2. A final version of "The Image and the Cry," a novel Cheney worked on for several years but was never able to publish.

3. Mrs. Cheney served for eighteen months as visiting professor at Japan Library School, Keio University, Tokyo, 1951–52.

4. In her November 11, 1953, letter to Sally and Robert Fitzgerald, O'Connor wrote: "I had a letter from the Cheneys and they were very pleased to have seen you, and thought everything very attractive, particularly the children" (*The Habit of Being*, p. 64).

5. Cheney worked on the public relations staff of Tennessee Governor Frank Clement, 1952–58.

6. Cold Chimneys had no central heat until 1957, and the Cheneys customarily moved to a Nashville apartment during the winter.

6. *To Brainard Cheney from Flannery O'Connor. TLS 1p.*

Milledgeville, 29 November [19]53

Dear Lon,

We are distressed you all didn't stop.[1] Eight o'clock would have been fine for us as we had just been to the

7:15 mass, which we always go to. I like to go to early mass so I won't have to dress up—combining the 7th Deadly Sin with the Sunday obligation. The next time stop and have breakfast with us. My aunt told me about the call the next week sometime. She lives in the upper stages of reality and seldom remembers to give any messages that come.

I don't want the story[2] back. My agent[3] said she sent it to the Atlantic but I doubt if they like that sort of thing. . . .

Yesterday I bought me a pair of black Polish crested chickens like nothing I have ever had before. I intend to get in the rare bird business yet.

The best to you both.

Flannery

[P.S.] I told T. F. Ritt of A.D. that he might write you about his magazine—something they started at Fordham a couple of years ago.[4] It was apparently a big mess and got quickly extinct but he is trying to revive it along better lines, with what success I wouldn't know.

1. The Cheneys had apparently made a trip to St. Simons.

2. O'Connor's "The Displaced Person," rejected by *The Atlantic* (see postscript to Letter 12), published in the *Sewanee Review*, 62 (October, 1954), 634–54.

3. Elizabeth McKee became O'Connor's literary agent in 1948.

4. Thomas Francis Ritt was a contributor of fiction to and editor of *A.D.*, a short-lived (four issues, 1950–52) literary magazine published by the A.D. Literary Association, Inc., first in Flushing, New York, then in New York City; there was no official connection with Fordham University.

7. *To Brainard and Frances Neel Cheney from Flannery O'Connor. TLS 1p.*

Milledgeville, 15 December [19]53

Dear Lon and Fanny,

My mother thinks I was mighty smart to get out of that blizzard when I did. Mrs. Stevens[1] came over this morning and informed us that it was six inches of snow in Nashville Tennessee at nine o'clock last night. She looked as if she had just got back from there. She always tells us every morning what the weather is in different parts of the country, giving exact time and location.

I had a lovely time as you must know.[2] We hope the next thing will be your stopping with us here, but all I can assemble in the way of guests is Mrs. Stevens. She always shows up when we have company anyway—with some unnecessary message—so as to get a look at them.

The trip back was very rough and punctuated by a little boy across the aisle from me who lifted his head from his paper cup every now and then to say in a hoarse voice, "Can't we go back on da twain?"

I'm enclosing that story[3] and always welcome any suggestions on how I could improve it. Merry Christmas.

Flannery

1. Wife of Regina O'Connor's dairyman tenant.

2. O'Connor visited the Cheneys in December, 1953. She wrote to Elizabeth and Robert Lowell (American poet, 1917–1977; with O'Connor in 1948, Lowell was one of four writers in residence at Yaddo, a writers colony in Saratoga Springs, New York), January 1, 1954: "I was in Nashville a couple of weeks ago visiting the Cheneys . . ." (*The Habit of Being*, p. 65).

3. O'Connor's "A Circle in the Fire," subsequently published in the *Kenyon Review*, 16 (Spring, 1954), 169–90.

8. *To Flannery O'Connor from Brainard Cheney, TL(cc) 1p.*

Cold Chimneys, January 2, 1954

Dear Flannery,

THE CIRCLE OF FIRE ["The Circle in the Fire"] is swell! We are so sorry that we didn't have you read it to us while you were here. Your restraint is finely discriminating.

Do hope the New Year begins well for you! We have had a pleasant Christmas.

We are moving in to town tomorrow—the 10 scuttles a day for four fires has caught up with me and it is virtually the same as living in the coal pits—smoke and soot everywhere. And, with all of it, we don't really keep warm when the weather is sure enough cold. Our address in town will be: Apt. 5, 2002 Terrace Place, Nashville, Tenn.—Please write! We'll be in town till April.

We did Christmas properly, making midnight mass—till 2 a.m.—then camping the night out in the town apartment, which happens to be right behind the

Cathedral, and returning for morning mass at 9 a.m. But come New Year's Eve and the Spirit of Paganism ensnared us. We set out to do it *quietly* and be home soon after midnight to be able to make mass—but somehow, I forgot to quit guzzling on the stroke of 12 and on top of that forgot to set the alarm clock—and instead of making mass, we only made a late breakfast served with whisky sours! Ah me, 'tis a hard row for the flesh!

I am hoping to sneak off for a week or even two, come Monday and try my hand at writing again. Our best,

Yrs.,

9. *To Brainard and Frances Neel Cheney from Flannery O'Connor. TLS 1p.*

Milledgeville, 1/17/54

Dear Lon and Fanny,

I have been reading The Conservative Mind[1] and just yesterday read your review[2] of it and was so proud to see you did him justice; also did justice to Brothers Biddle, Ross, et al.[3] I have been doing him some justice myself but in the short story form, having written another story about displaced persons,[4] this one with an equal-rights man in it. When I get through thinking about it, I want to send it to you.

The Fitzgeralds write that Italy[5] has its drawbacks—they say the rich there will do you in as quickly as the poor.

We aren't having any coal pit experiences here but our water pipes freeze and break with regularity and the cows don't run jump in the pond any more because it has ice in it. I will be glad to see the Spring. Perhaps that will bring you all to Lumber City by way of Milledgeville.

Yours,
Flannery

1. Russell Kirk, *The Conservative Mind. From Burke to Santayana.* (Chicago: Henry Regnery Co., 1953).
2. "The Conservative Course by Celestial Navigation," *Sewanee Review,* 62 (Winter, 1954), 151–59.
3. Cheney had taken exception to reviews of *The Conservative Mind* by Francis Biddle, in the *New Republic,* and Ralph Gilbert Ross, in the *Partisan Review.*

4. Apparently this became the second part of "The Displaced Person" in the revised, much longer version which was published in *A Good Man Is Hard to Find And Other Stories* (1955). See Letter 11.
5. Robert and Sally Fitzgerald had been in Italy since October, 1953.

10. *To Brainard and Frances Neel Cheney from Flannery O'Connor. ALS 1p.*

2/12/54

Dear Lon & Fanny,

Another report from the country.[1] I hope your albatross ["The Image and the Cry"] is well.

Yours,
Flannery

1. Perhaps a cover letter for "The Displaced Person" manuscript.

11. *To Flannery O'Connor from Brainard Cheney. TL(cc) 1p.*

Apt. 5, 2002 Terrace Place, Nashville, Tenn., March 15, 1954

Dear Flannery,

This is Andrew Jackson's birthday. I am not an admirer of Andrew's (though I don't breathe it out loud here) and I would be little inclined to celebrate in his memory, except that this holiday is giving me a chance to answer some long delayed personal letters—and first of all this one to you!

We dawdled over the idea of going down to St. Simons for a week this month, and I put off writing till we should decide—we were hoping that we might pick you up and take you on down with us—but we have been in such a swivet with this and that, nolo contendere, we're happy to even get our heads above water to stay here!

THE KING OF THE BIRDS is very fine indeed. I think that you make rich use of the medieval symbolism of the bird and that it succeeds as a symbol beautifully. I like the story. I am not, however, altogether sure that you get all of the dramatic impact possible out of your protagonist, the displaced man. It may be that my reading of the earlier treatment of this man (or the very similar character) in the DP story in which he was unsympathetically presented was so much in my mind that it affected my reaction to your presentation in this story. But his death did not wrench my heart, so to speak, as it should have, in the circumstances. I hesitate to suggest it, but it seems to me that he might have had just a little more build up—perhaps, just another touch or incident to reveal his charity.[1]

I have put aside all literary thought for the *season*—the political season. I finished work on the first section of my novel,[2] indulged myself in having a typist copy it for me—with the margins that she allowed, it ran 208 pages (and cost me more money than I had expected!). And now I have laid it by, to gather dust till after the primary election August 7th, I think it is. I am planning to take a leave of absence, then and try to get along with this interminable job—hope I may lay off till the first of the year, perhaps, and get it finished—maybe.

Letter from Caroline [Gordon Tate] recently spoke of Allen's trying for a renewal of his Fulbright—they were expecting to hear the decision momentarily—so they may remain another year.[3] Otherwise they should be returning early this summer, I think. She said they might come to Tennessee and pay us a visit, if and when they do come back.

This is all pretty contingent (with my present information) but we hope you can come up and join us at Smyrna, if and when they do—so that we may all be together for a spell.

Trust yesterday Georgia cyclones did not reach Milledgeville.

Please let us hear from you.

As ever,

1. "The King of the Birds" is the title O'Connor gave an essay she wrote, in 1960, about peacocks; it was entitled "Living with a Peacock" when it appeared in *Holiday*, 30 (September, 1961), 52–53, 55, then reprinted under O'Connor's original title in *Mystery and Manners: Occasional Prose*, Sally and Robert Fitzgerald, eds. (New York: Farrar, Straus & Giroux, 1969). Here, however, O'Connor obviously used "The King of the Birds" as a working title for a story she had sent Cheney—a story she later incorporated into the earlier version of "The Displaced Person" (published in the *Sewanee Review*, 62 [October, 1954],

634–54). See Letter 9, paragraph 1 and note 4. The final version of "The Displaced Person," published in *A Good Man Is Hard to Find and Other Stories* (1955), is much enlarged and revised to include the famous peacock symbol. (See Roy R. Male, "The Two Versions of 'The Displaced Person,'" *Studies in Short Fiction*, 7 [Summer, 1970], 450–57, for an informative account of the combining of the two parts of the story.)

2. "The Image and the Cry." See Letter 5.

3. Caroline Gordon and Allen Tate were in Italy in 1953–54; Tate was Fulbright Professor at The University of Rome.

12. *To Brainard and Frances Neel Cheney from Flannery O'Connor. TLS 1p.*

Milledgeville, 11 April [19]54

Dear Lon and Fanny,

You were certainly right about the story ["The Displaced Person"] and I have operated on it and improved to some extent and sent it off to the Botteghe Oscure lady[1]—who writes me that they will certainly miss the Tates.[2] So I presume they are coming back. I haven't heard from Caroline [Gordon Tate] in a long time.

Ralph McGill[3] was out here to see us last week and we thought he looked like a hant—reducing, or rather done reduced. But we hadn't seen him in two years so that might account for the shock.

We are hoping maybe Easter will bring you down this way.

Yours,
Flannery

[P.S.]—Monroe Spears[4] is going to print "The Displaced Person." The Atlantic kept it 4 months & decided it wasn't their dish.

1. "The *Botteghe Oscure* Lady was the Princess Marguerite Caetani (née Chapin), an American woman married to an Italian nobleman, who lived in Rome and edited and published a literary magazine called *The Botteghe Oscure*—a title meaning *The Dark Shops*, and called this because the Palazzo Caetani was located on a street called the Via delle Botteghe Oscure. There was some talk at some time about her publishing something from Flannery's work, but this somehow never came about. M. C. was a friend [of] Caroline Gordon's, too, and the Cheneys no doubt met her if they came to Rome while Caroline was there" (letter from Sally Fitzgerald to the editor, December 28, 1984).

2. The Tates were leaving Italy.

3. Ralph McGill (1898–1969, editor and publisher of the *Atlanta Constitution*, was a long-time friend of the Cheneys.

4. Monroe Spears was editor of the *Sewanee Review*.

13. *To Brainard and Frances Neel Cheney from Flannery O'Connor. TLS 1p.*

Milledgeville, 20 May [1954]

Dear Lon and Fanny,

I am certainly distressed to have to forego the visit for this weekend—that I already had the ticket for—but we are hoping now that you all can come down and spend next weekend (beginning Friday—28th) with us and bring Ashley. We have been wanting you for a long time and we do hope you can make it. I'll write Ashley in Louisville[1] but in case he is with you, please issue the invitation. The major sport around here of course is killing flies but you might find it restful before a campaign.[2] Let us know when we can expect you and do try to come.

Yours,
Flannery

1. Ashley Brown's home was in Louisville, Kentucky.
2. Reference is to Cheney's involvement in Tennessee Governor Frank Clement's reelection campaign.

14. *To Brainard and Frances Neel Cheney from Flannery O'Connor. TLS 1p.*

Milledgeville, 8 June [19]54

Dear Lon & Fanny,

We are still sorry you all couldn't make it but should the campaign abate a little, maybe you could take off for a short escape. We would be so glad to have you any time. The weekend I planned to come to Nashville, a friend of mine who was on his way to Denmark to live elected to pay me a visit and there was no way to stop him—otherwise I would have.

We have just survived high ceremonies here. The Stevens' (dairyman's) daughter, age 16, 9th grade, got married and my mother let them have the reception here. It was quite a wedding with bridesmaids in six flavors, children with dripping candles, and a cadaverous preacher in white pants, blue coat, and black and yellow striped tie. My mother always prepares for the wrong accident—she was expecting a hole to be burned in her tablecloth. But somebody set a wet punch cup on her Bible. All the guests were MITES, and their relatives.

The D.P. [Displaced Person][1] has bought himself an automobile. It cost $125 and he is paying for it $5 a month. A model A Ford with the back taken off behind the front seat. It's a moving skeleton and the gas is fed from a tube on the steering wheel. He gets in it and is rapt to the third Paradise.

I hear nothing from the [Allen] Tates or the [Robert] Fitzgeralds.

Yours,
Flannery

1. A Polish refugee and his family, the Matisiacks, hired by Regina O'Connor as tenant farmers in early 1952. There are numerous references to the "D.P.s" in O'Connor's letters to the Cheneys as well as in the collected letters in *The Habit of Being*.

15. *To Frances Neel Cheney from Flannery O'Connor. ALS 1p.*

Sunday [1954?][1]

Dear Fanny,

Barring mortal accidents I will be along Friday at 1:02 on Flight 254.

The grim pictures arrived. That face over the "fiery Flannery" caption looked like an old potato the mice had been at. My mother said: "I have seen you when you looked just like that," and put them hastily away. Thanks anyhow.

Yours,
Flannery

1. It has not been possible to date this letter with certainty; but the closing and the subject matter are consistent only with others written during this period.

16. *To Frances Neel Cheney from Flannery O'Connor. TLS 1p.*

Milledgeville, 2 May 1955

Dear Fannie,

I was real glad you liked Mr. Head and Nelson.[1] I guess Mr. Head is a kind of Peter but it is harder to gin up Nelson's character so he could be a respectable representative of the Christ Child. I guess it's more like Peter and Little Peter. Anyway, my trouble is I can never think of these high matters until after I have written the story. While I am writing my mind is always on the lowest common denominator, calculating the vulgar possibility, etc.

I asked Harcourt Brace to send you all a copy of my collection [*A Good Man Is Hard to Find and Other Stories*] and want you to see particularly what I did to that one called The Displaced Person (I practically made a novel out of it) and a new one called Good Country People, that the Tates like.

If you will send me Mr. Fugikawa's[2] address (& the right way to spell his name) I would like to get them to send him a copy of the collection.

I would certainly like to come to see you all, whenever it suits you, but my mother informs me it is indecent for me to do all the visiting. We are wondering if when school is out you won't be coming to Georgia and if so we do insist that you stop for the night if you can, but if not at least for a meal. This month I can't go anywhere, having been discovered by several ladies' clubs of Macon. My mother has a Chamber of Commerce approach to literature and she thinks that I must address all these DARs and Book Review Groups whenever called upon. The trouble is it takes me two or three weeks of hard labor to amuse these girls for five minutes and somebody told me that the only two books sold in Macon anyway are the Bible and Eneas Africanus. The last one I talked at was on April 23 and one of the ladies told me that it was a very important day—the birthdays of William

Shakespeare, Harry Stillwell Edwards, and Shirley Temple.

We enjoyed Ashley [Brown] and company and asked him all about you. When I was in Macon the last time, I met a Mrs. Coke who knows you and Mrs. Jessup.[3]

How is Lon's albatross?[4]

Affectionately,
Flannery

1. Characters in "The Artificial Nigger," first published in the *Kenyon Review*, 17 (Spring, 1955), 169–92; collected in *A Good Man Is Hard to Find and Other Stories* (New York: Harcourt, Brace and Company, 1955).

2. Masanobu Fujikawa, Tokyo librarian and teacher, former student of Frances Cheney; the Cheneys had taken Fujikawa to see O'Connor in Milledgeville.

3. Lee Cheney Jessup, Cheney's sister who lived in Nashville.

4. Cheney's novel-in-progress, "The Image and the Cry."

17. *To Brainard and Frances Neel Cheney from Flannery O'Connor. TLS 1p.*

Milledgeville, Tuesday [July 19, 1955]

Dear Lon and Fannie,

I was greeted by my mother with the announcement that there were two new peachickens, which brings the total to 9. Hedwig[1] officiated at their hatching. She is supposed to be my assistant.

I certainly had a wonderful time and enjoyed everything I did in Nashville[2] but mostly seeing you all again. Whenever I leave from a visit to my 87 yr old cousin, my mother says "Don't forget to tell her you enjoyed what you had to eat." However I enjoy the company so much when I visit you that I forget what I have to eat and at my 87 yr old cousin's the food is about all there is to remember. My mother was very pleased with the fan and fanned vigorously all last evening. She is going to write you.

That address for Cross Currents[3] is 3111 Broadway, NYC 27 and you should start with the Summer issue as it has several things in it in line with what you are thinking on currently.

I am sending along my Dom Chapman letters.[4] I

haven't looked at it in a long time but I used to be very fond of it.

The plane I came on was 40 minutes late because they had a big argument with a passenger and couldn't leave Nashville until they got him off the plane—which took 35 minutes. My mother said posted on the bulletin board in Atlanta was "40 minutes late on account of headwinds." Now I know what headwinds are.

Love,
Flannery

1. Hedwig and her brother Alfred were children of Regina's tenant farmers.

2. On July 22, 1955, O'Connor wrote to Catherine Carver, her editor at Harcourt, Brace and Co., about *A Good Man Is Hard to Find and Other Stories:* "I have just got back from a weekend in Nashville and met the people who run the local bookstore there and they informed me they were selling a lot of copies of it" (*The Habit of Being,* p. 91).

3. *Cross Currents: A Quarterly Review to Explore the Implications of Christianity for Our Times.* In an April 1, 1961, review in the diocesan paper *The Bulletin,* O'Connor wrote, "Of the many magazines in America published through the initiative of Catholics, the one which makes the most important contribution to Catholic intellectual life in this country is . . . *Cross Currents*" (reprinted in *The Presence of Grace and Other Book Reviews by Flannery O'Connor,* compiled by Leo J. Zuber, edited with an introduction by Carter W. Martin [Athens: The University of Georgia Press, 1983] pp. 112–13).

4. Presumably *The Spiritual Letters of Dom John Chapman* (New York: Sheed and Ward, 1935). John Chapman (1865–1933), fourth Abbot of Downside, was a Benedictine historian and exegete who had taken Anglican orders in 1889 but joined the Catholic Church in 1890; Dom Chapman wrote several treatises on the problems of spiritual life and on mysticism.

18. *To Frances Neel Cheney from Flannery O'Connor. TLS 1p.*

Milledgeville, Georgia, 3 August [1955]

Dear Fannie,

That decidedly ain't me except in the picture which looks like an ad for acid indigestion. People in Nashville will wonder what you fed me. As for Mr. Morrisey, he sure missed his calling. He ought to work for Photoplay or Snappy Story—to make a divebomb out of the old oaken bucket!![1] My my.

Our big pump is broken so we are temporarily using the small one and as the water is questionable, I am having to take typhoid shots, an interesting diversion for the mid-summer. Also we are being beseiged by a scorpion and his family and chattels who live in the shrubbery and are penetrating the house through various cracks. The old man is about six inches long and the son one and a half. I prefer the old man. If one bites you, you don't have time to get to the hospital. Nobody has been able to tell us how to get rid of them.

The total peachicken crop is sixteen so far but I am hoping to urge it up to twenty.

Please give my regards to Sue Jenkens [*sic*][2] and Caroline [Gordon Tate].[3] I wish I could get up again this summer but with typhoid shots, plus my new medicine,[4] I think I had better stick close to the Scientist.[5] The new medicine is doing fine so far and it is wonderful for the first time in five years not to have to give myself a shot every day.

Lon:

I see that one of the foremost snake handlers just died of a bite. His name was Hensley and I have heard him breathe fire over the radio.[6]

Love,
Flannery

1. A photograph of O'Connor which appeared in the Nashville *Tennessean,* Sunday, July 31, 1955, p. 4-E. Ralph Morrissey, book editor for the *Tennessean,* interviewed O'Connor during her visit with the Cheneys and wrote a feature story and review ("No Moonlight and Magnolias") of *A Good Man Is Hard to Find and Other Stories.* Morrissey was a photographer, as well, and took a number of photographs of O'Connor at the Cheney's house.

2. Sue Jenkins Brown was a friend of the Tates and the Cheneys. She and her husband, William Slater Brown, had a house, called Robber Rocks, in the Tory Valley area, along the New York-Connecticut border, near Sherman, Connecticut, for many years as "writers area." The Cheneys visited Sue Jenkins Brown at Robber Rocks several times. (Hart Crane once lived with the Browns, an experience documented by Sue Jenkins Brown in *Robber Rocks: Letters and Memories of Hart Crane, 1923–32* [Middletown, Connecticut: Wesleyan University Press, 1969]).

3. According to a letter dated June 10, 1955, to Sally and Robert Fitzgerald, O'Connor spent a weekend in early June in Connecticut with Sue Jenkins and Caroline Tate (*The Habit of Being,* p. 85).

4. This is the first mention in these letters of O'Connor's lupus. The medicine to which she refers is Meticorten (*The Habit of Being,* p. 96).

5. O'Connor's whimsical title for her doctor, Atlanta physician Arthur J. Merrill.

6. An allusion to Cheney's play, "Strangers in this World," which is about snake-handlers. See Letter 2, note 2.

19. *To Frances Neel Cheney from Flannery O'Connor. TLS 1p.*

Milledgeville, 7 September [19]55

Dear Fanny,

I must say Mr. Dale Francis' communication didn't rejoice me any. I wrote him a real polite letter though and *thanked* him for his high opinion and told him I was a born Catholic. I thought maybe after that he would write them and correct it but he didn't even answer my letter. It doesn't make any difference except that people do believe that if you have been brought up in the Church, you write ads if you write anything.[1]

You should see Hazel Motes[2] picture on the front of the British edition of my book.[3] It came out last month, put out by somebody named Neville Spearman who is apparently always just on the edge of bankruptcy. This one will probably push him over the edge. Anyway, here is the British conception of Mr. Mote's face (black wool hat on top); also the rat-colored car is there—all this in black and white and pink and blue, the book itself being an unbelieveable orange.

Tell Lon I am reading Peter Drucker.[4] With my total non-retention this is not going to do me much good but it is very impressive to me as long as I have the book open. Did you get to Michigan? It seems I am going to Michigan next spring, to Lansing to talk to the AAUW [American Association of University Women]. The lady[5] asked me if I would talk on the significance of the short story and I all but told her over the telephone that I didn't know what the significance of the short story was. Then I figured I would have ten months to find out, so I am going to Lansing in April.

Would you send me Caroline's Princeton address?[6] That is, if she has not left there.

I'll be pleased to see the picture[7] when you get [a] chance to send it. Remember me to Pauline[8] and Sue [Jenkins].

Love,
Flannery

1. A man named Dale Francis wrote a letter (in response to James Greene's review of *A Good Man Is Hard to Find and Other Stories,* "The Comic and the Sad," in *Commonweal,* July 22, 1955, p. 404), published in *Commonweal,* August 12, 1955, p. 471, in which he said that O'Connor was a Roman Catholic *convert.* In her June 8, 1958, letter to Cecil Dawkins, fellow Southerner, writer, and Catholic, O'Connor said of Dale Francis' "convert" remark: "He thought somebody told him so, or some such thing, and ever since anybody that writes anything, announces I am a convert. This wouldn't make any difference except that I think there is usually a difference in the way converts write and the way the born-variety write. With the born variety the point of view is more naturally integrated into the personality, or such is my theory" (*The Habit of Being,* p. 287).

2. Protagonist of *Wise Blood.*

3. *Wise Blood.* (London: Neville Spearman Company, 1955).

4. Peter Drucker (1909–), economist, writer, educator. Probably *The New Society: The Anatomy of the Industrial Order* (New York: Harper and Brothers, 1950), a copy of which was in O'Connor's library (see *Flannery O'Connor's Library: Resources of Being,* Arthur F. Kinney, ed. [Athens: The University of Georgia Press, 1985], p. 84).

5. Mrs. Rumsey Haynes, head of the Lansing, Michigan, chapter of the AAUW.

6. Caroline Gordon Tate's permanent residence was in Princeton, New Jersey; she had been a lecturer in creative writing at Columbia University in New York since 1946.

7. This may be a reference to another photograph taken by Ralph Morrissey.

8. Pauline Turkel had a summer place near Sue Jenkins in Tory Valley, and they were close friends.

20. *To Frances Neel Cheney from Flannery O'Connor. TLS 1p.*

Milledgeville, 29 September [19]55

Dear Fanny,

Here is the picture[1] but I want you to come see the original.

Since you last heard from me my state of affairs has changed considerably—I am on crutches and will have to be on them a year or two. Right now I feel like the Last Ape. It requires a major decision for me to swing across the room. All this is on account of a bone condition in the hip, which has been coming on for a couple of years. They say if I keep the weight off it entirely for a year or so, I may be able to save it—otherwise, I will spend my old age charging people in my wheel chair. While this might have its advantages, I think I will try the crutches for two years anyway. I tell my mother she had better take out insurance on me and on all the people I trip and kill while I am on these things. There is always something crashing now in my wake. Of course this is not such an inconvenience for me as it would be for a sporty type. I can still throw the garbage to the chickens (though I am in danger of going with it) which is my favorite exercise.

I know those young pacifists[2] would have scared me to death.

We hope there is a chance of you(?) all(?)'s coming to see us this fall. Do let me know.

Love,
Flannery

1. Probably a snapshot of O'Connor's self portrait in oil; such a photograph is among the correspondence in the Vanderbilt University Library collection of Cheney/O'Connor letters.
2. Anti-nuclear war demonstrators protesting in Nashville.

21. *To Frances Neel Cheney from Flannery O'Connor. TLS 1p.*

Milledgeville, 4 October [19]55

Dear Fannie,

If you are willing to stash me away downstairs and to remove any low altitude vases you have set about, I would love to come on the weekend of the 14th. I'll practice going up and down our front steps, telling myself these are plane steps. I am getting a lot more used to the use of three legs but I still huff and puff. Two people in town who use them have come out to see me to tell me how to do—one of them told me how on them she had broken her hip, had two concussions, split her face open, and knocked out her front teeth. The other one was more cheerful, though she informed me (unasked) that there was no possible way to walk like a lady on them.

I don't want my coming to see you to interfere with your coming to see me. We are expecting you just the same.

I liked the review in the TLS[1] but the one in the Manchester Guardian was a little weird, said the scoffers won and that the hero was focused throughout in a gaze of devoted lunacy. I have just about decided that is the way I will focus everything from now on.

When I get my ticket I'll let you know when the plane

arrives. You are mighty nice to ask me and I am yours with a gaze of devoted lunacy.

Love,
Flannery

1. An anonymous review, entitled "Grave and Gay," of *Wise Blood*, in the (London) *Times Literary Supplement*, September 2, 1955, p. 505; the reviewer described O'Connor as another Southern writer, "whose gifts, intense, erratic, and strange, demand more than a customary effort of understanding from the English reader," and went on to say that O'Connor "may become an important writer."

22. *To Frances Neel Cheney from Flannery O'Connor. TLS 1p.*

Milledgeville, Georgia, Sunday [October, 1955?]

Dear Fannie,

The 15th will be wonderful and I will be there at the airport at 1 P. M. which I hope is not too inconvenient an hour. The D. P. [displaced person, Mr. Matisiack] is now established in the Upper House and my mother says she looks forward to Peace.

Love,
Flannery

23. *To Frances Neel Cheney from Flannery O'Connor. TLS 1p.*

Monday [October, 1955]

Dear Fannie,

My friend, Mrs. Boeson, in Nashville sent me your review[1] of my stories [*A Good Man Is Hard to Find and Other Stories*] out of the Banner and I am real pleased. I mean real pleased. It is one more joy to get several plain statements after all the bunk I have been reading. I am particularly glad you said that about these not being impressionistic sketches as the lady who reviewed it for the Atlanta Journal[2] informed the public that these were plotless little gems, slices of life, pearls, said she, that "needed to be strung together" in order to have a meaning. She was the garden editor, I understand. Nothing but my other-worldly attitude saved me from apoplexy. Anyway, I am mighty much obliged to you and am looking forward to seeing you all on the 15th.

Love,
Flannery

1. *Nashville Banner*, July 1, 1955, p. 23. See Appendix B.

2. Frances Cawthon, "True to Life: O'Connor's Book a 'Must' for South," *The Atlanta Journal and Constitution*, June 5, 1955, p. F-2.

24. *To Brainard and Frances Neel Cheney from Flannery O'Connor. TLS 1p.*

Milledgeville, 18 October [1955]

Dear Lon and Fannie,

I certainly did enjoy myself—as usual—and I have a high regard for your plunder room. You all had better hurry and come to see us as one peachicken succombed in my absence. I don't think my being here would have prevented the inevitable occasion for him but I want there to be some left when you get here.

After eating that large breakfast with you, I got on the plane and was presented with a shrimp cocktail and a filet mignon, snap beans and a baked potato. I started to say in a loud voice like Mr. Head,[1] "I eaten before I left," but I thought better of it and ate what they gave me. After (as the Easter [*sic*] Air Line insists on saying) *deplaning*, I ate again with mother, but I practically haven't eaten since.

Alfred[2] has the earache so his staring to the side has a pained concentration in it right now. My mother dispenses aspirin and Sal Hepatica to all alike.

I enjoyed meeting Russell[3] and wish I could have stayed for the lecture. I also wish I could smoke cigars.

We are looking forward to seeing you.

Affectionately,
Flannery

1. A character in "The Artificial Nigger."

2. Alfred was one of the children of Regina's tenant farmers.

3. Russell Kirk (1918–), conservative author and lecturer, wrote *The Conservative Mind* (1953), which O'Connor admired (see *The Habit of Being*, p. 110).

Kirk was a visitor at the Cheneys the weekend of O'Connor's visit. She had hoped to hear Kirk lecture at Vanderbilt, but missed the date. Kirk's account of his meeting with O'Connor, "Memoir by Humpty Dumpty," is published in *The Flannery O'Connor Bulletin*, 8 (Autumn, 1979), 14–17.

25. *To Flannery O'Connor from Brainard Cheney, TL(cc) 1p.*

Cold Chimneys, Smyrna, Tennessee, October Twenty-fourth [1955]

Dear Flannery,

We have had what seems to us a WONDERFUL idea. It could be called innocents in Rome, or the true story of the three wisemen—two of whom were women.

We will fly to the Eternal City for the month of December if you will go with us? Caroline (T) [Tate] wants Fannie to come over for the last month of her sabbatical season and she wants to go, but she says she won't go without me. Well you know, I'm not so hot as a sightseer: I once went with F. to see New York and spent the week [in] a speakeasy. But I don't mind sightseeing, if I've got the right companionship—what I want is companionship and I'm choosey. I [*sic*] so I told F. that I wanted to oblige her but I wouldn't go unless you would come along for me to talk to, while she and the sightseers went down into the catacombs and such places.

SERIOUSLY, Flannery, won't you? We would go in a minute, if you'll go with us? We could catch a plane out (PanAmerican, I guess) around November 28th to December 1st and get over there in a matter of 18 to 20 hours—you can take a coach plane and save about $200 on the round trip fare I'm told. Old grandmother Caroline is at the other end to get us some inexpensive pension to stay in, as she says, right around the corner from the A. Academy.

And after watching your expert tripping up and down Eastern Airline steps, with various and sundry paraphernalia in your hands, why I haven't the ghost of a doubt but that you could manipulate the PanAm planes without a bobble. And, now, with that new medicine that goes down the simple oldfashioned route of the gullet, why, even if you had to take along an extra suitcase full of them pills, it would be no inconvenience.

Maybe you would like to stop with the Fitzgeralds? Any, some, or all of your time? We could and would be delighted, also, to take you there, too—though not for all of your time, God wot!

Anyhow, when you admitted to me (as we were on the way to the airport as you were leaving the other day) that you had been thinking somewhat of a trip to Rome, too, why it raised my interest one hundred per centum—and when the governor today wished me the time off to go and Godspeed, why that simplified my complications that might have stood in the way.

With the three of us I think it would be a real lark, or maybe it would be more pious to liken it unto a pilgrimhawk. Anyhow, we would get culture no end, and maybe, even a little religion, out of it.

If Regina needs any reassuring or bucking up in the matter, and you think I could help, let me know.

Nothing much has happened since your departure. Russell K. [Kirk] had his sessions (a fair turnout for the public one)[1] and he didn't have to talk long to his Segregationists: in the midst of his speech they got a call from the AP [Associated Press] asking them what they were going to do about the "Memphis ruling" and this so excited them that they never did get back to R's speech.[2]

Our love, in Christ's Name,

1. Russell Kirk's Vanderbilt lecture, October 17, 1955.

2. Cheney was at odds with many of his conservative friends in the Agrarian tradition who favored a return to the values of the old South, particularly in the matter of Segregation. On October 17, 1957, Federal Judge M. S. Boyd ruled in Memphis to accept the Tennessee State Education Department's plan to gradually admit Negroes to white colleges.

26. *To Caroline Gordon Tate and and Brainard and Frances Neel Cheney from Flannery O'Connor. TLS. 1p.*

Milledgeville, 2 December [19]55

Dear Caroline [Gordon Tate] & Lon & Fannie,

I reckon you are all in Rome now, pilgriming and so

forth and I do wish I was too. When you all were arriving in the Holy City, I was arriving in Atlanta, the state capitol, to address a luncheon of the Ga. Writer's Association. I have now got to be famous enough to address this body. I set two down from Miss Lillian Smith who asked me to visit her on her mountain top.[1] I allowed as how my infirmity prevented my going to the mountains right now. I sat next to a librarian named Miss Eunice Costa (?) and whenever I find myself in the company of a librarian, I say in an impressive voice, "Do you know my friend, Mrs. Cheney?" At which they always say yes and accept me as a blood brother. After the talk, one lady shook my hand and said, "That was a wonderful dispensation you gave us, honey." Another lady said, "What's wrong with your leg, sugar?"

My mother has got another family on the place along with the D. P.s [displaced persons, the Matisiacks] now. They are sort of half way between poor white trash and good country people—Mr. Buford May and his wife, Mayrene, and their two children with leaky noses and no shoes. My mother remarked to Mr. and Mrs. May that since they could smoke cigarets, she thought they could put shoes on the children, at which Mr. May told her with dignity, that smoking cigarets was a Habit. They have nothing but a red automobile and one suitcase. They make the Matisiacks look like John D. Rockefellers.

I hope when you come back you'll be prepared to tell me what a cattycomb is like. I met a man at the thing in Atlanta who had a heavy French accent. He said, "You haf been on the left bank, haf you not?" and all I could think of was: I stay on the left bank of the Oconee River, Brother.

Affectionately,
Flannery

1. Lillian Eugenia Smith (1897–1966), a celebrated writer who lived (on a mountain) in Clayton, Georgia.

27. *To Flannery O'Connor from Brainard Cheney. TL(cc) 2pp.*

February 17, 1956

Dear Flannery:

Your image has been much in my mind's eye, somewhat as if you were in another revolving door being moved in the opposite direction. My own revolvement has been keeping me pretty dizzy.

First, with my means of support: on my return to Nashville the first of the year,[1] I had no assistant and a month's accumulation and I have been solidly occupied with it ever since. Moreover, a couple of efforts to get a new assistant have proved unproductive. So I am still caught in the work routine.

On top of that I had the diversion of a weekend in Louisville where the Little Theater was producing an old play of mine—the one about snake handling.[2] Soon after my return, Red (Robert Penn) Warren came to town nosing into the segregation situation through Tennessee, Mississippi, Arkansas and Louisiana, and I strung along with him while he was in Tennessee and Mississippi—partly in professional capacity and partly for the fun of it. I was edified and enjoyed it all very much, but it kept up the whirl of the revolving door.[3]

I've had a few indirect sideline notes from Ashley Brown and Tom Carter via Fanny about their trip and pleasant weekend with you. I certainly wish we might have gone with them.

To get down to the business of this letter, if it has any, the man who produced my play in Louisville, John Caldwell, (of FLORIDA AFLAME fame)[4] has a wild idea that sounds interesting to me and I thought it might interest you, and it is perhaps no wilder than some other of his ideas that have been productive. The idea is entitled a Provincial Theater which he would give locus either here or Sewanee, and it would be, I understand, somewhat in the nature of a dramatic workshop in which we would write and produce plays—subsidized by the Ford Foundation with all rights for commercial production and profits reserved. He has had a nibble on his idea from some man of the Ford Foundation who said to him to get together an interested group to work out a prospectus to present to the Foundation. He, Red Warren and I gave it some discussion over highballs the other evening, and decided to try to give the Ford Foundation an opportunity for investment. At Red's suggestion, and at our agreement, it was decided that the initiating group should be a carefully selected one with a view to a certain amount of compatability in their idea and attitude toward the dramatic art, their philosophical position, their balance and agreeability. On the basis of these considerations we developed a list which would, of course, include you. I might say here, parenthetically, that between Warren and I, we already have more fiction writers in the group than anybody else. But then, why not? Most of us would agree to write some drama, if we could be assured of a good wage for our time—it's so much easier than writing fiction, anyhow.

Anyhow, we would like to get you into the planning bunch to see that this thing takes on a sound form and direction. Others on our list of prospects are Andrew Lytle, Francis Ferguson, Eudora Welty, a man at Harvard named Robert Chapman, the dramatic director at Vanderbilt, Joe Wright, Alfred Starr and his brother, Milton, and Peter Taylor.[5]

Our present plan is for us planners to gather here in Nashville either around the middle of March or the middle of April. At least those dates have been suggested to me by Caldwell. And I'm trying to begin to negotiate on that basis. I'm going to assume that you will join us and which of these would suit you better, and if neither, make your own suggestion.

Fanny joins me in love.

Sincerely,
Brainard Cheney

Miss Flannery O'Connor
RFD
Milledgeville, Georgia

1. Cheney had taken a brief leave of absence from his public relations staff job with Tennessee Governor Frank Clement.

2. "Strangers in this World: A Folk Musical." Music, Charles N. Bryant; choreography, Joy Zibart; direction, John Caldwell. Produced, Louisville, Kentucky: The [University of Louisville, Belknap Campus] Theatre, January 26–28, 1956. Originally produced at Vanderbilt University, February 6–9, 1952. See Letter 2, note 2.

3. Out of this experience, Warren wrote an article, "Divided South Searches Its Soul," *Life*, 41 (July 9, 1956), 98–9+; and a book, *Segregation: The Inner Conflict in the South* (New York: Random House, 1956).

4. "Florida Aflame," written and produced by John Caldwell, was an outdoor "pageant drama" depicting the history of the Seminole Indians in Florida. Performed from January 22 through April 17, 1955, in a new ampitheatre overlooking Tampa Bay in Safety Harbor, Florida, "Florida Aflame," was intended to stimulate tourist trade.

5. Andrew Lytle (1902–), professor at the University of the South, editor of the *Sewanee Review*, novelist, literary critic; Francis Fergusson (1929–), professor of comparative literature at Rutgers University, drama critic, author of *The Idea of a Theatre* (1949), a fundamental text in America dramatic criticism; Eudora Welty (1909–), Mississippi short story writer; Robert Chapman (1919–), drama scholar at Harvard University; Joe Wright (1918–), professor of drama and theatre director at Vanderbilt University; Alfred (1898–1957) and Milton Starr (1896–1976), owners of a chain of movie theatres, Vanderbilt connected personal friends of the Cheneys, who regarded them highly as cultivated men with a great interest in writers and artists; Peter Taylor (1917–), short story writer.

28. *To Brainard and Frances Neel Cheney from Flannery O'Connor. TLS 1p.*

Milledgeville, 18 February [19]56

Dear Lon & Fannie,

A recent communique from the [Robert] Fitzgeralds informs me they are freezing so I congratulate you on getting to and from Italy when you did. Ashley [Brown] and Tom [Carter] visited us in the worst possible weather but it is very fine again, the peachickens have eaten my Mama's first cosmus and I plan to have the first goose egg of the season for breakfast tomorrow—one goose egg for breakfast and you practically don't have to eat the rest of the day.

I have just got through reviewing a book[1] for the Diocesan rag, The Bulletin. A book of short stories from the Catholic press and I have decided the motto for fiction in the Catholic press should be: "We guarantee to corrupt nothing but your taste."

I have also just got through writing a story about a lady who gets gored by a bull.[2] I get so sick of my novel [*The Violet Bear It Away*] that I have to have some diversion.

Thanks for the ballad. I'll have to look at the Yale Review.[3] I read about the Governor's reception of the Gentleman's Committee with great glee. Here at Christmas we had a parade that Santa Claus rode in. He rode in a truck crammed full of black and white children all mixed up together. The next day somebody asked the local representative if he wasn't going to wire [Georgia] Gov. [Marvin] Griffin. "Hell no," said he, "he'd call off Christmas." So that's the way it stands around here.

Happy George Washington's Birthday.

Affectionately,
Flannery

1. *All Manner of Men*, edited by Riley Hughes (New York: P. J. Kenedy and Sons, 1956), included in *The Presence of Grace and Other Book Reviews by Flannery O'Connor*, pp. 13–14. This review was apparently the first of 120 separate reviews (of 143 titles) O'Connor wrote, between 1956 and 1964, with few exceptions for local diocesan papers.

2. "Greenleaf," first published in the *Kenyon Review*, 18 (Summer, 1956), 384–410.

3. On their excursion through West Tennessee and Mississippi "to survey the segregation situation" for Warren's *Life* magazine article, Cheney and Warren stopped at the University of Mississippi, where they listened in on a round-table discussion by eleven students. One of the students had written a ballad parody of the celebrated Till case. (Emmett Till was a young black man murdered in Mississippi in 1955. The white man accused of the crime was tried and acquitted; he later sold his story, complete with confessional details, to William Bradford Huie for a magazine article.) Frances Cheney felt that the student's poem was a parody of the Australian ballad, "Waltzing Matilda," which had received critical explication by William Powers in "Waltzing Matilda," *Yale Review*, 43 (Summer, 1954), 497–510. Cheney sent copies to several of his correspondents.

29. *To Brainard Cheney from Flannery O'Connor. TLS 2pp.*

Milledgeville, 19 February [19]56

Dear Lon,

I'm much interested in the theater idea[1] and would like to be among those present—though if there's anybody who knows nothing about the theater, it's me. Anyway, I'm always willing to assist the Fords, Guggenheims, or Rockefellers to spend their money. March and April would both be bad times for me to come as I have to give a talk in Atlanta on the 16th of March and I am supposed to spend the week of April 23rd in Michigan. Every time I try to get out of the engagement in Michigan[2] I appear to get deeper into it. The trouble is you have to write what you are going to say and that takes a lot of time.

Ashley [Brown] told us your play ["Strangers in this World"] was a great success in Louisville and sent me a picture of you and Fannie and Joy [Zibart] and the [Tennessee] Governor [Frank Clement] and some others.[3] I wish I could have seen it. Right now, we are missionary territory for a troup of Jehovah's Witnesses. They are after our D.P.s [the Matisiacks] and they arrive on Sunday morning with literature. The D. P.s bow and grin and accept the literature although they can't read it. Last week my mother met them and told them these people were Catholics and very well taken care of by their own Church; she stood by until they had departed.

I hear from a friend at Notre Dame that Russell Kirk was last seen there. At that time the Conservative Review[4] was two weeks distant—which is where it always appears to be.

Couldn't you and Fannie come down some weekend? The weather is good now and we hanker for company. Thanks for including me in the theater project and I hope the planning party will be sometime when I can come.

Affectionately,
Flannery

1. Apparently O'Connor's interest was not simply polite. She wrote to her agent, Elizabeth McKee, on March 15, 1956: "Some friends of mine in Nashville have a plan afoot for the establishment of a Provincial Theatre. I might eventually be interested in adapting some of my things for that—myself" (*The Habit of Being*, p. 146).

2. At the Lansing chapter of the AAUW. See Letter 19.

3. Photograph was probably from *The Louisville* (Kentucky) *Times*, Saturday, January 28, 1956, p. 6.

4. Title under which Russell Kirk intended to publish a magazine, actually

published under another title, *Modern Age: A Conservative Review* (see Russell Kirk, "Memoir by Humpty Dumpty," *The Flannery O'Connor Bulletin*, 8 [Autumn, 1979], 14–17).

30. *To Flannery O'Connor from Brainard Cheney. TL(cc) 1p.*

February 27, 1956

Dear Flannery:

This is to forward to you a brief statement of the theater project drawn up by Caldwell.

It seems, too, that the time and place for our planning meeting must remain uncertain until after a preliminary visit on the part of Caldwell and others to the offices of the Foundation in New York on March 20. Red [Robert Penn] Warren thinks that it may turn out that we will have to have our meeting in New York in the shadow of the Foundation offices and that they will sieze upon this opportunity to spend money in meeting us there. Personally, I will not grouse against such subsidizing.

A more decent letter will follow.

Sincerely,
Brainard Cheney

Miss Flannery O'Connor
RFD
Milledgeville, Georgia

31. *To Flannery O'Connor from Brainard Cheney. TL(cc) 1p.*

May 9, 1956

Dear Flannery:

Forgive me for being so belated in sending you notice of time and place for the playwright's theater project meeting. I only found out yesterday I was to do some notifying in the matter. If you can make it, please do by all means. I am enclosing a carbon of the letter I have just gotten out to Francis Ferguson, which will give you all the dope as I know it.[1]

The "capture" of the FUGITIVES on Vanderbilt campus was a very spectacular triumphal return of those expelled 30 years ago.[2]

We are very eager to see you and will count on your being in New York.

Sincerely,
Brainard Cheney

Miss Flannery O'Connor
RFD
Milledgeville, Georgia

1. This letter is among the Cheney correspondence in the Vanderbilt University Library archives. It details the progress of the theatre project idea (first mentioned to O'Connor in Letter 26) and informs Fergusson of a May 14, 1956, meeting in New York City between the project group members and a representative for the Rockefeller Foundation.

2. A reunion of the Nashville Fugitive poets took place May 3–5, 1956, at Vanderbilt University. See *Fugitives' Reunion: Conversations at Vanderbilt, May 3–5, 1956*, Rob Roy Purdy, ed. (Nashville: Vanderbilt University Press, 1959).

32. *To Brainard Cheney from Flannery O'Connor. TLS 1p.*

Milledgeville, 11 May [19]56

Dear Lon,

I wish I could get to the New York meeting but that is too far away for me at this point and on crutches I intend to confine myself to the rural districts. I am much interested in this project, however. Some man is supposed to be coming down here to see me who wants to talk about making some of my stories into a movie but I look on this with a chill eye.

We hope you will be planning a trip in this direction before politics begins to get hotter. I am currently entertaining two orphan-enfant/chukar quail in a box under my feet at this typewriter and it is interfering with my powers of communication.

Love to you both,
Flannery

33. *To Brainard and Frances Neel Cheney from Flannery O'Connor. TLS 1p.*

Milledgeville, 21 June [19]56

Dear Lon & Fannie,

I'll be delighted to show up on the 29th on that plane that gets in at 1:02. By now I feel like an old hand at getting up and down plane steps and as I have recently found out that crutches are to be a permanent addition, this is all very well. I'll be looking forward to seeing you and Caroline [Gordon Tate] if she makes it.

Yesterday the incubator produced the first four peachickens of this season so my sense of well-being is at its height.

Love,
Flannery

34. *To Brainard and Frances Neel Cheney from Flannery O'Connor. TLS 1p.*

Milledgeville, 3 July [19]56

Dear Lon & Fannie,

I am planning to paint, draw, or somehow perpetrate, a memorial of my visit. It will depict the buff orpington hen dining with the goose and the wren. This ought to be a natural subject for me as I have all the models in the backyard. Anyway I'll send you the results, if any, of this project. I certainly had a good time as I always do and I'll get back to my novel [*The Violent Bear It Away*] with renewed vigor after the change.

Regina was supposed to have Hedwig spend three nights with her but Miss Hedwig attended a double feature twice, a total of five hours in the local theatre, on the afternoon before she was to render this service and was thus unable to. She came over with a long vague face, Regina said, and said she felt like she was "almost going to vomit" so Regina told her to go home and do it and send Alfred.[1] Alfred is non-conversational but he loves to visit so Regina said she sat on the porch with

Alfred until she was blue in the face and finally asked him if he didn't think he ought to go up and go to bed. He said well he would but he wasn't sleepy yet, so she said well wouldn't he like something to eat and he said well what did she have. So she said she fed him for the next half hour and that made him sleepy. The next two nights she told him not to come until he was sleepy. He is fifteen. She always seems so glad to have me back.

My two Polish crested chickens jumped on her the first time she opened the door to feed them, as they have been trained to do, but she said they didn't do it twice. They looked very depressed I thought when I got back but I have about got them into shape again.

Love, and thanks again for letting me come.

Flannery

1. Hedwig and Alfred were children of Regina's tenant farmers.

35. *To Flannery O'Connor from Brainard Cheney. TL(cc) 1p.*

July 19, 1956

Dear Flannery,

Will you let your name appear on a dummy committee for the distribution of that essay of mine, A NEW "CROWN OF THORNES" FOR THE DEMOCRATIC PARTY?[1] I am also asking Caroline Tate, Ashley Brown, Tom Carter, Fanny and my sister, Lee Jessup.

I am resorting to this recourse because I was unable to get it published in a periodical before the Democratic National Convention. Either I will publish here through a local printer or through Henry Regnery, who has offered to do it for me on a cost-plus basis.

The chief reason for my using a dummy committee—which I will call the Committee for Renewing the Democratic Party, or something of the sort—is that I must publish under a soubriquet or anonymously in order not to embarrass Governor Clement before the Convention. The article is, of course, freely critical of the Democratic Party as well as the Republican Party and could prove embarrassing for him if my name was connected with it. I intend to by-line it A Life Long Democrat.

I believe you are familiar with the argument of the essay and the position I take. I don't have a copy of it at the moment, but as soon as I get it in proof form I can send you a copy, if you want to read it before getting on the committee. As you can imagine, I am in a terrible swivet in preparation for the Convention which Our Boy will keynote.[2]

Hope we can all get together after the Convention. Fanny joins me in love.

Sincerely,
Brainard Cheney

1. Cheney had tried, unsuccessfully, to publish a political essay, "A New Line of Goods for the Democrats," first in Russell Kirk's proposed *Conservative Review*, then in the *Yale Review*, and finally in the *Virginia Quarterly Review*. There was interest in the piece, but Cheney wanted it published in time to influence national politics in the election year, so he asked Kirk to help persuade Henry Regnery, the conservative publisher, to publish it in pamphlet form, at Cheney's expense.
2. Tennessee Governor Frank Clement gave the Keynote Address at the 1956 Democratic National Convention.

36. *To Brainard and Frances Neel Cheney from Flannery O'Connor. TLS 1p.*

20 July [19]56

Dear Lon & Fannie,

I'll be real pleased to have my name on the dummy committee—never been on a dummy committee before but it sounds mighty congenial. I'd love to see the essay when it's printed but I certainly don't have to see it before hand.

I'll be sitting with my ear glued to the radio when Brother Clement makes his oration. May St. Thomas balance Billy Ghrame [Graham].

After the convention, please plan to come down here. It is high time I was doing the entertaining.

Cheers,
Flannery

37. *To Frances Neel Cheney from Flannery O'Connor. TLS 1p.*

Milledgeville, 26 July [19]56

Dear Fannie,

Thanks for your word about the bull. The man down the road from us had a bull that was always getting out and running his head through the fender of the truck, couldn't stand trucks. Our bull was of a different nature—the contemplative type. His name was Paleface and he sat all day on a hill where he could look down and see the Fords go by on the highway. He is now tinned beef. We are going artificial.

Lon called up the day before we got our telephone and that afternoon I went in and tried to get him but after I had tried three times his secretary or somebody allowed as how he had been called out of town. Our telephone number is 2-5335. I run in all directions everytime I hear it ring.

Would you please tell me in your capacity of Liberryan just what encyclopedia I should buy? Is there a better one than the Britannica? I find I need me a reference set as all I have is The Book of Knowledge for 1898, containing pictures of little boys in sailor suits etc looking at the stars.

It will have to be "Pigs of Andalusia." I hope you saw Mr. Dupee's little piece in Perspective USA where he said that my mother raised hogs and I raised peacocks.[1] I tell my mother that everytime this new telephone rings and it's for her and she's not here, I am going to say "Mama's out slopping the pig," and let it go at that. She won't allow a pig, a goat, or a dog on the premises.

Love,
Flannery
F. O'C
Committee Transfusion Dem. Party

1. F.W. Dupee, "Letter From New York," *Perspectives, USA*, No. 14 (Winter, 1956), p. 154. O'Connor's "The Life You Save May Be Your Own" was published in the same issue of *Perspectives, USA*, pp. 64–75.

38. *To Flannery O'Connor from Brainard Cheney. TL(cc) 1p.*

July 27, 1956

Dear Flannery:

Here's the pamphlet that "The Committee" is distributing. I sent out 700 copies.

If, by remote chance, anybody should inquire of you who the "Life-long Democrat" is, please just say that his identity is a confidential matter until after the November election.

Many thanks.

Sincerely,
Brainard Cheney

Miss Flannery O'Connor
Milledgeville,
Georgia
Same letter to:Carolina Gordon
Ashley Brown
Tom Carter
Lee Jessup

39. *To Frances Neel Cheney from Flannery O'Connor. TLS 1p.*

Milledgeville, 19 August [19]56

Dear Fannie,

All my subconscious has come up with this past week is Prahhhshuss Lord, take my hand and lead me awnnnnn![1] Anyway this is just to extend that invitation again if you all are thinking of coming in this direction, which we certainly hope you are.

Love,
Flannery

1. Reference to the final words of the Keynote Speech made by Tennessee Governor Frank Clement at the 1956 Democratic National Convention in Chicago: "Precious Lord, take our hand. Lead us on!"

40. *To Frances Neel Cheney from Flannery O'Connor. TLS 1p.*

Milledgeville, 29 August [19]56

Dear Fannie,

Lady Irene[1] is with the compliments of Ashley [Brown]. Maybe she and Russell [Kirk] can get together when they both get back to Michigan.

We are still hoping to see you all here before school begins.

Love,
Flannery

1. Joking reference to a clipping and picture from the *Louisville* (Kentucky) *Courier,* sent to O'Connor with instructions that it be forwarded to Mrs. Cheney—apparently to poke fun at Kirk for being such an Anglophile.

41. *To Frances Neel Cheney from Flannery O'Connor. TLS 1p.*

Milledgeville, 23 September [19]56

Dear Fannie,

S. Beckett[1] seems to be able to get praise from all quarters, no matter how opposed. There was a highly praiseful review in the last Cross Currents taken from the Jesuit monthly, Etudes.[2] I would like to see it[3] for Bert Lahr[4] more than any higher reasons though.

I have just sold "The Life You Save May Be Your Own"[5] for a television play to be put on (I think) by the General Electric Playhouse.[6] People with TV sets tell me this is a program conducted by Ronald Reagan but I don't know if that means that Ronald Reagan is going to get to be Mr. Shiftlet or not. I have got my money anyway and now I am going to try and forget about it, although that is mighty hard to do, thinking all the time that R. R. may be Mr. Shiftlet and that they will probably let him and the idiot daughter live happily ever after in a Chrysler convertible. I don't know when it's going to be and I don't want to know. With the proceeds, I have bought my mother a new refrigerator, the latest model with every attachment. It spits the icecubes at you, the trays shoot out and hit you in the middle, and if you step on a button, the whole thing rolls out from the wall.

Next week I am doing a Harnet Kane[7] in Macon for the ladies of the Catholic Parish Council on the daring subject: What is a Wholesome Novel?

I have just received ten pamphlets from Ashley [Brown] about the Unity School of Christianity—prosper and be healthy through Christianity. I have a mental picture of him examining the culture of California in minute detail.[8]

Let us hear from you when you have time and we still hope you'll get in this direction this fall. I hope the Tennessee Repertory Theatre prospers?[9]

Love,
Flannery

1. Samuel Beckett (1906-), Irish-born French novelist, playwright, poet.
2. Review by Raoul Josbin of the original version of Beckett's play, "Waiting for Godot," in *Cross Currents: A Quarterly Review to Explore the Implications of Christianity for Our Times*, 6 (Summer, 1956), 204–07. Originally appeared in the Jesuit monthly, *Etudes*, July, 1953.
3. "Waiting for Godot."
4. The Broadway production of "Waiting for Godot," which opened April 19, 1956, starred Bert Lahr and E. G. Marshall.
5. O'Connor's short story, originally published in the *Kenyon Review*, 15 (Spring, 1953), 195–207; included in *A Good Man In Hard to Find and Other Stories*.
6. O'Connor sold the television rights to the story to Revue Productions (*The Habit of Being*, p. 175). The CBS-TV film adaptation, on "Playhouse of Stars," starred Gene Kelly, Agnes Moorehead, and Janice Rule, and was broadcast on March 1, 1957.
7. Harnett Thomas Kane (1910-) was a Louisiana journalist, novelist, and writer of non-fiction books about his home state.
8. Brown was an instructor at The University of California, Santa Barbara, 1956–59.
9. See Letters 27, 29–32.

42. *To Flannery O'Connor from Brainard Cheney. TL(cc) 2pp.*

1221 Eighteenth Avenue, So., Nashville, Tenn.,
October 14, 1956

Dear Flannery,

We tried to make a sortie upon the TV world to see "THE LIFE YOU SAVE etc." but somehow got the wrong cue.

We were most disappointed—but maybe not as much as we would have been, if we had seen what they *dun to it*. Anyhow, we hope you got your price and that the refrigerator is all it was represented to be.

Yep, I know about that Unity School of Christianity. I am the ghost for a projected volume on Clement and his religion, to be called something like GOD IS MY PARTNER (though I think somebody has already beat us to that title) and the publisher has sent me a whole armload of the magazine put out by UNITY. It is called, GOOD BUSINESS. It pretty well puts grace on a per centage basis and, as you might say, God in the sky co-pilot's cockpit.

Your recklessly made invitation to *drop by* your mamma's house (and working hideout) is about to catch [up] with you. This is a WARNING. As soon after the General Election voting day (November 6th) as possible, I am departing this world (politics) for So. Ga. and the turn of the century to pitch a long threatened novel and will call upon you at or near Milledgeville—especially to learn about "What Is A Wholesome Novel," among other things—because I want this one to be wholesome. Also, I (and Fannie with me) want very much to see you.

I will tell you all about the TENNESSEE THEATER'S mishaps and prospects when I see you.

I will say that our Gatlinburg appearance before the PTA state board was a complete flop, but we have realigned our forces and are now taking a different tack.

Looks like the Democrats are going to be an uncomfortably close second runner this time. I shouldn't admit that I am not convinced that we are not going to win. But I console myself with the hope that maybe it would be just as well and mabe the *peepul* will appreciate us more when they do get democracy back in the saddle—and maybe we will appreciate being back in the saddle more—though that is a lot to hope for. It is even more extravagant to hope that we may begin to see what we need so much to begin to see—and that is a bigger-better Party is not going to be able to give us a bigger-better means toward future ends that it does not even admit the existance of—of—of—ff—oo!

In these days it's hard to be a Democrat—about the only thing that makes it possible for me to be a Democrat is to think of trying to become a Republican.

It helps, too, to think about the STATES RIGHTERS.

We have been talking to some UNITARIANS tonight: nice people—and honest, but young, and religiously very blank.

I am a sodden sinner—this isn't a confession, it's a chronic state that I only half work at. Mercy, Mercy, mercy—we're so black down South—and I'm blacker than most people in Tennessee, because I come from Ga.

I'm also lazy. But I hope to get out of that some by going on the wagon and steaming myself up for this 30-day spree on the whywho—of course I've grown pretty doubtful about myself—I was, it seems so wrong in my last abortive effort! But then I was also damned, then! We send our love—and your wonderful mother, too.

Lon

43. *To Brainard and Frances Neel Cheney from Flannery O'Connor. TLS 1p.*

Milledgeville, 18 October [19]56

Dear Lon & Fannie,

We are much cheered to hear that you are actually going to enter Georgia. Plan to spend the night or the week-end or whatever suits you with us and we will all mourn the near miss of the Democrats together. I signed off paying any attention to it after the Prachas Lord speech and am just waiting for another four years.

Unfortunately I don't know what a wholesome novel is either; I am never informed on the subjects I discuss. I did tell them that the average Catholic reader was a Militant Moron. They sat there like a band of genteel desperados and never moved a face muscle. I might have been saying the rosary to them.

The award from the Georgia Writers[1] consists of a "handsome scroll with the achievement award *seal*" on the bottom of it. This is like the Good Housekeeping Seal of Approval. The harmful effects of my work have been found to be less than 1% and now no patriotic Georgian need feel any danger in reading it.

You haven't missed that television program yet as it hasn't been yet, but I certainly hope to miss it myself. They tell me it will be either on the GE program or the Schlitz Beer program. I think the Schlitz Beer would be more in keeping.

We are both looking forward to your visit. Just drop us a card when.

Love,
Flannery

1. The Georgia Writers' Association Annual Award.

44. *To Flannery and Regina O'Connor from Brainard Cheney. TLS(cc) 1p.*

Lumber City, Ga., December 3, 1956

Dear Flannery and Regina,

Never such comprehensive succor and solace before extended me in one week-end! Soul and body! And however short I may have fallen of my opportunity for feasting my soul, I more than made up for in a bodily fashion. Even this evening I was still on soup: I've neither needed nor wanted a meal since I quit Andalusia Farms.

Too, I enjoyed so much our tour of town and country!

If you will pardon my dull way of always bringing shop talk into my letters on practically any subject or occasion, Flannery, I would like to offer a footnote. It is only that I can never remember these things when I am discussing my efforts—especially when I've made a bull, as I did on the beginning of Chapter One of IBMBTTO.[1] Originally I had begun it with action (ie, dialog) but perceiving that I wanted the accent to be not on the subject matter of the meeting but on the ritual, this steps attitude became a sign. And I fell into the error of trying to substitute attitude for action, without even realizing it! Until you pointed it out. And I think you entirely right in suggesting, that I begin with the preliminary action of

Adam, bringing him to the foot of the steps. Thanks no end!

As ever,
Lon

1. IBMBTTO was an acronym for "I Bent My Back to the Oppressor," Cheney's working title for the novel which became *This Is Adam* (New York: McDowell-Obolensky, 1958).

45. *To Brainard Cheney from Flannery O'Connor. TLS 1p.*

Wednesday, Milledgeville [December 1956]

Dear Lon,

We hope you'll stop by for the night or a meal anyway or whatever is convenient on your way back to Nashville. I'd like to keep up with IBMBTTO and hope you'll let me see it again. Your visit was not only enjoyable for both of us (me & Regina) but profitable for me as I have made a new ending onto my story[1]—that I think is better—giving the old man time to realize that he's not getting anywhere fast.

Tomorrow I have to go to Macon to give a talk at Wesleyan [College] and after that I will go back to my own long haul.

Cheers and please try to stop by again.
Flannery

1. "A View of the Woods," subsequently published in the *Partisan Review*, 24 (Fall, 1957), 475–96.

46. *To Brainard and Frances Neel Cheney from Flannery O'Connor. TLS 1p.*

Milledgeville, 3 January [19]57

Dear Lon & Fannie,

I was mighty sorry that I couldn't get up or you all down last weekend but I did enjoy talking to you over the telephone. I meant to inquire for IBMBTTO but the telephone disorganizes me. Anyway, I hope it enjoys a prosperous new year.

If you all have the stomach for it, you can view "The

Life You Save May Be Your Own" on the Schlitz Playhouse of Stars, Friday, Feb. 1st[1] at 9:30 P.M. New York time but something else your time. Starring Brother Gene Kelly. Who announces that there will be no singing and dancing in this but that he is going to ACT, a thing which he has had no opportunity to do in the movies. He also says, "the story is a kind of hill billy thing in which I play a guy who *befriends* a deaf mute girl in the hills of Kentucky." Underlining mine. Another announcement described it as "Flannery O'Connor's backwoods love story." I don't know whether I should see this thing or not but my mother insists we are going to and she has notified all the kin and I know they are going to think that the TV version is much better than the original.

The enclosed Christmas card came from the Georgia Trappist monastery [at Conyers] and made me think of Fannie.

Affectionately,
Flannery

1. Actually, March 1, 1957.

47. *To Frances Neel Cheney from Flannery O'Connor. TLS 1p.*

Milledgeville, 7 January [19]57

Dear Fannie,

I'll love having the missal[1] and will write Norman Berg[2] today. I had thought that sometime I would meet him at some of the Grim Functions I attend in Atlanta but he always manages to escape them. I asked one girl whose editor he is why he wasn't at the Ga. Writer's Asso. Meeting and she said, with pride, "*He* wouldn't be found dead here."

I haven't heard from Caroline [Gordon Tate] in ages but none of the reports of her are very happy.[3]

My mother said your description of Ashley [Brown] was superb. (I hadn't thought she had looked at him that hard.) I hope he's recovered, but this is a bad time for colds. I have lost seven peachickens in the last six weeks.

The most intelligent one just didn't come down out of the tree one morning. He sat up there all day and at sunset, he dropped off the limb, dead. That one had imagination.

Thanks for the congratulations[4]—I figure they have to get around to everybody eventually and now I am off the list.

Cheers,
Flannery

1. Perhaps the *Parish Holy Week Missal,* Leonard J. Doyle, ed. (Collegeville, Minnesota: Doyle and Finegan, 1956), which is among O'Connor's journals and magazines in the Flannery O'Connor Room at Georgia College (see *Flannery O'Connor's Library: Resources of Being,* p. 81).

2. Norman Berg was an editor for the MacMillan Publishing Company; he was MacMillan's Atlanta representative.

3. A reference to the marital troubles of Caroline Gordon and Allen Tate.

4. For the 1956 Georgia Writers' Association Award.

48. *To Flannery O'Connor from Brainard Cheney. TL(cc) 1p.*

1221 18th A.S., Nashville, Sunday, [January] Thirteenth [1957]

Dear Flannery,

Congratulations on getting some measure of your just dues in the two short story collections of the year[1]—I see by Richmond Beatty's column[2] that you are one of three to make both collections!

The [seeds] of your polite conversation are now about to be reaped by you in grim sheaves of paper!

Herewith are the three chapters I did down in Georgia on that novel (IBMBTTO). I finally edited and copied them. I haven't been able yet to get going again—too much interference, but I'm still optimistic.

The first chapter is still not good, but I hope roughly what I am aiming at. It won't get written finally til the last one is done, anyhow.

To repeat, briefly: I plan to use the ritual at the steps between Lucy Hightower and Adam Atwell as a rhythm of sorts throughout the book, ending with it, I hope, for a total significance. I hope 250 pages will do it: the present action to take place over a spring, summer and fall—Adam to become the Christian hero; but Lucy is light, as well as the object of his anima, sublimated. Her story is that of the exile who finally rejects her return, rejects in triumph.

Do hope we can get to see each other again before long!

Right rough season for me just now—but things will get better.

F. joins me in love.

As ever,

1. For "Greenleaf," in *Prize Stories 1957: The O. Henry Awards,* Paul Engle and Constance Urdang, eds. (Garden City: Doubleday, 1957) and in *The Best American Short Stories of 1957,* Martha Foley, ed. (Boston: Houghton Mifflin, 1957).

2. Richmond Croom Beatty's January 13, 1957, book review column, "Under the Green Lamp," in the Nashville *Tennessean.*

49. *To Brainard Cheney from Flannery O'Connor. TLS 1p.*

Milledgeville, Georgia, 16 January [19]57

Dear Lon,

I have just finished reading these three chapters and I certainly think you ought to be pleased with what you have done. The 2nd and 3rd chapters are wonderful. The farther you get into this, the more your writing seems to relax and become natural sounding. I would forget about the first chapter until the rest of it is written. Right now it (the first chapter) seems to me to suffer from what must be a "thematic preoccupation" on your part, but it seems a lot better than it was when I read it here. I reckon that when you think too much about this from the thematic angle, your images get over-extended and flamboyant, but when you just have your mind on what is happening at present, then you get everything down there right. If you keep on like you are going, I think the whole thing should turn out just right. I hope politics won't interfere with this novel, and when you get some more done, I'd love to see it.

A letter from the Fitzgeralds say that Robt. is about to come over to take the Chair of Poetry at Notre Dame for the 2nd semester—I gather this is what Allen [Tate] let drop OR SOMETHING.

I have been busy writing an article for AMERICA,[1]

which I feel very silly writing but which was requested. Supposed to be about 1800 words on the subject of the Church and the fiction writer, which is something you can't say anything about in 1800 words, but nevertheless, I try.

Thank Fannie for sending the missal to me. I wrote Norman Berg a letter and thanked him.

My mamma is thinking about getting herself a Hungarian family. If she does, we will have a mighty elaborate mixture [of tenants and farm help].

I wish my novel [*The Violent Bear It Away*] were coming as good as yours.

Cheers,
Flannery

1. "The Church and the Fiction Writer," *America*, 96 (March 30, 1957), 733–35.

50. *To Brainard and Frances Neel Cheney from Flannery O'Connor. ALS 1p.*

Tuesday [1957]

Dear Lon & Fannie,

If you all have the stomachs for it, you can view the TV adaptation of "The Life You Save" on the Schlitz Playhouse of Stars on Friday night, March 1. I am convinced it will be nothing you'll recognize.

The displaced person [Mr. Matisiack] has just quit and we are in the market for some good country people.

I am thinking of going to Notre Dame to talk on the 15th of April. Robt. [Fitzgerald] seems to think you all may be there???

Affect—
Flannery

51. *To Brainard and Frances Neel Cheney from Flannery O'Connor. TLS 1p.*

Milledgeville, Georgia, 5 March [19]57

Dear Lon and Fannie,

Robert has made a reservation for me at the Morris

Inn for Sunday April 14. I wish I could come to Nashville and go up with you all but I think that would be too much of a trip for me. By the time I got ready to give that talk on Monday, I would be done already wo' out. He says he will meet me in Chicago Sunday afternoon, the talk is Monday afternoon and I'll leave early Tuesday morning. I am mighty glad you all are going and I hope this is the same hotel you'll be at. Robert said it was right next to the campus.

I want to go look at all them Cathlick interleckchuls as you don't often see none around here.

Cheers,
Flannery

52. *To Brainard and Frances Neel Cheney from Flannery O'Connor. TLS 1p.*

Milledgeville, 13 March [19]57

Dear L&F,

Well I feel as if I will be bringing my own audience with me to Notre Dame. In every dead silence I will certainly expect you to stomp and cheer. I am only used to idiot audiences so this is going to be rather a strain on me. I wrote Robt. and told him I would come if they weren't expecting me to be W. K. Wimsatt Jr.[1] or somebody. Robt. allowed it should be aimed to fit the student mentality so I feel a little better about it. At all the Methodist and Baptist institutions that I normally talk at around here, I quote St. Thomas prodigiously and as the audience is never too sure who he is, it is always much impressed. I am going to have to think of a new angle for this occasion.

I stood the tv show a good deal better than I am standing taking the local congratulations for it. Every old lady in town has told me how sweet she thought it was and one old lady said, "That story really made me think!" I didn't ask her what. Everybody around here thinks I have arrived at last.

Don't speak ill of the Book of Knowlege.[2] I grew up on a 19th century edition of it that had belonged to my grandmamma when she was a little girl. I particularly remember the illustrations about a young man of about six in a sailor suit and round hat. He stood on a wharf and watched a ship come in. In each illustration the ship was bigger. He therefore came to the conclusion that the world was round. He did this without assistance. I was mighty impressed and will never forget the Book of Knowlege. I reckon it's deteriorated though.

Our D.P. [displaced person, Mr. Matisiack] has gone and we are fixed up with some PWT [Poor White Trash] and it is a big relief. English is flowing freely for the first time in three years.

According to Ashley [Brown], Russell [Kirk] is now going to get out a quarterly.[3]

Affectionately,
Flannery

1. William Kurtz Wimsatt, Jr. (1907–75), prominent literary theorist, critic, scholar.
2. See Letter 37.
3. See Letter 29, note 4.

53. *To Flannery O'Connor from Brainard Cheney. TL(cc) 1 p.*

Smyrna, Saturday night: June 22, [19]57. (Address still: 1221 18th a.s., Nashville)

Dear Flannery,

It's been a long time since we've had any communication! I don't know who owes who what, in the turnabout of correspondence—but it's been a long time.

When our plans to get to Notre Dame failed we were so disappointed that we fell into silence. We seemed all at once to run out of both time and money, what with my being sick for a week and our paying out more than we expected on renovating the house and our income tax.

We had thought to have a housewarming come June, with you here to occupy your renovated quarters, etc. The hitch has been we haven't been able to get the contractor to quite finish up and get out. Now he has actually got the renovation of the two rooms about complete, but we also got him to do some ménding on the rest of the house:

screens, window blinds, mend windows, etc. And we can't seem to get him going.

Now we have suddenly discovered that the Village [of Smyrna, Tennessee] is going to get gas after all (by mid October) and we must get the heating man started putting in central heat! It looks like the summer is going to be consumed in renovation, too!

But we are not going to wait til all of the mending is done to have you up for a week-end and a party—if we can get You here?

How are things going? We are so eager to have word of you. We have seen no close friends in so long! How comes the novel [*The Violent Bear It Away*]?

I put Fannie on the plane this am for Kansas City, where she will remain til next Saturday, being a "power" in the politics of the A.L.A. [American Library Association], and, I suppose, lobbying (as we would call it in my trade) for the interests of Peabody [College].

Last evening a McDowell Obolenski man[1] was in N. [Nashville] for dinner with us and we saw the jacket for Andrew Lytle's new novel—it looked fine. Title: THE VELVET HORN, which, to me, has a more interesting sound that its allusion actually lives up to.

Had a trip to Lexington, Ky., here with Red [Robert Penn] Warren a couple of weeks ago and it was a delight, to be sure: he was looking at caves.[2] Incidentally he read the stuff I had rough[ed] up on my novel [*This Is Adam*]—if I had had any pride of authorship at all I wouldn't have let him see it in the shape it was in—I hadn't even read it over myself. He stomached it, however, and gave me some sound corrective advice—I had let the biographical material take me a little off course and was suffering some from its private content for me.

I have revised and am here (in the country by myself, in hope of getting it read and edited in the next couple of days.) When I get it in shape, would you be long-suffering enough to read it for me? There will be roughly 150 pages of it—ten chapters, I believe—of which you've already seen the first three.

When I get it in shape, I think I may send it to my

agent and see what she can do about getting me a contract—and even an advance! If I had a couple of thousand advance, I'd take off three months and finish it. It is so frustrating to work as I am trying to work now.

How about a visit with us around the middle of July? I'm sure we'll have this place habitable by then.

Lytle and his family should be in the neighborhood sometime soon.

F. joins me in love,

as ever,
lon

1. David McDowell, of publishing company McDowell-Obolensky.
2. In preparation for Warren's novel, *The Cave* (New York: Random House, 1959).

54. *To Brainard Cheney from Flannery O'Connor. TLS 1p.*

Milledgeville, 24 June [19]57

Dear Lon,

I'll be highly insulted if you don't send me those 150 pages to read when you get them ready. You are making progress with it all right. I have been making a little progress with mine [*The Violent Bear It Away*] lately but nothing like any 150 pages. If I could just get me 150 pages I'd feel like I was at least going to have a novel sooner or later.

David McDowell [of McDowell-Obolensky publishing company] said he'd send me a copy of Andrew Lytle's novel [*The Velvet Horn*]. I read the galleys for Robie Macauley's stories which they are going to bring out. That book is going to be called The End of Pity and there are some mighty good stories in it.[1]

Since my mama's D. P.s [displaced persons, the Matisiacks] left, we have been enduring the trials of poorwhite trash to such an extent that she has about decided to convert to beef. We got rid of the last tribe a few weeks back after finding out that the man was selling milk out of the cans between here and Eatonton and also taking the gas out of the truck and selling that and suchlike antics. Now she has no help but the negroes and as she says they have to mind her and she has to mind them so they get along peaceably. They live across the road but come over here every night and spend the night and also cook over here—but they keep up the other establishment for social purposes.

July is going to be a bad month for me to go anywhere as we are going to be swamped with visiting kin and at the end of the month I have to go to Athens to give a lecture to the old girls at a writer's conference. The last time I did this one old soul said, "Will you give me the technique for the frame-within-a-frame shortstory?" Anyway, maybe we can get together, if not in July in August. What are the odds for your getting down here? We'd certainly love you to come and have plenty of room as the visiting kin always elect to stay in town with Sister [O'Connor's aunt].

I forget if I wrote you about my Notre Dame visit. Anyway, it was very pleasant. Robert [Fitzgerald] met me in Chicago and Tom Stritch[2] met me and Robert in South Bend. I liked Tom Stritch very much. He wrote me a few weeks ago that he had just put Robert on the plane for eventually Milan. Poor Robert had to rush back to move all the little Fitzgeralds to their summer castle. The audience for the lecture was mostly graduate students and their wives with a sprinkling of seminarians who looked like football players in the wrong costume. Your and Fannie's presence would have added greatly to my cheer.

Does anybody ever hear from Caroline [Gordon Tate]? It was good to hear from you and do not neglect to send me the novel when you get ready.

Affectionately,
Flannery

1. New York: McDowell-Obolensky, 1957.

2. "Thomas Stritch was one of Flannery O'Connor's most cherished friends. He was, as well, a friend of the Cheneys and of the Fitzgeralds. Flannery greatly enjoyed his company, and he was the one who in a sense introduced her to the pleasure to be found in music, when he sent her a large number of records from his own vast collection, very late in her life. Tom was the nephew of an eminent American ecclesiastic, Cardinal Stritch of Chicago, and a mainstay for decades at Notre Dame, where he held a Chair in Communications. A Tennessean, he was also appealing to her by reason of his Southernness, even though he had lived in

Indiana for many years" (letter from Sally Fitzgerald to the editor, December 28, 1984). There are numerous references to Tom Stritch throughout *The Habit of Being.*

55. *To Brainard Cheney from Flannery O'Connor. TLS 1p.*

9 July [19]57

Dear Lon,

I think this [Cheney's novel] couldn't be coming better. You have really got the relationship between Adam and Mrs. Hightower in there in a concrete way, without stating it, and that's what you want to do.

Only one or two things occurred to me: that scene where Adam faces the men in Duke's office seems to me to happen too quickly. I mean he gets there too quick. It seems to me that could stand some kind of preparation because it's a very important scene. If it were led up to a little slower, the reader'd realize the importance of it more.

Then occasionally you seem to let the omniscient narrator talk like Adam (He was filled with wonderment etc) or at least it seems to be the omniscient narrator; anyway there's some confusion about who it is. Caroline [Gordon Tate] is always telling me that when the om. nar. talks like anyone of the characters or uses colloquialisms that you lower the tone. When you get through with this, I'd go through it with an eye to such things as it would improve the quality of the writing.

Also, occasionally there is an image that sticks out and becomes too noticeable. Such as those freckles standing out as if on stems. Maybe my literal imagination but I keep seeing the stems. It's too much. Also the one about his mouth being as tight as the door of a dutch oven or something. I don't know what the door of a dutch oven looks like but no matter that image don't work. This is not the kind of book that will depend on such things so anything like that that sticks out, I'd just remove it. When in doubt, operate, according to Dr. O'Connor. Which may be why she can't accumulate more words on her own behalf.

I think the new title[1] is probably better than the other. Anyway I think you have nothing to worry about with this novel. It is on the way at a great rate.

We have just bought a Santa Gertrudis bull and he is expected at the end of next week. My mamma looks forward to the day when she will be in the beef business. For a while she will have to be in the dairy business right on but at least we have the foundation now for the other. All the Santa Gertrudis I have seen are so impressive as to be plumb overwhelming. We are just hoping he will stay on the place. A man was here the other day who he [*sic*] had a bull that you couldn't keep in the federal penitentiary.

We are expecting Ashley [Brown] Saturday and wish you all were coming too. Any time you can make it, we want you to come.

Affectionately,
Flannery

1. After "I Bent My Back to the Oppressor," Cheney experimented with "A Soft Answer" and "Long was the Furrow" before deciding on *This Is Adam.*

56. *To Frances Neel Cheney from Flannery O'Connor. TLS 1p.*

19 July [19]57

Dear Fannie,

Nymphettes scare me to death; however, I enclose a variation on the theme, which should be read carefully and meditated on. I particularly like the fact that this girl's measurements are the same as Gina Lollabrigida's but she is only 5 feet 2; also that she writes poetry; and that nothing so far has got her down.[1]

Cheers,
Flannery

1. According to Mrs. Cheney (in a January 28, 1985, interview in Smyrna, Tennessee, with the editor), "We had both read Nabokov's *Lolita* [Paris: Olympia Press, 1955] and 'nymphettes' was a frequent word in our vocabulary. I believe she enclosed a newspaper clipping." The newspaper clipping, an article from *The Atlanta Journal and Constitution Magazine* ("Jill Is a Big Girl Now," by Olive Ann Burns), was about Jill Pepper Feldser, a precocious Atlanta girl who, at the age of two, had been taken to Hollywood to become a movie star and who now, at eighteen, wanted to sing on Broadway.

57. *To Brainard Cheney from Flannery O'Connor. TLS 1p.*

13 August [19]57

Dear Lon,

I wish I could get up to NY to swell your ranks for the Rockerfellers[1] but it would be too much for me. I don't favor NY in August. The pollen comes in there August 15 and don't leave for three weeks. It seems to me I had some letters once from John Marshall about what I had done with my Rockerfeller money, etc., but I didn't realize he was the man that gave it out. Anyway, keep me posted how it turns out; and if you all are to be seeing Miss Caroline [Gordon Tate] give her my best. And when you get through with this trip we hope you'll be coming to Georgia.

I recently sat next to Ralph McGill at a luncheon and he asked about you all. I had to go to a thing called The Southern Writers' Conference in Athens. It was about as Southern as the southern part of Madison Avenue.

How is the novel [*This Is Adam*]? Mine [*The Violent Bear It Away*] is somewhat better than usual so I am trying to stick with it. I saw Walter Sullivan's[2] unfavorably reviewed in the NYTBR [*New York Times Book Review*] this week but it sounds as if the movies might be the place for it.

Keep us posted.

Affectionately,
Flannery

1. Reference is to Cheney's continuing effort to get funding for the Tennessee theatre project. See Letters 27, 29–32, 41.

2. Novel by Vanderbilt University professor Walter Sullivan, *Sojourn of a Stranger* (New York: Holt, Rinehart and Winston, 1957).

58. *To Flannery O'Connor from Brainard Cheney. TL(cc) 2pp.*

November 4, 1957

Dear Flannery:

Pardon my use of dictation as a method of getting a letter written to you. And also the semi-official look it will have.

We have been thinking about you practically daily and talking about you, but we haven't gotten around to doing much else. We had a rather harrassing summer because we never did actually get into the house at Smyrna. However, we have finally got it complete and have begun occupancy—in an off-and-on manner.

The new natural gas heating system works. Believe it or not, those 12-feet ceiling rooms can be heated.

Also, your bedroom, which is now where the old kitchen used to be and adjacent to the downstairs bathroom and connected with it. And if I do say so, it's quite the fanciest room we ever put together. We do hope you'll like it. And we're all set to have room-warming rites and ceremonies.

But before I go any further, listen to this. It's all set for a Yuletide house party composed of yourself, Allen and Caroline Tate and James Waller,[1] who will be in and out (he will have to spend some of the time with his brother in Nashville), but we won't take *no* for an answer. The house will be in full readiness for the occasion with adequate heat and other supplies. We have heard recently from Caroline, who is still counting strong on this get together. And I intend to write Allen to refresh his mind in a few days. But he was the one to suggest it in the first place, so I am counting on his being here.

It looks like McDowell, Obolensky is going to bring out my novel that's in the making: THIS IS ADAM. At any rate, they've agreed to advance me $1000 to finish it on. I'm aiming at getting going on it the first of the year. My time between now and Christmas is so much committed already that I don't suppose I could get started earlier.

I am eager to have news of how work goes on your novel. And what the news is with you, your mother and the other members of the family.

Fannie joins me in love.

As ever,
Brainard Cheney

1. James Muir Waller (1900–71), a long-time friend of the Cheneys, was an economics professor at the University of Georgia. Waller graduated from Vanderbilt University in 1922 and had many friends among the Agrarians, the

"Twelve Southerners" who published the symposium, *I'll Take My Stand* (1930); he contributed an essay, "America and Foreign Trade," to a second symposium of Agrarians and others who favored a decentralized economic and political structure, *Who Owns America?*, Herbert Agar and Allen Tate, eds. (Boston: Houghton-Mifflin, 1936).

59. *To Brainard and Frances Neel Cheney from Flannery O'Connor. TLS 1p.*

Milledgeville, 6 November [19]57

Dear Lon & Fannie,

I have been just before writing you to ask what chance there was of you being in this neighborhood this season—as I remember that last year about this time you were hereabouts. We were wondering if you all couldn't get down for Thanksgiving? My Canada goose got so mean we had to wring his neck and he is now in the deepfreeze waiting on us to have the proper company to serve him. He nearly broke my wrist and I said: This rascal has bit me for the last time. I have made up for his loss by buying myself three Chinese geese. They just came today and are very odd looking, but their dispositions seem calm. Anyway, consider coming to help us eat the other one.

The Christmas get-together sounds fine to me if the Lord is willing when the time comes. I have an Asian flu shot in me so I expect to remain hale.

That is certainly fine about the $1000 to finish the novel and that is a lot of advance so they must think highly of it. I have laid off mine for a short spell while I write a story ["The Enduring Chill"]. The story is not so hot but it is like a vacation in the mountains to me.

The latest item with us is that my wealthy 88 year old cousin in Savannah wants to give my mother and me a pilgrimage to Rome this spring. The Monsignor from the Savannah diocese is conducting it and my cousin is determined we shall go. My mother is all for it. I am not so sure I can stand it—17 days of Holy Exhaustion—but I suppose this is the only way I'll ever get there. My mother and me facing Europe will be just like Mr. Head and

Nelson facing Atlanta.[1] Culture don't affect me none and my religion is better served at home; but I see plenty of comic possibilities in this trip. We are to stop in Dublin, London, Paris, Lourds, Rome and Lisbon long enough to smell them. I'll hope to see the [Robert] Fitzgeralds.

My book of stories just came out in England.[2] The publisher changed the name of it to The Artificial Nigger and on the jacket there's a picture of a giant granit African being tortured or something.

Let us hear from you and do plan to come to see us.

Love,
Flannery

1. O'Connor's characters in "The Artificial Nigger."
2. *The Artificial Nigger and Other Tales* (same contents as *A Good Man Is Hard to Find and Other Stories*. [London: Neville Spearman Company, 1957]).

60. *To Frances Neel Cheney from Flannery O'Connor. TLS 1p.*

Milledgeville, 17 November [19]57

Dear Fannie,

We wish you all could come but if any other time comes up that you could, please let us know.

Right now we are recuperating from a little wind last Thursday that took about all the roof off the barn and several out-buildings. Beinst neither my parent or me or any of the help landed in nearby trees, we are very thankful. Also my mother figures she will gain on the insurance as some of the roofs would have fallen in if they hadn't been blown off. She's an accomplished seer of the bright side.

I would be much obliged if you would jot down on the enclosed card whatever address Caroline [Gordon Tate] is currently receiving mail at. I have the 145 Ewing St. but that doesn't seem to reach her.

Edified by the clipping. The best one I have seen lately was a report of a talk a gentleman in Atlanta from the telephone company gave to the Young Business Men's League on the necessity for the liberal arts in education.

The liberal arts was about people, he said, and it was *people who did business.*

Cheers,
Flannery

61. *To Brainard and Frances Neel Cheney from Flannery O'Connor. TLS 1p.*

Milledgeville, 10 December [19]57

Dear Lon & Fannie,

I was fully counting on coming until a few days ago when I began to get dizzy. Investigation proved that I had got an overdose of the new medicine I am taking and it will be some time before this wears off and the dose can get regulated. This is the latest one out—Medrol, a great improvement over the last and worth experimenting around on. However, I wish it didn't have to come at Christmas. Anyhow, I am sending a fruitcake in my place and possibly a story ["The Enduring Chill"] also, that I have in production right now, and would like yr. opinion on.

I was going to bring you some peacock feathers to go against your yellow walls. I think they are too long to mail. Next year I will have 7 cocks shedding tails instead of one and I should be able to go into some kind of business. My mother claims the feathers we have sitting around create moths. I claim they do not. Impasse.

She is currently taking Jack, the colored milker, to the dentist everyday to get his new teeth fitted, or to get the impressions made for them. He told the dentist he didn't want anything but "pearly white teeth." The dentist asked him what did he mean by pearly white and he said he meant he wanted them like the pearl on the handle of a pistol; also he wanted a gold crown on the front. Regina tried to talk him out of it because it would cost him fifteen dollars extra for a gold crown, but he said he wouldn't spend his money for no ordinary looking teeth. So it is arranged for them to be pearly white and one gold crown near the front. We are as anxious for them to come as he is.

I hope you all will have a fine Christmas and am distressed I'm not going to get to see you.

Affectionately,
Flannery

62. *To Flannery O'Connor from Brainard Cheney. TL(cc) 1p.*

Cold Chimneys, Smyrna, Tennessee, January 2, 1958

Dear Flannery,

Your new pages for THE ENDURING CHILL[1] came after Caroline [Gordon Tate] and Allen [Tate] had departed, bearing with them the mss. of the story. C. took it along to have at hand when she wrote you her more detailed criticism—including the suggestions of others.

The revisions, as read separately seemed in line with what we were suggesting. But it would be too much to attempt a judgment, without rereading the whole story.

I am forwarding the pages you sent us on to Caroline as of this morning. Would have done it sooner, but we have been in a swivet getting Fannie moved back to town and me *redistributed* in the country. Too I had a hard couple of days to put in again at the office, before signing off for my two months leave.

I might disclose, too, that my writing just at this moment, is due to the fact that I fired a fell [*sic*] back this morning, when I tried to begin reading over my novel mss. [*This Is Adam*]. I found that I still have not recovered from my Christmas indulgence (I suppose that's it) plus a congenital inhibition at warming up on a cold manuscript. I am putting the awful moment off til afternoon.

Too, I plan to lunch with Tommie Stritch—so I have come back into town for that.

Again, we all missed you so much! But here's for blessed New Year with successes of all sorts. And, for ours, the hope that we do get to see you before too long.

As ever,

1. See Letter 66, note 1.

63. *To Flannery O'Connor from Brainard Cheney. TL(cc) 1p.*

Cold Chimneys, Smyrna, Tenn., Feb. 5, 1958

Dear Flannery,

'Tis a hope that things gang glee with thee! (To make what use I can of my rusty scotch!)

'Tis a hope wi' method i' the madness.

For instance are you busy preparing for your European tour?

Or are you making tracks on your novel and don't want to be bothered?

Or are you feeling the weight of years, worries and waggrambraus and don't want to be bothered?

Or you?

If ye be, say so quick—

For wee Lonnie and Fannie have a mind to pop ye a call—if 'tis convenient?

Please be candid and speak freely, or we'll be terribly hurt.

But if you have nothing better to do, come February 15 (Saturday) and 16 (Sunday) coming, we would so love to come down and see you?

I haven't asked the schedule yet. We can let you know more exact, when we find out if it suits.

I have been going great guns on a rough first draft of THIS IS ADAM. (I took off Sat.-Sun. and overrelaxed, if you know what I mean—and I am just now out of it again). As long as I think I am going where I am aiming for and doing it well enough to pass muster first blush reading, why I'm moving full-steam-ahead. It is my enthusiastic hope (and probably very incautious of me to voice it) to have finished the unread rough draft by the date mentioned above. It won't be ready to see the light of day then. But I hope to spend the last two weeks giving the mss. a cold reading. Before I call on my friends to help me get it in shape.

Caroline [Gordon Tate] writes me that she [is] trying to advise you with that last short story, THE ENDURING COLD ["The Enduring Chill"]—is sure you are going to bring it off, but feels it baffling. I think it is a terrific story—and I sure hope [it] is going well?

Fannie joins me in love to you and Regina both.

As ever,

64. *To Brainard and Frances Neel Cheney from Flannery O'Connor. TLS 1p.*

Milledgeville, 8 February [19]58

Dear Lon & Fannie,

Well cheers! I don't believe it but we will absolutely be expecting you on the 15th. Let me know what hour of the day you will arrive so I will know how many geese and steers to take outen the deepfreeze. This is great and I hope the weather will be an improvement on what it is this minute. Last night the wind blew open the gates and I woke up to hear a horse calling me from the front steps. The other morning we looked out the window and found a neighbor's mule drinking out of the bird bath. All this has set my mother into action and she is at the moment out supervising the building of a cattle gap with hollow tile.

I hope you'll bring Adam [*This Is Adam*] along with you. As for me I am making progress on the story ["The Enduring Chill"] but I don't speck it is finished yet. It is much improved however.

We are both certainly looking forward to this long-awaited visit. Will you be driving or what?

More & extended cheers,
Flannery

65. *To Brainard and Frances Neel Cheney from Flannery O'Connor. PCS.*

Saturday [February 8, 1958]

Dear L & F,

It just occurs to me that I said we'd expect you on the 15th but can't you come on the 14th? It would make it easier on you if you are driving. We'll expect you on Friday 14th anyway.

Cheers,
F

66. *To Brainard and Frances Neel Cheney from Flannery O'Connor. TLS 1p.*

Milledgeville, 4 March [19]58

Dear Lon & Fannie,

We were mighty sorry the visit was cut off. We spent a week in the hospital and when we came home my mother had to go right to plumbing. She is getting to be a master plumber. Maybe you all can make it before we go on our trip [to Italy]. We will be here every weekend but the Easter weekend when we may go to Savannah. The doctor said I couldn't go on the pilgrimage—too much—7 places in 17 days. So we plan to go spend a week with the [Robert] Fitzgeralds in Levanto and then go to Lourdes and Rome with the group. I am already feeling how glad I will be to get home. I discover myself to be one of those awful people who prefer plumbing to art, but then you can carry the art around in your head but not the plumbing.

I sold my story to Harper's Bazaar.[1] It's much improved though it still needs to be hit in a few spots.

I hope your novel [*This Is Adam*] is coming along according to schedule. I abandoned the schedule on mine [*The Violent Bear It Away*] long ago.

Cheers,
Flannery

1. "The Enduring Chill," *Harper's Bazaar,* 91 (July, 1958), 44–45, 94, 96, 100–02, 108.

67. *To Frances Neel Cheney from Flannery O'Connor. TLS 1p.*

Milledgeville, Georgia, 6 July [19]58

Dear Fannie,

I am supposed to pass these [recipes?] on to you. The gourmet [Regina O'Connor?] is at it still.

I have found out for sure I am not adjusted to the modern world. I have been taking driving lessons from the Driving teacher at the local highschool and after fifteen dollars worth of instruction, I grandly flunked the driving test—not the written one, the one where you drive. I did bring the patrolman back alive, but he didn't seem to think that was enough. He said, "I think you need sommo practice." This coming Wednesday I have to go try again.

We are hoping that the visit we missed from you in February, you may make this summer. If there is a possibility please let us know.

I hope the novel is progressing. I think mine is.

My love to you both,
Flannery

68. *To Flannery O'Connor from Brainard Cheney. TLS(cc) 2pp.*

Smyrna, Tennessee, July 12th, Saturday [1958]

Dear Flannery,

This letter has been long projected and several times begun. Here's hoping for better luck this time!

We enjoyed so much your recent word! It was great to have it directly from, if not the horse's mouth, then the automobile horn!

We are sure that you are going to learn to drive, and well—just don't let them buffalo you about it—Especially with their gobbledegook. And remember everybody hits a few things they are not aiming at during their days of lesser familiarity with the craft.

We are eager to have a detailed account of the

European trip from you, directly. And we may take you up on the visit, when F's summer school is over.

I have just undergone a change that may (in one respect, at least) facilitate this. I have just resigned my political job.[1]

It's like this. Officially (on account of my long and still cordial relations with [Governor Frank] Clement) I am resigning because I want to devote my full time to my own writing. A thing true, true! I've always wanted to, but couldn't figure out how to eat along with it—which I must admit I haven't figured out this time, either.

But. The political fact is that I cannot stomach the Clement candidate for Governor. One Buford Ellington. It is the matter of his pitch on Segregation. I didn't know he was going to do it, til he made his opening speech. He made a backhanded invitation to the Ku Klux Klan, et al to the effect that he would close down any school at their behest before they would let it be desegregated. That may be necessary in Mississippi, or Georgia, but it isn't in Tennessee. It is an open invitation to lawlessness in Tennessee, and the rule of behind-government-pressure of the violent elements. Ellington is a Mississippi redneck and I don't aim to be a party to the rise of Mississippi redneck-ism in Tennessee!

I am working undercover (because of my personal relations with Clement) for another candidate now, but I won't be very active. And after the election I will be out of politics.

You ask about the novel (THIS IS ADAM). Well it is set for September 23rd publication. Things move along swiftly with this young outfit, McDowell Obolensky!

Too, I am just out of the hospital, as of this morning. It was like this. I had a real hard down stomach ache and I went to see my doctor. While there he gave me some medicine—a nitro-glycerin pellet, he said. Instead of relieving me, I got worse. I don't know whether the pill did it or not, but I broke out in a cold sweat, nausea, etc, and my blood pressure plummeted downward, or so he says. He laid [me] on a sofa, like of [*sic*] was a soft-boiled egg, gave me a shot in the arm, and wouldn't let me even move my head, while he called an ambulance and got me a hospital room.

Well, of course, that sort of stirred up my immediate friends and relations. And I was pretty uneasy myself that first night. I couldn't think of any convincing reason why I couldn't have a heart attack, or die, either! Except for God's mercy. And that, sometimes, is mysterious.

Well by morning (and a cardiogram, etc) it was pretty sure it wasn't my heart.

Then the doctor seized upon my bloated lower abdomen. I told him just gas (please pardon this gruesome detail) but that didn't satisfy him. It took him two days and consultation with a surgeon (who also saw me four times) to abandon his hypothesis.

By this morning the swelling was gone and the pain and he had to sheepishly agree with sheepish me.

But it was a humdinger—a $200 stomach-ache. I couldn't afford another one, however.

It caused F. to cancel her trip out to San Francisco to a library convention (she had her ticket, new clothes and everything). And for that I feel real guilty. She seems to enjoy conventions so much—and of course, a trip to San Francisco is a treat, for any reason almost.

She now pretends that she only wanted an excuse not to go! But I know better.

She is really submerged with summer school this summer. It is truly hard on her. Only the prospect of her being able to turn the school back to Bill Fitzgerald[2] in September is pulling her through. She takes it all so hard.

We are both very eager to see you. Picked up a Harper's Bazaar in a women's clothing place (where I had gone with F. to select clothes for her trip!) and saw in it THE ENDURING CHILL. Didn't have a chance to read it. But—I am delighted that you have published it and I intend to read it as soon as I can lay hand on the magazine.

And glad to have the word of progress with your own novel [*The Violent Bear It Away*]. That's fine!

F. joins me in love to you all.

As ever,
Lon

1. Cheney resigned from Tennessee Governor Frank Clement's staff, June 30, 1958.

2. Bill Fitzgerald was director of the George Peabody College Library School for several years during the fifties and sixties; Mrs. Cheney was acting director, 1956–58 and 1961–63.

69. *To Brainard and Frances Neel Cheney from Flannery O'Connor. TLS 1p.*

Milledgeville, Georgia, 3 August [19]58

Dear Lon and Fannie,

I don't know when your school is out but I want to reissue my invitation for you to pay us the visit we missed last winter. I hope you haven't had any more pseudo-heart attacks. You must be in good form as that piece in the Sewanee on the Toynbee situation[1] was very fine. I say Amen to that a couple of hundred times.

Me, I am licensed now to operate a motor vehicle in the state of Georgia. I have knocked down one state highway sign advising me to go 15 miles an hour; otherwise no damages.

Our D. P.s [the Matisiacks] are coming back to work here again. In the meantime they have acquired a television set so we think they may be better satisfied.

Thanks for the Obolensky [McDowell-Obolensky, publishing company] catalog. I'm waiting to read the book [*This Is Adam*].

Cheers,
Flannery

1. Brainard Cheney, "The Crocodile or the Crucifix: The Politics of Syncretism, Toynbeeism, and Revelation," *Sewanee Review*, 66 (Summer, 1958), 507–18.

70. *To Flannery O'Connor from Brainard Cheney. TLS(cc) 2pp.*

Smyrna, Tenn., October 4th [1958]

Dear Flannery,

He lived in storm and strife his heart had such desire for what proud death may bring, or words to that effect. I feel like that disillusioned mother who believed that her boy could be President, after sending her third one forth to the jug.

On the publication of my first book [*Lightwood*, 1939], I, in my innocence, was astonished at all of the attention and publicity that it got. To be sure, it didn't result in any great sales. But for a long time I was sure it might have. So with my second [*River Rogue*, 1942], and its almost-success was fraught with just-missed-it-here-and-there stories. Though they never did finally pay off anywhere.

I wished I believed in paradoxes. But I don't. This novel [*This Is Adam*], apparently, has completely missed fire (except for the firing that I did with my own resources hereabouts). And I wish I could believe that such an ill-omened beginning might mean eventual success.

What is obvious is that my fine feathered friends of McDowell Obolensky did not get books out to reviewers and dealers and retailers in time for them to get ready for publication date. Even Donald Gordon who does the rating for the book trade (does all of them) did not get one in time to rate it. No New York reviewer got one in time evidently. And the dealers here didn't get their books in time to read it before putting it on sale.

It is (the old brownstone town house of Obolensky) [a] fine place to go and have a cocktail and gab (I was never in the Plymouthrockyandcold place of Houghton Mifflin but once and that was but to shake a few cold hands and hear old man (I'll think of his name later) ask me if they were wearing shoes in the South yet). But I am wondering what else they do. In early July I sent them a list of all of the *race* publications which I got from this Southern news bureau (you know, both sides) with the suggestion that they circularize them with a special pitch. They all said they thought it was a good idea. But I got a letter from the publicity manager this week, in response to my inquiry, that she is working on that letter but she hasn't got it out yet.

(The old man I was referring to above was Tichenor.)

Ah, well, ah well! I shouldn't have started this letter to you this morning, as you see.

We had a gay and pleasant time at your house last month. Though, I can't but feel a little disappointed that we didn't get to see more of you. Our one sally out of town of the summer turned out rather oddly. The only reason sufficient to make it possible for us to get away was in order to go down to see you. But we spend more time everywhere else, even at a chance pause in Clinton, S.C. to get a cup of coffee (where we ran into a P.C. [Peabody College] English teacher Fannie knew) than at Milledgeville.

The worst part about it is that I spend my days now frittering away my time—autographing a book here and butting in on a tv program there. And I can't get back to work. Can't even command the release, the whateverittakes to settle down to work!

Yesterday (or the day before) I was introduced to the manager of the Methodist bookstore, who said: "Oh, yes, I feel like I know Mr. C., through his books. I haven't had a chance to read this one yet. But I enjoyed THE VELVET HORN [by Andrew Lytle] so much."

And on Monday I talked to the girls of the Donelson Arts Guild (on the Fugitives) who all brought me their cute little placards (that that original girl, the president had thought up all by herself) they were wearing on their bosoms, saying: THIS IS ALICE, THIS IS EMILY, etc.

(Of course with all of that originality, I shouldn't expect too much for my honorarium. Besides it was an honor to get to speak to the Donelson Arts Guild! But I didn't expect them to have the guts to hand me five dollars.)

After my tv appearance, I was shocked to be stopped on the street by a couple of acquaintances who had seen the show. As it turned out they were shocked, too: They had cut on to see the World Series: the Show was sharing half its time with the W.S. I guess I should count that a break!

What I set out to ask you is: Have you got a copy of THIS IS ADAM from McDowell Obolensky yet? They were supposed to have gone out about three weeks ago, but now I wonder.

The [Bill] Fitzgeralds got back from their two-years

junket Saturday a week ago. And that is one big relief for us. Fannie & I and a crew of the most-good-for-nothing cleaners I ever saw worked on the house for two days trying to get it in order. F & I quit it at 10:30 p.m. on the night before the Fitzgerald advent of the following morning, resigned to the notion that what we had not got done we wouldn't be able to do before they arrived anyhow.

And we are once more consolidated on living quarters here at Cold Chimneys and, My What A Relief! We hope it will be economical, too.

We do so much want to see you!

We do wish you would come up to see us. Can't we plan a trip for you? Any time that would suit you would suit us.

F. joins me in love to you and Regina.

As ever,
Lon

71. *To Brainard Cheney from Flannery O'Connor. TLS 1p.*

Milledgeville, 5 October [19]58

Dear Lon,

I have just finished your novel [*This Is Adam*] and I certainly do like it. It's a real accomplishment and I am interested in hearing more about this other one you are writing that carries on the theme of this one.[1] There was a very favorable review of it in the Savannah Morning News, favorable but not very perceptive, so I won't send it.[2] I wish mine [*The Violent Bear It Away*] was going to be as good.

Nothing goes on around here except the trials of 100 cows. My mother has her a new hired man who cost her $200 last week in broken machinery. I suspect he will soon be back at the saw mill.

I have the makings of a deal to sell the city of Atlanta a pair of peafowl. If I could get into the business it would be more profitable than writing.

We wish you all would come to see us again.

My love to you both,
Flannery

1. Cheney planned a trilogy of novels, the first of which was *This Is Adam.* His next effort, "Quest for the Pelican," which was never published, would occupy him for the next three years.

2. Lucy B. McIntire, "Debt Owed to Simple Folk of South's Plantation Days," September 28, 1958 [n.p.].

72. *To Brainard Cheney from Flannery O'Connor. TL 1p.*

Milledgeville, 6 October [1958]

Dear Lon,

[David] McDowell didn't send me a book [*This Is Adam*] until a few days ago. I read it at once and now Regina is reading it. She keeps saying, "This sounds exactly like Lon talking," and she appears to be enjoying it very much. Whatever McDowell didn't do, they also didn't proofread it. They didn't review it in the Atlanta Sunday paper so I have written a letter up there to the girl who writes the literary column and I expect her to see about it.

I sure wish I could get up but we still haven't found us a driver. A couple of years ago you were down here around Thanksgiving. If there's any chance of you and Fannie being around this Thanksgiving, let us know and plan to have dinner with us.

Following the Donelson Arts Guild,

This is Flannery.
Cheers

73. *To Brainard Cheney from Flannery O'Connor. TLS 1p.*

Milledgeville, 12 October [19]58

Dear Lon,

The girl I wrote to on the Constitution[1] about your book wrote me that when she asked the book editor [Sam Lucchese] about it, he said, "Sorry, honey, but it was about niggers." This seems a trifle odd for the supposedly liberal Constitution. Anyway, Mrs. Lochridge wants to do a column on you and sneak in something of a review in that and she said she would call you up. I sent her your address.

Cheers,
Flannery

1. Betsy Lochridge, O'Connor's acquaintance at the *Atlanta Constitution*. (Mrs. Lochridge subsequently published, in the *Atlanta Journal* and *Atlanta Constitution Magazine*, November 1, 1959, pp. 38–40, an interview with O'Connor at Adalusia Farm, "An Afternoon With Flannery O'Connor.")

74. *To Flannery O'Connor from Brainard Cheney. TLS(cc) 1p.*

Smyrna, Tenn., Oct. 22, [1958]

Dear Flannery,

Your report from Mrs. Lochridge about the CONSTITUTION book editor came as a shock—especially THE CONSTITUTION. And, too, [Ralph] McGill [*Constitution* editor and publisher] I do count an intimate friend.

So I took the liberty of writing him and I now have a reply. I am enclosing copies of both letters.

I did not say who my informant was, or how the information came from the paper.

But, if it will not embarrass you, I would like to give my source?

Already I have had corroboration: Norman Berg (Macmillan's Atlanta representative) with whom F. rode up to Louisville today to a librarians convention, told me this morning that he was (I think he said lunching) with Lochridge and something came up about me and my book. And she told him about going to the book editor in my behalf and reported the same as she did to you. Except more. She said the book editor at first said he thought I was a negro. But said he wouldn't review it anyhow, because it was about negroes.

Also, they seem to lay it on the publisher, too! I'm sure that Mack [Ralph McGill] didn't know anything about it. But I'm dubious about the book editor.

This may be a teapot tempest. But the Constitution's attention happens to be important to any sale I might have on this book.

I am still trying to get along with that political essay about which I spoke to you when I last saw you.[1] Seems like old INTERFERENCE keeps getting me. But, with F. in L'ville, I should finish it this week.

What is the word with you?
Best of luck!

As ever,
Lon

1. On October 9, 1958, Cheney had written Russell Kirk about an essay he hoped Kirk might publish in *Modern Age:*

> . . . I [have] turned up what I regard as the most important political perception I ever fell upon.
>
> I have been (off and on) working it up in an exploratory piece (I've got about a dozen pages roughed out). The idea, oversimply said, is this: the *colored man* (as a political fact and symbol) is not an extension of the *common man,* but will—in time—supplant him. By colored man I mean to take them all in, not indigenous to Western Society. It will be [my] argument that the colored man cannot be embraced under the democratic tradition, but only under the Christian tradition. Though, of course, there will be a desperate try to make him the common man. The South has a peculiar place in this, but it is an American and world-wide problem.
>
> If you want it I would like to know? I will let you see a first draft. But if not, I will shop elsewhere with it. For I do want to publish it. (Carbon of unpublished letter from Brainard Cheney to Russell Kirk, in Vanderbilt University Library, Special Collection.)

Cheney discussed this idea with a number of people, but the essay was never published.

75. *To Brainard Cheney from Flannery O'Connor. TLS 1p.*

Milledgeville, Georgia, 24 October [19]58

Dear Lon,

I suspect the white man in the woodpile is the book editor but I don't want you to quote me as your source because I am afraid it might cause the Lockeridge [*sic*] girl trouble. She is struggling to make a living there and her boss is the book editor and it was probably indiscreet of her to write me this. Anyway I wouldn't want it to get back to the CONSTITUTION that it came from her. Norman Berg is her editor at McMillan.

If I were you I'd write brother [Ralph] McGill and tell him that you have it from two sources that you can't name and that since they have no objection to reviewing this kind of book that you will send him a copy at once so he can review it. Every time there is a Georgia writer who writes so much as a limerick collection, they review it, with firecrackers and tin horns.

Ashley [Brown] wrote he had seen a favorable review

by J. Saunders Redding in the NY Herald Tribune.[1] Redding is a very nice Negro whom I met at Yaddo.[2] Also there was a good review in the NY Times.[3]

I hope you get this settled to your satisfaction but please don't bring the Lockeridge [*sic*] girl into it. If you mention my name they will know she was the one [who] told me because she is my good friend up there.

Let me hear how it comes out.

Cheers,
Flannery

1. "A Negro Named Adam and the Problem He Inherited," *New York Herald-Tribune Book Review,* October 12, 1958, p. 5.
2. See Letter 7, note 2.
3. Orville Prescott, untitled review under heading "Books of the Times," *New York Times,* October 10, 1958, p. 56.

76. *To Flannery O'Connor from Brainard Cheney. TLS(cc) 2pp.*

Smyrna, Tenn., November 10th, Tuesday [1958]

Dear Flannery,

This, we hope, as the saying used to be, finds you well?

It is also a little forewarning.

But before I forget it, let me thank you for your concerned letter about the Constitution staff member. I had already talked to [Ralph] McGill when I got it. But there was no mention between us of who either you or Norman Berg might have talked to. Incidentally, he, McGill, seemed to take a pretty dim view of his book editor. He had got no word of my book, before the letter I wrote him. The idea of censorship, he said, was absurd. He sent me word that he himself has reviewed it. It was to have appeared Sunday. I haven't got hold of a Constitution as yet to see.

We have been busier than birddogs. F. is just back (Sunday night) from an American Library Assn. board meeting in Philadelphia, where she spent half of last week and she has been working night and day this week to catch up with home work! I don't see why she does it, but she does!

I finished some time ago the first draft of the common man vs. colored man essay and have since been trying to get squared away to begin a novel. But I wanted to confer with my publisher [David McDowell] first. And, this afternoon late, I found that he was not coming down here; so, I've decided to go up there [New York]—day after tomorrow.

The ulterior element in this letter, of which I have already forewarned you, is we would like to take up up one [*sic*] your casually polite invitation to come to Thanksgiving dinner. Only we can't get there for Thanksgiving dinner. And we wonder if it would do all right, if we came about the same time on the next day, which is Friday?

Please, if it doesn't suit in any way—or if you don't feel like company just now, why we'll never forgive you if you don't say so. We can come most any old time! It doesn't have to be now. The question is would it suit, if we got there around lunch time on Friday, the 28th, and staid till the next morning?

F. is calling me to quit this tap-tapping, she is going to bed. And I've certainly already done my worst and it's time to quit.

As ever,
Affectionately [Handwritten]
Lon

77. *To Brainard Cheney from Flannery O'Connor. TLS 1p.*

Milledgeville, 21 November [19]58

Dear Lon,

We will love to have you have dinner with us Friday and stay overnight. There is only one thing. Our cousin is dying in Savannah—the one who gave us the trip to Lourdes—and we may have to go down there at any time. Let me know where you will be Tuesday, Wednesday and Thursday so that if I have to call or wire you not to come I can. I am supposed to go to Birmingham Monday, talk on Tuesday, and come back Wednesday but I may have to call that off too, but write where you will be to Regina in case

I am in Birmingham. We certainly want to see you and I am hoping that my cousin will hold on until after Thanksgiving. She is ninety so there is not much chance of her getting better.

I didn't see Ralph's [McGill] review in last Sunday's paper but maybe it will be in next. I am glad he is doing something about it. Their book page is no good anyhow.

We will hope to see you Friday. Unless you hear from me please plan to come.

Love,
Flannery

[Handwritten] P.S. If we are not here Friday and you are coming through Milledgeville anyway, the place to eat here is The Sanford House, right up from the bus station. It may be closed but I don't think so.

78. *To Brainard Cheney from Flannery O'Connor. ALS 1p.*

Sunday night, 11-23-[19]58

Dear Lon,

We will expect you Friday and to spend the night. Our cousin died tonight and the funeral is Monday so we will be here waiting for Friday.

We are really looking forward to this.

Flannery

79. *To Brainard and Frances Neel Cheney from Flannery O'Connor. TLS 1p.*

Milledgeville, Georgia, 2 December [19]58

Dear Lon and Fannie,

We were certainly sorry you couldn't get here but we are going to expect you sometime during the Christmas holidays. Let us know when.

The letter from Caroline [Gordon Tate] today was pretty bad. It doesn't look like you can do anything for them but pray.[1]

My good news that Caroline is talking about is that

the doctor is letting me walk around the house a little without my crutches. He says the bone is beginning to recalcify. Last year they told me this wouldn't happen. My mother talked to the Archbishop at Cousin Katie's funeral and told him about this and he said, "Ah, seeing the Pope did her some good."

Where is the review Ralph McGill was supposed to write? I haven't seen it. I think he should make haste and come through.[2]

Cheers,
Flannery

P.S. I met a friend of Fannie's at Birmingham-Southern—Howard Creek—who asked to be remembered. I am supposed to read at Vanderbilt at a symposium April 22–23.

1. Reference is to the marital troubles and impending divorce of Caroline Gordon and Allen Tate.

2. McGill's review, "A Georgia Story: 'This Is Adam' Idea Came 30 Years Ago," appeared in *The Atlanta Journal* and *The Atlanta Constitution*, December 14, 1958, p. 16-E.

80. *To Flannery O'Connor from Brainard Cheney. TLS(cc) 1p.*

Smyrna, Monday, 15th [December 1958?]

Dear Flannery,

This is to say thank you again for everything!

My stay at Andalusia Farm was certainly a well fed one: body, mind and spirit. And, under the inflexibility of your pastor, I even got back to Dublin (driving 50 miles before day) to mass on Monday to keep the feast of the immaculate conception.

Please tell Regina how much I enjoyed everything.

Got back here by the hardest on Saturday afternoon, driving from Valdosta. And with a boil on the end of my nose from all the fine Georgia hospitality—too much for my poor man's stomach!

Here's wishing you both a truly sacramental Christmas. And thanks again for such a good time!

As ever,
Lon

81. *To Frances Neel Cheney from Flannery O'Connor. TLS 1p.*

Milledgeville, 28 December [19]58

Dear Fannie,

My mother and I have spent the holidays identifying reptiles we have met. The next time we kill us a snake, we'll be intellectually on top of it. Thank you hugely for that contribution.[1] We have spent the holidays staying close to home to prevent bloodshed on the place. One of the negroes bought himself a gun for Christmas apparently for the pleasure of threatening his wife. She came over the other night and said she was scaird to go home because he had promised to git her. My mother had to induce him to bring the gun over here to spend the night. She also delivered a sermon on thou shalt not kill during the Christmas time, which was touching and had some effect.

I only walk without the crutches a very little bit so I am not going to have to give up the advantage of looking mean.

I hear you have a Lolita in your backyard.[2] That must be interesting.

The best new year to you both.

Love,
Flannery

1. Perhaps a Christmas present book Mrs. Cheney had sent O'Connor.
2. See Letter 56, note 1. This reference is otherwise obscure.

82. *To Brainard Cheney from Flannery O'Connor. ALS 1p.*

Friday [February? 1959]

Dear Lon,

Enclosed please find yourself.[1] We were surprised to learn you all had moved to Shelby, Tenn. The next time you come this close come to see us.

I am going to the University of Chicago for a week Feb-9–14 to give two workshop classes and a public reading. The fee persuadeth me.

Cheers and to Fannie,
Flannery

1. A feature article about Cheney, written when he was in Atlanta autographing copies of *This Is Adam:* Yolande Gwin, "His Mama 'Done Told' Him All About Adam," *The Atlanta Constitution,* January 29, 1959, p. 15. Gwin gave Cheney's address as Shelby instead of Smyrna.

83. *To Flannery O'Connor from Brainard Cheney. TL(cc) 1p.*

Smyrna, Thursday 11th [February, 1959] [misdated]

Dear Flannery,

Thanks!

Maybe we should move to Shelby, Tennessee: it would be easier to spell. I suppose it should be said in extenuation of the relaxed manner in which Yolande did her story that she took down her notes at a cocktail party at which Wade[1] and I were trying to warm her up to her assignment.

Chicago at this season is not my idea of pleasure. Still I can't think of anything that would persuade me to brave the Windy City so much as a fee, just at this juncture.

I am back from New York after 16 days of *experiencing* it. Outside of a hangover and a cold, I can't tell yet what I got out of it.

But one anonymous aphorism: "The Southerner don't care how close the Negro gets to him, just so he doesn't get too high; the Northerner doesn't care how high he gets, just so he doesn't get too close." For all of my introductory letters and two weeks of hectic pursuit, I was not able to meet a single Negro socially!

But the *big news!* Caroline [Gordon Tate] reported to me that you have finished your novel [*The Violent Bear It Away*]? Or aren't you letting it out yet? I saw C. 3 times while I was there—one time, too many. But I will save that til I see you. Apparently A. [Allen Tate] is going through with the divorce. He's filed it.

Every wish for a successful Chicago sojourn!

Love from us both,

1. Clint Wade was a public relations man Cheney knew in Nashville; he did some work for David McDowell's firm.

84. *To Brainard and Frances Neel Cheney from Flannery O'Connor. TLS 1p.*

Milledgeville, Georgia, 22 February [19]59

Dear L & F,

. . . .

I am still picking at the novel [*The Violent Bear It Away*], though for all practical purposes I suppose it is more or less finished. When I get a readable copy, I want to send it to you and see what you think. I am not sure about it. Too close and can't see it. Caroline [Gordon Tate] says it works. I hope she is right.

Is that invitation to stay with you for the Vanderbilt thing[1] still good? It seems an imposition. I would have to come on the 21st and leave on the 24th (April), and twice I will have to be in Nashville—on Wed. afternoon for the reading and on Thursday morning at 9:30 for some kind of meeting with students. He (Randall Stewart)[2] said I didn't have to be on the symposium. It's on modern poetry and I don't know nothing about modern poetry. Consider these inconveniences before you get yourself stuck with a guest and let me know.

The Ford Foundation has just given me $8,000, or will over the next two years. What they don't know is that it's going to last me eight years. I ain't accustomed to living like a Ford. Robert Fitzgerald also got one and Miss K.A. [Katherine Anne] Porter.

Cheers and my love to you both,
Flannery

1. The annual Vanderbilt University literary symposium, April 21-24, 1959, at which O'Connor was to read.
2. Chairman, Department of English, Vanderbilt University.

85. *To Frances Neel Cheney from Flannery O'Connor. TLS 1p.*

Milledgeville, 5 March [19]59

Dear Fannie,

The Allen Hotel[1] don't appeal to me a bit. You are stuck.

Tell Lon I was recently in Davison's Book Department [in Atlanta] and Adam [*This Is Adam*] was on the first table by the door. I was gratified.

My mother is fixing to have a timber auction. It was going to be held at the lawyer's office but the lawyer said that timber men liked to have room to move around where they could spit, so she is having it here. Otherwise we are becalmed.

Cheers,
Flannery

1. The Allen Hotel, located not far from the Vanderbilt campus, had probably been proposed by the literary symposium organizers as a lodging for O'Connor.

86. *To Frances Neel Cheney from Flannery O'Connor. TLS 1p.*

Milledgeville, 10 April [19]59

Dear Fannie,

I have me a reservation on Flight 206 for Tuesday the 21. That gets to Nashville at 1:30 PM, which is a very inconvenient hour so if you all can't conveniently meet me then, I'll just set there and wait for you and any time will do. I'll have to go back on Friday at 9:15 AM. I wish I could stay longer but the Lord is not willing. My mother has to come in town to sleep when I go off and this leaves the place to the wolves at night. The negroes got in a big full Wednesday night and Regina had to ask Jack to hand over his switchblade knife so she would know he wasn't going to put it into any of the rest of them. He always hands his weapons over very docilely. Then my mother says, "Let's not have any more unpleasantness tonight," and they go on off. All near-killings she refers to as "unpleasantness."

I am looking forward to the visit, though not the literary chores.

Love,
Flannery

87. *To Brainard and Frances Neel Cheney and Lee Jessup*[1] *from Flannery O'Connor. TLS 1p.*

Milledgeville, 25 April [19]59

Dear Lon & Fannie & Lee,

I am now back from being the woman of the hour [at Vanderbilt] to being the woman of the barnyard. I returned to a hen who had just hatched fifteen chickens and my cup runs over. I certainly enjoyed all my time in Nashville (Smyrna, that is) and thank you all for the superabundance of hospitality. I'll hope to sleep in that elegant room again with all that marble.

. . . .

My mother is fine and was glad to get back into her own bed. She averted several unpleasantnesses while I was gone and the staff seems to be doing as well as usual. I have told her about that kind of eggs you make and she proposes to try some. When I return from going somewhere I always relate what I have et on the trip and in this way we enlarge the possibilities of our table.

My love to you all,
Flannery

1. Lee Cheney Jessup, Cheney's sister who lived in Nashville.

88. *To Frances Neel Cheney from Flannery O'Connor. ALS 2pp.*

Sunday, May 17, [19]59

Dear Fannie,

The Baron[1] is in Milledgeville and I am highly obliged to you. I have almost finished the first volume and will send it along when I finish it. You are contributing greatly to my education. I see nobody has checked these books out since 1954. Them Tennessee theologians must all be Baptists.

Cheers,
Flannery

1. Mrs. Cheney had sent O'Connor two volumes by Baron Friedrich von Hügel, *The Mystical Element of Religion as Studied in Saint Catherine of Genoa and Her Friends* (London: J. M. Dent, 1908, 1923), a classic study in mysticism. O'Connor's

interest in von Hügel (1852–1925), Italian-born British Roman Catholic religious writer, is evidenced in two book reviews she had written, June 23, 1956, and August 31, 1957, for *The Bulletin:* reissues of *Letters from Baron Friedrich von Hügel to a Niece* (Chicago: Regnery, 1955) and *Essays and Addresses on the Philosophy of Religion,* Vols. 1 and 2 (New York: Dutton, 1950). Noting that von Hügel "is freqently considered, along with Newman and Acton, as one of the great Catholic scholars," she spoke of his "vigorous, intelligent piety" and his "always measured and intellectually just tone" and felt his works deserved a wider reading among Catholics. (See *The Presence of Grace,* pp. 21–22, 41–42.)

89. *To Flannery O'Connor from Brainard Cheney. TLS(cc) 1p.*

Smyrna, Sunday, May 24th [1959]

Dear Flannery,

This for a word about the after-glow of your visit. And to mention specifically and [*sic*] subject that we devoted some talk to while you were here.

Do hope you got home, without having suffered any lasting setback from the excesses, verbal and otherwise, or the Symposium!

Fannie & I did enjoy your visit so much! The only lack we found on reflection was in not having you read THE ENDURING CHILL[1]—or learning more about the prospects for you[r] novel.

To our subject of talk: Caroline [Gordon Tate] has written me a letter—date of May 12—that reads like she may be on her way out of the labyrinth. The whole tone and tenor seems like her old self. And its big and most wholesome news it seems to me is this: "I had a slight misfortune in that line, myself, the other day. I was lying in bed with a bad hangover and I said to myself that I was not as young as I once was and it behooved me to take care of myself and I decided I would just stay in bed all morning. Unfortunately I had put the typewriter on the night table. As I recall, I sort of turned over in bed—and the first thing I knew I had eight pages of THE NARROW HEART[2] written. Had another whack at it later and I now have twelve pages, so I am committed. The gaff, as my father would say, has been slipped home."

About the postscript I am less sure, but at least it is the self-conscious gesture connected with the effort:

"I am seeing Fr. McCoy Wednesday—redoubling my efforts to see if I can't find some way to give Allen [Tate] a divorce."

If the two of them could make up their minds to accept a separation, it would seem to make more sense to me. But who am I to know!

I am doing along, but still all is tentative. Next week (this week, I should say: Sunday, this being) I hope to do chapter eight [of "To the Victor"], when, it is my plan, to then turn back and give the whole screed a *cold* reading, to see whether I think I am getting a novel into words, or not. I hope to feel [a] lot better about it after that.

Fannie is taking a day off to run over to see her brother in Newberry, S.C. But otherwise, I suppose we won't recognize the end of school spring and the beginning of school summer.

She joins me in love,

As ever,
Lon

1. O'Connor's story, subsequently published in *Harper's Bazaar,* 91 (July, 1958), 44–45, 94, 96, 100–02, 108.

2. "The Narrow Heart: The Portrait of a Woman" Caroline Gordon Tate planned as the second part of a double novel of which *The Glory of Hera* (Garden City: Doubleday, 1972) was the first. "The Narrow Heart" was not completed.

90. *To Brainard and Frances Neel Cheney from Flannery O'Connor. TLS 1p.*

Milledgeville, 14 June [19]59

Dear Lon & Fannie,

Volume II of the Baron goes back to you tomorrow. I wouldn't say I had been too enlightened by reading it once, but I can always say I've done it. As the old ladies in elementary education say, thank you for sharing this reading experience with me, you and the jint liberries.[1]

My mother had her timber auction and got about $25,000 more than she expected to get so she is very pleased. It was held on the front porch and I observed from behind the door. After the saw timber was sold, they were debating what they would do with the tops, etc., and one of the bidders said, "There ain't going to be none. He's going to have to cut the pine needles to come out."

A note from Sue [Jenkins] Brown said she guessed I had heard the news from the House of Tate, most of it doleful. I haven't heard anything much.[2] My editor [Robert Giroux] was down and he had been talking to [a friend] who, it appears, introduced the current woman to Allen [Tate]. [She told him] if the girl thought Allen was going to marry her she had another thought coming. Caroline wrote me too she had started the book but I haven't heard anything since then.

As to me and my book [*The Violent Bear It Away*], I am making progress or have that delusion and when I get a clear copy, hope to send it to you for yr comments. I hope you and yours [Cheney's novel, "To the Victor"] is coming along.

Fannie White[3] asked me to get Lee Jessup's address for her. Will you send it to me?

Affectionately,
Flannery

1. The Joint University Libraries was a separate corporation (1936–79) operated through a contractural agreement by three Nashville institutions: Vanderbilt University, George Peabody College for Teachers, and Scarritt College for Christian Workers.

2. Caroline Gordon and Allen Tate were separated; Tate was seeking a divorce.

3. Fannie White and Mary Jo Thompson operated the Sanford House, a tearoom in Milledgeville, where O'Connor and her mother regularly ate their noon meal.

91. *To Flannery O'Connor from Brainard Cheney. TLS(cc) 1p.*

Smyrna, Tuesday [Summer 1959]

Dear Flannery,

Thanks to you and to Regina for a delightful two days!

And thank Fanny White, too, for the pie, when you see her—it was delectable.

(Incidentally, that number for my sister's street address is: 3313 Hobbs Road, Nashville, etc.)

Your renovation on the house is quite exciting—I am

eager to see the finished results. I hope there are no major unpleasantnesses along the way.

I had quite an exciting time at the monastery at Conyers[1]—after I found it and found the driveway into it! But, at any rate, after I had encountered a couple of brown brothers, one of whom carried my request to see Fr. Paul Bourne[2] to the prior, I was told to wait in the retreat house sitting room.

In a short time he appeared. We talked and then he took me on a tour of the building. I found him quietly and almost imperceptibly engrossing and endearing. When we parted it was enthusiastic.

And enthusiastic about the building, too! It was quite a job—the way they are polishing down the concrete arches in the chapel to look as smooth as dressed stone! And the windows!

And Fr. Bourne's garden, too! He gave me the name of the grass and that of the company to get it from—the grass inside the court. Did you inspect it? It is a wonderful carpet grass—I had never seen any like it before.

And his rock that spouts water!

We talked about his friend, your mutual friend, Bill Sessions,[3] although I do not know him and even about the possibility of organizing an H.O.C. (Historically Orthodox Christian) Theater.

(I think, it was my mentioning your name that worked the magic, with the prior.)

Got in here at 6 p.m. So what with getting lost for a while in Atlanta, I made pretty good time.

A letter here from Fannie tells me that she spent week-end at Robber Rocks[4] with Sue [Jenkins Brown]—and is to see Caroline [Gordon Tate] for lunch Wednesday.

Thanks again to you both for an uncommonly good time.

As ever,
Lon

1. The Holy Ghost [Trappist] Monastery at Conyers, Georgia, outside Atlanta.
2. O'Connor was quite impressed by Fr. Paul and had suggested the Conyers

stop to Cheney. There are numerous references to Fr. Paul Bourne in *The Habit of Being*.

3. William Sessions, a Georgia educator and writer, was a friend and correspondent of O'Connor's. A substantial group of letters to Sessions were published in *The Added Dimension: The Art and Mind of Flannery O'Connor,* Melvin J. Friedman and Lewis A. Lawson, eds. (New York: Fordham University Press, 1966), 209–225; and a number of O'Connor's letters to Sessions are included in *The Habit of Being*.

4. Sue Jenkins Brown's home; see Letter 18, note 2.

92. *To Flannery O'Connor from Brainard Cheney. TL(cc) 2pp.*

Smyrna, Sunday [late July? 1959]

Dear Flannery,

THE VIOLENT BEAR IT AWAY has carried me off altogether!

Congratulations! It is a very powerful story. It's strong stuff.

Fannie and I, after reading it, have argued it back and forth. We seem to agree about it generally, but not altogether.

But first, let me say, that your metaphor on p. 40: "A burning arm slid down Tarwater's throat etc." is terrific! It is bold, dramatic and very humorous—one of the best you—or anybody else—ever got off.

The quality holds up, the humor is no where strained or overdone. And I think you get away with the little girl evangelist to a remarkable degree.

Our reservations and/or questions are these.

Fannie wonders if Old Tarwater and his Commitment, in the first and second chapters, is not repeated too often—does it grow a little wearying for the reader.

I had already read the first chapter, so it came as second reading for me. I did not get first impact with this reading. Hence, I don't feel that I can well judge about this.

My question is the ending. Frankly, to me it seems a little obscure. I don't argue that it should be less obscure.

Perhaps, you want it ambiguous enough for the various readers to give it their own interpretations.

F. and I have argued this at length. She does not agree with me.

As a strict constructionist (the character can only act in the terms of the story) it seems to me that Tarwater: "His singed eyes, black in their deep sockets, seemed already to envision the fate that awaited him but he moved steadily on, his face set toward the dark city, where the children of God lay sleeping."-------IS heading toward expiation (as society demands) of his murder of the feeble-minded boy, OR

A career of murdering and/or baptizing idiot boys—?

You have introduced, with significance, the girl evangelist. But she does not seem sufficiently tied up with Tarwater and his intentions to be descriptive of the envisioned "fate."

And prophesy—but what prophesy? Old Tarwater was (according to the record) a failure as a prophet—that is his prophesy didn't come true. There is his hunger for the "bread of Life"—this may be revealed to others, perhaps, but it is not prophesy.

GO WARN THE CHILDREN OF GOD OF THE TERRIBLE SPEED OF MERCY. I, frankly, am not sure what this mercy is, nor its speed—beyond the speed with which the young Tarwater "mercifully" murdered the idiot boy—in which, he was (as I took it) doing to death his old uncle (psychicly [*sic*], or spiritually)?

Some allusions in the context of the story have escaped me, I'm afraid.

If you don't mind, I'm going to hold on to your mss. copy, until I send you my stuff ["To the Victor"] to read. I would like to have it by me for any comment or explanation you want to make. For a few days at least.

I hope to get you a copy of my stuff before the week is out. I still have to get part of it copied. F. read it over yesterday. Was not enthusiastic about it. And she made some suggestions, with which I agree and want to put into effect before I send it to you. I should be able to put it in the mail—if my old secretary will type it with her usual dispatch—by Friday.

We are gradually moving toward the end of summer school and our departure for Ireland. F. is holding up by the hardest. And I'm not doing much better.

But the prospect of the trip is cheering and helps us to hold on.

I am now rereading Red [Robert Penn] Warren's latest THE CAVE[1] for review. I will reserve comment until I see you.

Incase we don't see you before we go, we will bring you a report on the O'Connors and perhaps, the Flannerys, too?

We are now slated for an interview with "Dev"![2]

F. joins me in love,

As ever,

1. See Letter 53, note 3.

2. Eamon DeValera (1882–1975), U.S. born President of the Republic of Ireland. The Cheneys got an appointment for the interview through a Peabody College student of Mrs. Cheney whose brother was a guard at DeValera's house.

93. *To Brainard and Frances Neel Cheney from Flannery O'Connor. TLS 1p.*

Milledgeville, 5 August [19]59

Dear Lon & Fannie,

Thank you both for reading the book. About the end: I meant that Tarwater was going to the city to be a prophet and the "fate" that awaits him is the fate that awaits all prophets or as the old man said, "the servants of the Lord can expect the worst." I reckon on the children of God doing Tarwater in pretty quick. What he means by the speed of mercy is that mercy burns up what we are attached to, the word is a burning word (see Vol II Baron Von Hugel)[1] to burn you clean, etc. The old man was successful as a prophet when he did what the Lord told him to, ie, when he stole Tarwater and raised him up to be a prophet. The boy finally answers his call, and he also baptizes Bishop, so what the old man predicted and hoped for is fulfilled even if not in the way he foresaw. More concerned here with the spirit of prophecy than with right predictions. I think you take too abstract a view of it. What I am concerned with is that what Tarwater does is believable. Maybe you didn't read the first chapter again. I added a lot to it. The old man's commitment may be repeated too often but I felt if it wasn't in there good, Tarwater's subsequent actions wouldn't be believable.

In an earlier draft when Tarwater smears the dirt from his uncle's grave on his forehead, I had "as if to annoint himself." Caroline [Gordon Tate] said I didn't need that, that it was evident that he was annointing himself with the dirt; but I think now I better add that like I started to in the first place. It might indicate more clearly that he is going to the city to take up the prophet's work.

Ashley [Brown] called up the other night from Columbia, S.C. where he was being interviewed for a job. He said he thought Caroline [Gordon Tate] was in a terrible condition but not to mention it to her or anything about her present troubles when I wrote. Seems she has turned against practically everybody, and I guess is wound up. He says he listens to her and that is about all anybody can do.

Marge Cluny [*sic*] and her Augusta kinfolks[2] came over and spent one Sunday afternoon with us and we enjoyed them and hearing about you all. Congratulations on being a graduated water skier.

I'll be on the lookout for your manuscript and thanks again to both of you for reading mine.

Love,
Flannery

1. See Letter 88, note 1.
2. Marge Cooney, a pianist who travelled for Community Concerts for many years, was a friend of the Cheneys.

94. *To Brainard Cheney from Flannery O'Connor. TLS 2pp.*

Milledgeville, 12 August [19]59

Dear Lon,

For a novel that is as topical as this one ["To the Victor"], I think it is pretty successful. I didn't lose interest at any point, but I felt the need of a few things.

1. It seems to me that more often than he does Hightower ought to pull this up off the level of action and be reflective about what is happening. I think we ought to have Hightower's character more firmly in view in the beginning and throughout. We ought to be aware at all times that his interest in this is on what it means and that he is not just a miscellaneous busybody on the governor's staff. The opening paragraph is good but I think after it you ought to have Hightower reflect on the whole story and then begin to tell it. I think you jump into the action too quickly after the first paragraph or so. With material that is this topical, you have to keep the interest lifted to keep it from being merely sensational. Hightower ought to reveal his own character, I think. The reader ought to gather that he is what Ashley [Brown] called you one time—a smoke-filled room boy who comes in when the smoke has been cleared out. I feel Hightower himself is important because everything is strained through him. His role is like Marlow's in Conrad.

2. pp 10, last line. Make it plain that this is a photograph of himself. This is not clear as you have it.

3. No need for Hightower to get so coy everytime he gets around Maggie. You lower the tone at your peril. Keep old Maggie out of those low-cut dresses. I wondered what a Tenn. county principle's [*sic*] wife was doing in an evening dress on election night when they weren't going out of the house. Chap. 3. pp 11, I think those tears are too much.

4. Chap 4. pp 8—that "bee breaking away from its own stinger" doesn't work.

5. The flogging is a trifle hard to accept when all we get is its being reported in the station. If Hightower could be on the scene when she is taken away from the hoodlums, this would make it more believable and give it some reality. You don't want to overdo it, but I feel you need something more here.

6. Chap 7 pp 10—don't use words like "puzzeledly."

7. Chap 9 pp 15—think it is bad having their faces have a "brain-washed" look. Also I think the governor would be more acceptable if he had a few recognizable faults, maybe some of that vulgarity that the real one has. Hightower seems too uncritical of him. I think he should admire him with a few more reservations.

8. Where Missie tells her tale at McNamara's she seems at first stilted and then suddenly rather loose and slangy. I see this as in part intentional but still it doesn't quite work. I don't know but what it might work better if you had Hightower narrate most of her story in his words and have it direct from her only occasionally.

9. When she talks to Hightower alone, her talk is more natural but don't have her use a bogus word like *boohoo* when she means cry. You want pathos here and you ain't going to get it out of a word like that.

10. I think the courtroom scene is very successful. However, I would leave out that stuff about the rosary beads. Catholic writers must always avoid plugs for the Church. That about her mother's being a Catholic is all right because it isn't tacked on gratuitously.

11. Chap. 13, pp 4. I find it hard to accept that Hightower would lift her up on her toes and say, "My god, Missie, you're in the family." Again this may be the fault of not knowing enough about Hightower and what he might or might not do.

12. Chap. 13 pp 5—Boling's way of expressing himself doesn't seem too natural to me.

A good many of these points are just quibbles and

things that stuck out as I went along. The main thing to me is Hightower and what I say in pint [*sic*] 1.

I think Leblanc is very well done and I think the line of action is good and altogether I think essentially you've got it in the bag.

The summary of the rest of it hasn't come but I will mail this to be sure you get it before you go. I will send the ms. back tomorrow, as our postoffice is closed Wed. afternoon.

Let us hear how you stand the Irish[1] and I would like to know if any of this criticism you can agree with. I do think it will be a good novel when you get through with it.

We've invited the Wests[2] to bring Tommie Stritch down next week. If you see him, tell him we hope they will come.

Love,
Flannery

1. The Cheneys vacationed a month in Ireland, returning home on September 24, 1959.

2. Conn and Robert West were personal friends of the Cheneys; he was an English professor at the University of Georgia.

95. *To Brainard Cheney from Flannery O'Connor. TLS 1p.*

Milledgeville, 12 August [19]59

Dear Lon,

After seeing the summary ["To the Victor"] I get a better idea of what you are up to. The summary makes me feel more than ever that you had better get Hightower's character down in some forceful way, from the beginning. The book is really Hightower's quest and you need some preparation early in the book for the fact that he is eventually going to get himself seduced and have a new vision. Seems to me that in the beginning of the book he ought to meditate over what has happened, perhaps refer to his seduction in such a way that the reader won't know fully what he's talking about then, but will realize with recognition when he comes to it.

You will sink the theme better if you emphasize

Hightower; the racial problems should be there not for themselves but for Hightower. It seems to me you can take the curse off the topicality that way and still make your points about the race situation.

When you get the rest of it finished, you may want to trim out some of what you have in this first part. Chapter Ten provides some explanations. The political summary in the first pages of the chapter will probably be skipped by the reader. It would be better if you could get that in some other way.

The summary deepens it considerably for me. Maybe I can say something more intelligent when I see the whole thing. Anyway I like it and I think you will really have something here when you work it out to the end.

Let us hear from you and we hope you have a fine trip [to Ireland].

Affectionately,
Flannery

96. *To Flannery O'Connor from Brainard Cheney. TLS(cc) 1p.*

Smyrna, Tenn., 8–16, [19]59

Dear Flannery,

On the comment on *To the Victor:*

You couldn't be more right! (Using T. [Tom] Stritch's favorite phrase.)

I so appreciate what you say about bringing Marse and his character and background and comment on his experience more into the topical story. It is the thing I felt it needed, too. But I have been uncertain about it. I was afraid at the outset to bog it down with it. You know I never tried to do an I story before. I was conscious of the hazards of this (I think) rather sloppy technique.

It was of great importance to have you tell me this. Now I think I can go ahead and do what ought to be done to—as you say—lift it out of topicality.

I agree with your other incidental criticisms, too.

We are getting set.

F. is finally over with her social academic and

psychiatric duties at Peabody and, exhausted, is at the same time relieved. We are at the packing stage and I think we will make it by the time the 10 o'clock (Braniff) plane leaves tomorrow morning.

We'll bring you a report on the Auld Sod and your kin.

Thanks a million!

Love, as ever,
Lon

97. *To Brainard Cheney from Flannery O'Connor. TLS 1p.*

Milledgeville, 3 September [19]59

Dear Lon,

Sent off the blanks recommending you for the grant[1] today and enclose you the carbon. My advice is to get as many people as you can to recommend you as the more people nominate you, the more chance you have of getting one—I presume.

I haven't heard anything from or about Caroline [Gordon Tate]. I hope she has not gone up in steam.

When you all get back we want a visit from you with a total-recall account of your trip [to Ireland].

Love to you both,
Flannery

1. Cheney had asked O'Connor (and others, see Letter 99) to nominate him for a Ford Foundation award in an August 20, 1959, announced program to assist "creative writers, dancers, directors in the professional theater, and theater architects and designers."

98. *To Brainard and Frances Neel Cheney from Flannery O'Connor. ALS 2pp.*

Sunday [September ? 1959]

Dear L&F,

This is just to inquire if you got away from the Irish safely. I wrote you c/o Am. Exp. Dublin to say I had sent in your nomination for the Ford but you probably didn't get the letter.

Fannie, if you are showing all those Japanese[1] the

dear old Southland, bring them by Andalusia and we will pass them some Social Tea biscuits and coca cola.

Cheers,
Flannery

1. Japanese library faculty and students who were visiting Mrs. Cheney at Peabody College.

99. *To Flannery O'Connor from Brainard Cheney. TLS(cc) 1p.*

Smyrna, September 29, 1959

Dear Flannery,

This sheet was in my typewriter, when Fannie brought in the mail awhile ago, with your note. And before this goes any further, let me say, Thanks a million for your help with the Ford Foundation. I got your letter in Dublin, o.k. It was handsome of you—however, undeserved.

And I have another thing to thank you for—at least your indirect efforts (even if you are not a member of the Georgia Writers Association?). I have just been notified by a Mrs. Raymond Massey of Atlanta that THIS IS ADAM has been selected for the association's 1958 award—Just look where the Georgia outcast has got to!

About the Ford award: looking into the political horse's mouth—it seems that I have some help. Joe Wright (Vanderbilt Dramatics Director) also wrote them in my behalf. And when I got back to NYC, John Caldwell (who is partners now with George Hammond, who is on the F. Board, Fine Arts) and Vivianne F. Koch Day (they had both been asked to recommend) recommended me. Looking into the political horse's mouth is usually unprofitable for me, but anyhow, and however it comes out—about all has been done that, perhaps, could be.

I was very inspired about the theater while I was in Dublin—the source of this inspiration was, chiefly, Ray McAnally, Abbey Theater producer and a very engaging young man (about 35) with whom (and his wife, Ronnie) we formed a warm relationship.[1] Too, my inspiration comes in part, from what they do in Dublin through small private theaters—the maturist [*sic*] acting I saw and the finest I saw in such a theater.

I have some nebulous thoughts, born of this *Inspiration* that I wish to kick around with you in time. Too, I cannot put down here in type what I saw and felt about Ireland—it is still coming to me. But I count my visit there an important experience. I suspect that Ireland is tremendously important in the world today—and I doubt (at least I didn't meet him) that many people there yet have that suspicion.

We were charmed and highly entertained—despite the fact that I was twice down with a kidney attack—last in Dublin where the doctor barely got me up to get on the plane for home!

And your Uncle Padraic O'Connor up in Galway has the most charming statue to him in the park I ever saw—he seems to be about the most popular of Ireland's recent story tellers.

More later. F. is calling me to duty at the wheel of the car, and so to town. Our best.

Love,
Lon

1. Cheney communicated his enthusiasm for O'Connor to his new friends, the McAnnallys. He sent them a copy of *A Good Man Is Hard to Find and Other Stories*, and on November 9, 1959, wrote them, "I think [O'Connor] is the most important young writer of fiction in America today" (unpublished letter in Vanderbilt University Library, Special Collections). He also told them he had read the Irish Constitution and had left his copy with O'Connor to read.

100. *To Brainard Cheney from Flannery O'Connor. TLS 1p.*

Milledgeville, 4 October [19]59

Dear Lon,

Well I am glad you have arrived at the ultimate distinction & are going to be recognized as a Georgia Writer. You will receive a paper scroll tied up with a yellow ribbon and will be expected to shake the hands of numerous old ladies. This occasion will bring you to Georgia so can't you plan to come on down here, before or after—that is the both of you—and give us an account of your Irish trip? I think Ashley [Brown] and Caroline [Gordon Tate] are coming for the weekend of the 23rd

(October) so don't come then as you would have to sleep in the barn. I don't know when the Ga. Wr. thing is.

I have just got through correcting proofs which is very discouraging as I see all the awful things wrong with it. It seems dull and half-done. Print is much too clear.

I hope you are getting on with yours ["To the Victor"] now.

It sounds as if you have a pretty good chance at the Ford with all those folks recommending you. Maybe you can go back to Ireland and work near one of those theatres.

Cheers,
Flannery

101. *To Flannery O'Connor from Brainard Cheney. TLS(cc) 1p.*

October Eleventh [1959]

Dear Flannery,

The GWA [Georgia Writers' Association] scroll conveyance is to occur on a Saturday night, October 31st—barring the interference of witches and haunts.

So though it will put you and Regina to come strain, some added strain, it won't I take it put me in the barn, if I accept your invitation for that week-end—to wit, November 1st, a Sunday. And with deep sympathy for your added strain, I herewith nevertheless accept your kind invitation.

This bids fair to be a rough fall for you all, on the literary circuit!

But I do so much want to see you. Fannie does, too. But dang it! She's got to set out this week-end to be gone a month, a bevy of visiting Japanese librarians. She tenders her heartfelt regrets.

Incidentally, I have been notified by Ford Foundation that I have been nominated. Just how much that means I don't know, for I still have to be voted on by an anonymous *panel*—supposedly on the basis of my statement of "purpose" and such like. Andrew Lytle tells me he has been nominated, too.

You have my mortal sympathy in your proof-correcting. There's nothing so deadly, nor disappointing and on the whole frustrating, I think.

It has been harder than usual for me to get down to work again—had my first real work day yesterday (Saturday) only to get interrupted again today! It's really hard to beat this game.

If the 31st is not convenient, let me know.

F. joins me in love to you both.

As ever,
Lon

102. *To Brainard Cheney from Flannery O'Connor. TLS 1p.*

Milledgeville, 14 October [19]59

Dear Lon,

We'll be looking for you on Nov. 1. Does this mean you will try to make Mass here or go in Atlanta? Here it is at 7:15 and 11:15. We go early. If you want to drive on down Saturday night, just let us know. Anyone coming on the premises unexpected in the night is given the silent treatment while my mother calls the sheriff, but if we are prepared to expect you, we will let you in.

You don't have to worry about interference from witches and hants at the GWA [Georgia Writers' Association]. They are all members and participate. Mrs. [Raymond] Massey called me up the other night and asked me to talk at one of the meetings. I declined. She then offered to make it a night meeting (more glamorous). I declined. She then said, "Flahnury, deh, have you reached the stage where you accept pay for your talks?" "Oh yes," says I, "long ago." "Well," she says, "we will pay you." I declined. Told her I was going to have company that weekend, so don't let her know you are coming to Milledgeville and be the company as I made out I was going to have company all weekend. I congratulated her on their awarding the award to you and that ended our conversation on a cheery note.

We are looking forward to yr arrival at whatever hour.

Cheers,
Flannery

103. *To Flannery O'Connor from Brainard Cheney. TLS(cc) 1p.*

Smyrna, Tennessee, October Twentieth [1959]

Dear Flannery,

It is disappointing to think about, but I reckon that I had better not try to make mass in Milledgeville. I don't know what time I could decently get away from whatever demands are put upon me in Atlanta—and it would be a two-hour drive for me in the middle of the night and later than that when I got to Andalusia Farm. No. I'll not try it.

So I will make an early mass in Atlanta. I have a reservation at the Biltmore. I trust I can find a church in the neighborhood. With ordinary order and luck I should be able to make your place by Noon, or before.

After you failed her, Mrs. R. M. [Raymond Massey] called me (on Sunday) and gave me the business about participating. But she didn't get to the point of offering me pay—I might have weakened! She did say, however, "Would you like us to pay for your hotel?" I told her quick that it would be an utter pleasure. So maybe I did make something out of the encounter.

F. is real put out that she can't come! Anyhow, she joins in sending love to you both.

As ever,
Lon

104. *To Brainard Cheney from Flannery O'Connor. TLS 1p.*

Milledgeville, 9 November [19]59

Dear Lon,

Here is the Irish constitution back.[1] We are real glad you got to see Fr. Paul [Bourne].[2] He did get permission to come down with [William] Sessions and the lady from San Francisco last Saturday and I guess it was quite an outing for a Trappist. Anyway, he enjoyed your visit and was very pleased you asked for him. He brought Regina some plants and we sent him back with some nuts for the monks, which they can eat. It turns out he is a great admirer of Baron von Hugel.[3]

A letter from Caroline [Gordon Tate] seemed more or less cheerful.

We have put up the bottle of doubtful liquor for your next visit. Make it soon.

Cheers,
Flannery

1. Cheney had left with O'Connor a copy of the Constitution of the Republic of Ireland. See Letter 99.
2. See Letter 91.
3. See Letter 88, note 1.

105. *To Brainard and Frances Neel Cheney from Flannery O'Connor. TLS 1p.*

Milledgeville, 10 December [19]59

Dear Lon & Fannie,

Merry Christmas to you both and so forth. We are holding up well under a drizzle of relatives for the holidays, but otherwise have nothing to report. Caroline [Gordon Tate] reports that the doctor has found her to have thyrotoxicos apathetica; but whether this is a purely literary disease or not I don't know. Anyways, the best from Andalusia for the season.

Affectionately,
Flannery

106. *To Brainard Cheney from Flannery O'Connor. TLS 1p.*

Milledgeville, 6 February [19]60

Dear Lon,

There is no accounting for people who give away money. However, this must mean that you are to write novels and not plays and it is nobler to write novels than plays according to my deep feelings on the subject.[1]

I can't remember your last [novel-in-progress] title ["To the Victor"] but HEART OF MADNESS sounds too much like HEART OF DARKNESS maybe; but I am glad you are coming on with it.

We were visited by Ashley [Brown] three days last week. He had made Henry James' tour from Charleston through Florida. Ashley is on the road now more than Kerouac,[2] though in a more elegant manner.

Our room is finished and awaits guests. My mother was sorry she missed you all when you stopped over. She saw you coming in but didn't know who it was as Lee [Jessup] was driving.

I am steeling myself to gaze coldly at the reviewers who are going to trounce my novel[3] [*The Violent Bear It Away*]. One old lady has already started the ball rolling in the Library Journal with many unfavorable comments;[4] however, Andrew Lytle says it works and I, having written it, am inclined to agree with him. [Robert] Giroux says there is a favorable one in the February Catholic World.[5]

Cheers to you and Fanny and let us know if you are coming this way.

Flannery

1. Cheney did not receive the Ford Foundation award he had sought. See Letter 97, note 1.

2. Jack Kerouac, Beat Generation novelist, wrote *On the Road* (New York: Viking Press, 1957).

3. *The Violent Bear It Away* was published on February 8, 1960. New York: Farrar, Straus and Cudahy.

4. Dorothy Nyren, Untitled Review, *Library Journal,* 85 (January 1, 1960), 146.

5. P. Albert Duhamel, "Flannery O'Connor's Violent View of Reality," *Catholic World,* 190 (February, 1960), 280–85.

107. *To Flannery O'Connor from Brainard Cheney. TLS(cc) 1p.*

Smyrna, February 20th [1960]

Dear Flannery,

Here it [Cheney's novel-in-progress] is again, with a face lifting and a new name! And I hope more of a novel.

I'm not happy with the name, but I haven't been able to think of a better one yet.

I just told Fannie what was on my mind a few minutes ago and she said it would be damned, without that curse tagged on to it: NIGGER LOVER. I suppose the opprobrium would be rather too much to bear up under.

The irony would be pretty harsh, too.

By this time I don't know whether I like it or not.

I am zoomed up over TVBIA [*The Violent Bear It Away*] again—but what I have to say about it, I'll put in my review[1] and send you that.

Cleaning this one up was real bitter work. And I'm not too sure about the copying—I haven't done a line by line rereading. Hope you don't run into too many bulls.

We have had three snows this month! Most unusual for us—it's still on the ground.

But when spring comes, we hope you will feel like coming up to see us—What about it?

Must get this to the p.o. before noon—they shut tight here at the stroke of Twelve.

Fannie joins me in our best.

As ever,
Lon

1. "Bold, Violent, Yet Terribly Funny Tale," *The Nashville Banner*, March 4, 1960, p. 23. See Appendix C.

108. *To Brainard Cheney from Flannery O'Connor. TLS 1p.*

26 February [19]60

Dear Lon,

I have just finished your ms. and will write you a short note to get out my first enthusiasm. To tell you the truth when you told me what you were going to do with the last third of it, I thought: oh oh, it's going to get worse. But it has not got worse, it has got better. Once you get yourself on the stage and take over, interest never fails for the reader. I think the whole thing hangs together. I think you have pulled it off.

My only serious objection is in the last twenty or thirty lines—when he tells her that he is hungry and is going to eat the body of the Lord. This is very abrupt and being so unprepared for, it provokes laughter and not the emotion it should. I think you would do better to have him think to himself in his own head what it is he is hungry for—maybe a couple of paragraphs or maybe just one would do—then after thinking it, he could turn and tell Missie that he knows what she is after, but not say what because actually it can't be said to her. It will be enough here if the reader gets it.

I think you ought to be real pleased with yourself over what you have done here. I'll send the ms. back tomorrow or Saturday with a few details marked down that you might give a lick or two to.

I have just read a review of my book [*The Violent Bear It Away*] in Time[1] that is rather like having a dirty hand wiped across your face. They even bring in the lupus. Also read Mr. Donald Davidson's review in the NYTimes.[2] There is a good one from the Catholic pint [*sic*] of view in the February Catholic World[3] and a favorable one in the Saturday Review by Granville Hicks.[4] But I see it is going to get a nasty trouncing.

Well cheers for you. I ain't no critic but I sure like your book.

Oh. I hope Fannie wins out on your not calling it NIGGER LOVER but I don't like HEART OF MADNESS any better. Too many hearts of things lying around now.

My love to you both,
Flannery

1. "God-Intoxicated Hillbillies." *Time,* 75 (February 29, 1960), 118, 121.

2. "A Prophet Went Forth." *New York Times Book Review,* February 28, 1960, p. 4.

3. See Letter 106, note 4.

4. "Southern Gothic With A Vengeance." *Saturday Review,* 63 (February 27, 1960), 18.

109. *To Brainard Cheney from Flannery O'Connor. TLS 1p.*

Milledgeville, 27 February [19]60

Dear Lon,

Some further minor notes on your book:

page 9—I don't much think it's good to say "we of religious bent"—I don't know that you want to make the narrator's point of view so explicit there, you'll lose a lot of readers if you do. You might just say the part about original sin and let the reader draw his own conclusions.

page 18—boy to bear—transpose. I guess this is a typing error.

page 31—see ms.

page 44—one arm would do. I still think you overdo it here.

page 66—cliche

page 78—I'd cut out that "drooling like a bullfrog," etc.

page 122—see ms.

page 246—that "flags of true" image don't work, for me anyway.

The only other thing I can think of is this: *if I was you* I'd hit it another lick where Marcellus enters upon the scene where Missie is being stomped. You just report there that they had the woman on the ground. I think you ought to draw the picture more distinctly. Marcellus is telling this not just after it happened, but much later when the woman is an important part of his experience. It seems to me he would be more emotional here, dilate a bit maybe, and we could get a hint of his further relations with Missie. He wouldn't just say "the woman" was on the ground.

I think you have mighty well overcome the curse of topicality in this book, which was what worried me when I read it first.

Thanks for asking me up. Maybe when I get shut of

these talks[1] I can come. The last one is the 1st of May. I am thoroughly sick of hearing myself.

Cheers to you and Fannie,
Flannery

1. An upcoming lecture tour; see Letters 113, 114, 115.

110. *To Flannery O'Connor from Brainard Cheney. TLS(cc) 1p.*

Smyrna, March Fifth [1960]—and the coldest here on record!

Dear Flannery,

Thanks so much for reading it again, and so much thanks for your good criticism. I agree with you entirely. Have triggered with the final scene at the door, taking only the incredible sentence out of direct quotes and leaving the rest in. Though I have no idea that that is final.

I am still puzzling over a title.

Thanks too for the tear sheet from [the Atlanta] Constitution. It seems to be general, all right.

We are having our trouble here with a sit-in at lunch counter demonstrations. My sympathies are divided. Vanderbilt fired a Negro preacher-divinity student and one could assuredly say with justice on its side, but surely not charity. He had taken part in leading the demonstration, was guilty of talking too much—so that some of the demonstraters had it in for him, too—and advocated continued violations of the city ordinance—or at least current police interpretation of it.

Now that I see my comments on TVBIA [*The Violent Bear It Away*] in print they seem a lot of generalized spouting and very little about the book. I tried to cover too much ground and rather mother-hubbarded it. And I used every bit of space the editor would allow me, too.

At a party at Walter Sullivan's the other evening, Fannie led me up to Don [Donald Davidson] (I had not seen his review then) who, it seems, was saying that he couldn't understand it, and said "Lon knows—Tell Don what it means Lon"!!* * + #!! She can be awfully trying for me sometimes!

Anyhow, his review was respectful. I couldn't see that the Herald-Trib did much better.[1] Haven't seen *Time* or the good one you mentioned yet, but will look them up.

Fannie is calling me—we were on our way to the store to get Sunday groceries, when she got a long distance call from her old library pal, Bob Gitler,[2] in Chicago, so I put the empty bottles we were returning down and took up this letter—now Bob has hung up and she wants to go again.

Anyhow, it's enough of me for one time!

We send our best.

Lon

1. Coleman Rosenberger. "In A Bizarre Backcountry." *New York Herald Tribune Book Review,* February 28, 1960, p. 13.

2. Robert L. Gitler (1909–) was later Director of the George Peabody College Library School, 1964–67.

111. *To Flannery O'Connor from Brainard Cheney. TLS(cc) 2 pp.*

Smyrna, Wednesday, March Ninth [1960]

Dear Flannery,

This is to tell you that your publisher did not send a copy of THE VIOLENT BEAR IT AWAY to *The* [Nashville] *Tennessean* here (the book page that Dick Beatty runs). And he is disappointed. It does seem that they might have at that. Your chances of intelligent consideration with Beatty is [*sic*] far above average. Even sales here, I would guess, might be better than average.

I am casing a book (since I see the author every time I go to a party at Grace Zibart's)[1] by a lay divinity professor at VU.[2] I don't know whether he has a denominational connection or not, but he is obviously a professional protestant. I suspect that he is a follower of [Richard Reinhold] Niebuhr, since he (N.) is the editor of the series in which our friend (a Dr. Gilky) appears. Gilky has gone back to orthodox Christianity (insofar as doctrine is concerned) offering criticism of both

Protestant Liberals and Fundamentalists. A thing he does by liberally quoting from, among others, the Church Fathers from Iranaeus through Aquinas (here he breaks off sharply). Then says: "Protestantism can consistently appeal to no external authorities in religion; what a man cannot himself affirm to be true can have no real value or relevance to him."

I haven't finished it, but it would seem that he expects to cover up on his demarche to orthodoxy by the expedient of the Emperor whose nakedness the true believers would not remark. He is still awfully scientistic, except as to religious doctrine.

It is curious. And I will have to finish it to see what sort of accomodation, if any, he works out.

We are still snowed under—the seventh snow last night—four inches. Fannie finally got to town about mid day.

We are looking forward to May and your coming up.

F. joins me in love,

Lon

1. A Nashville friend; wife of Carl Zibart, a Nashville book dealer.

2. Langdon Brown Gilkey (1919–), theology professor at Vanderbilt University, 1954–63, wrote *Maker of Heaven and Earth: A Study of the Christian Doctrine of Creation* (Garden City, New York: Doubleday, 1959).

112. *To Brainard Cheney from Flannery O'Connor. ALS 1p.*

Friday [March 1960]

Dear Lon,

I am distressed they didn't send a book [*The Violent Bear It Away*] to the *Tennessean* but I will write and tell them to. If it's too late to review it, he'll have the book anyway.

I am currently in bed with the sore throat, which is why you are being subjected to my handwriting.

I liked your review very much and am obliged to you for doing so well by me. With [Donald] Davidson thinking it was a fantasy, I had about lost my faith in educated readers.

I have just received a review from the Boston Herald[1]

which announced that it is a real tragedy about an old man's inhumanity to a child. Sob.

It was snowing here this morning and we are all sick of the weather.

Cheers to you & Fannie
Flannery

1. Ruth Wolfe Fuller, "Inhumanity to a Child," *Boston Sunday Herald,* February 28, 1960, p. 40.

113. *To Flannery O'Connor from Brainard Cheney. TLS(cc) 2 pp.*

Smyrna, Tenn., April 4, 1960

Dear Flannery,

Look not upon the wine when it is red, nor upon the whiskey at any time—I think that Scripture should read. I don't have a head this morning, but my stomach feels somebody had been discarding old inner tubes and the like in it.

It was truly scandalous in me, here on Passion Sunday. But I was one of the honorees (there were a hundred more) of the T. [Tennessee] Library Assn. party for T. [Tennessee] authors yesterday afternoon. I fortified myself ahead of time. Then I consoled myself afterward.

And today my Scriptural readings and meditations are proving depressing.

Fannie had to take hers with her to town and school, poor wretch. But that may be a better way to forget about it. I have finished a first draft of a play (I CHOOSE TO DIE) as of Saturday. And that's not a title I would want to be fooling around with today anyhow.

And I have a letter of criticism (finally) from Red [Robert Penn] Warren on my novel, which I am calling current, THE PRESSURE ON OUR HEARTS—sounds more like a moral essay than a novel title, but how do you like it. Of course, I knew Red would not like my novel, nor my viewpoint—he being a Liberal Materialist, that was one reason I wanted his comment. He was even more radical than I had counted on. He said, in effect, throw it away and write another one. Still I hope to benefit some from his criticism. Just now, I'm not up to figuring out how! One thing, I'm going to give *Marse* [a] nickname and drop the Marse out of use—he said *they* (Meaning the LM's [Liberal Materialists] I take it) would throw rocks at me if I left in that petit nom. I'm thinking of giving him the nickname of Shorty—Shorty Hightower—a man of his build with Hightower for a last name would inevitably have been called Shorty.

We are at last having spring here—and none too soon! Fannie and I put in most of Friday afternoon puttering around the yard—but have had rain every day since.

How are you coming with your tours? And when will they be over? We are making plans for your coming up for a good long visit—and we hope you are making plans, too?

Best of luck!

Yrs.,
Lon

114. *To Brainard Cheney from Flannery O'Connor. TLS 1p.*

Milledgeville, 10 April [19]60

Dear Lon,

I guess that's what Red's [Robert Penn Warren's] reaction could be expected to be, but I still think it's a success. The name Marse seemed to me to fit in well with his interest in his overshoes. I would at least have him remember once in a while that his real name is Marcellus even if he must be called Shorty. After all, it's your book, it ain't Red's.

Keep thinking about the title. You'll get a better one if you keep thinking.

I wrote FS&C [Farrar, Straus and Cudahy, O'Connor's publishers] to send the book to [Richmond] Beatty, which they did, and he gave it to Walter Sullivan to review. Walter, as you will see, didn't do much with it, but don't mention I said so.[1]

I have just got back from Mobile and the Jesuit College. You would like it. I enjoyed myself very much and had a good audience. They begin their classes with Our Father, close them with the Hail Mary, are integrated and lapped in azaleas. I still have another talk in front of me, this one to a Catholic women's convention in Savannah. I am doing this one because I can't fast for lent and should do some extra penance. They are my version of the hairshirt.

I was mighty edified by the Rev. Pike.[2] Anything like this I am always glad to hear about.

Love to you and Fannie. Whyn't you all come to see us and christen our new room?

Flannery

1. "Violence Dominates Fresh Tale," The Nashville *Tennessean,* April 24, 1960, p. 13-D.

2. Probably a reference to a newspaper clipping about James Pike, controversial and iconoclastic Episcopal bishop.

115. *To Brainard and Frances Neel Cheney from Flannery O'Connor. TLS 1p.*

Milledgeville, 8 May [19]60

Dear Lon & Fannie,

I didn't get to complete the circuit afterall. I got to Mobile but not to Savannah for the anticipated hair-shirt talk as I broke out with a splendid case of hives about ten days beforehand. This was perfect timing. The doctor said I could not go. This is what you call an anticipatory illness and illustrates psychosomatic disease at its best. I hope that my carcus will bring off another triumph like this the next time it is necessary.

We have been having such a spate of company and still expect so many that I don't see myself a clear weekend yet to come to Nashville. When is the season up on you? I know I can't get there in May.

According to rumor Caroline [Gordon Tate] is busy doing research on herself in the Tate Archives at Princeton.

I'm glad the novel is out of your house and the play is

in and I hope the off-Broadway bidnis goes along.[1] I have a friend [Maryat Lee] trying to get up the money to put one on and to hear her tell about her trials makes me glad I'm not nothing but a novelist.

Fannie, quit malingering and have the hives instead. Much more dramatic.

Cheers,
Flannery

1. An off-Broadway production of Cheney's "Strangers in This World" which never materialized, despite considerable New York encouragement and months of effort.

116. *To Flannery O'Connor from Brainard Cheney. TLS (cc) 1p.*

Lumber City, Georgia, June 18th [1960]

Dear Flannery,

You made a not-very-serious-sounding inquiry about the possibility of our extending a May-time invitation to come to see us in Smyrna into a June-time one (Knowing, I trust, that the invitation is standing and perennial, anyhow). And I did not reply—at least, not til now. The truth was that you sounded so dubious and then the school-end season came on us, and Andrew Lytle & family came up to Sewanee to marry off their daughter Pamela—the publishing house of McDowell Obolensky blew up and David McD. [McDowell] came to Sewanee, too (to deliver a commencement speech)—etc, etc—just one thing after another (Including visits by Ashley [Brown] plus Carole Johnson,[1] and James Waller[2]). In on top of it all, I had suddenly to run off down here to see an old girl while I could see her. That I never did get around to writing you. Never did!

And the thing is that Fannie, too, had to run off and is now, I take it, in Montreal, Canada—whooping it up with the girls of ALA [American Library Association]. We both will be back on the 25th.

And what about making that invitation for July? July would be wonderful for us. We both plan to be there, and there is nothing planned, except what we may plan for the occasion of your visit?

And, oh, by the way—as usual, I am down in Georgia, and would surely hate to pass through (or into and out of again) the state, without seeing you? If it is convenient, I would come by on my way back? But do be brutally frank. I can understand, that you have not only a problem of finding time to work, but finding time to have company. And goldernit say so? I will be leaving here early Wednesday morning. Do very much want to see you and talk about several things. And could stop over Wednesday evening, if it were convenient. On the other hand, I would understand it completely and utterly if it was inconvenient?

Please let me know.

I seem to be on the uncharted waters in David McD's. pocket, with my last novel (HRTL) ["Hard Road to Love"]. And anybody's guess is as good as mine on what's going to happen.

Do hope this finds you well?

My affectionate regards to you and Regina,
Lon

1. Carol Johnson (1928–) contributed poetry, reviews, essays, and articles to the *Sewanee Review, Shenandoah, Commonweal,* and *Poetry.* She was a friend and correspondent of O'Connor's: "the only writer I ever initiated a correspondence with," O'Connor wrote to "A" (*The Habit of Being,* p. 184).

2. See Letter 58, note 1.

117. *To Brainard Cheney from Flannery O'Connor. TLS 1p.*

Milledgeville, 18 July [19]60

Dear Lon,

I do like the fish title better, but then I think anything at all would be better than Hard Road to Love. Keep on reading the Bible and you might find something better yet. I hope the new one is on the road. I find the whole idea of the new one very exciting.[1]

Tomorrow we are having quite a party to spend the afternoon with us—the Trappist Abbot, a Monsignor from the Atlanta diocese and a station wagon full of nuns from the cancer home in Atlanta.[2] They are going to bring their lunch and eat it on the road and then spend the afternoon with us. We invited them to lunch but the sister said she wouldn't think of it as then she couldn't bring as many as she wanted to. They may even stick in a couple of cancer patients. These sisters are writing a book which they want me to edit. I don't know what will come of it. Anyhow they are going to get quite a trip tomorrow. They are in the order founded by Hawthorne's daughter. I have just read that lady's biography. It might interest you. Theodore Maynard: "A Fire Was Lighted."[3]

I've been asked to go to Minnesota in October for a week and talk at four or five Catholic colleges—the which I plan to do. The Sisters who have asked me have the idea that I'm quite decripit and have asked if I would like to be lodged in their infirmary. I want to mitigate this reputation, but not too much.

Cheers to you and Fannie and if you get down this way before the summer is out, let us know.

Love to you both,
Flannery

1. Cheney envisioned a trilogy of novels, beginning with *This Is Adam* and ending, in the chronology of the story they would tell, with "Quest for the Pelican." The "new" novel Cheney would call "The Tiger Returns" (see Letter 139) and eventually publish as *Devil's Elbow* (New York: Crown, 1969).

2. Our Lady of Perpetual Help Home.

3. Theodore Maynard, *A Fire Was Lighted: The Life of Rose Hawthorne Lathrop* (Milwaukee: Bruce Pub. Co., 1948).

118. *To Flannery O'Connor from Brainard Cheney. TL(cc) 1p.*

Smyrna, Friday, Ninth [September, 1960]

Dear Flannery,

I've been aiming at this for weeks.

But somehow my letter-writing has been inhibited. I think, perhaps, it's because I haven't been writing—period.

We are trying to eke out the summer, while September lashes us with a fiery tail. It's been a frabjous season. Unplanned activities, guests, demands—

tomorrow I'm to join my fellow K. of Cs. [Knights of Columbus] at St. Rose church at Murfreesboro to help paint the church! You know, a neighborly old paint slapping-on. If they know what's good for them they won't turn me aloose with that paint brush! I painted the roof to this house. It took three painters to get that straightened out.

Currently Tom Stritch is here. He spent the night with me on Wednesday (Fannie had gone down to Newberry to visit her brother) and we sat late with the problems of the world, soared the highest mountains and saw into valleys that we could not see at all the next day. But we enjoyed ourselves. One incidental upshooting of our discourse was his opinion that the Catholic issue will not be important in the National campaign[1]—as a Georgian-Tennessean, I take a contrary view. Also I was on hand (a loyal pro) when Al Smith ran back there.

Tom is working on a memoir of his beloved uncle, the cardinal[2]—but I could not get a look at it—that is not yet. We spoke of you—almost called you up, until we looked at the clock.

The week before I had a brief visit from Russell Kirk[3]—working on an article for *Fortune* magazine. It was his view that, at the present, the unholy alliance between the secularists and the Baptists would beat Kennedy.

Fannie finally finished up summer school (19th, August) and we've been trying to do something about the place: patching, mending, plumbing, etc. This includes setting out 25 yellow pines: I mean it is to include it: the trees haven't got here yet.

Nothing has happened with me, literarily speaking. I have done the basic planning for my next novel, but haven't worked up steam (nor acquired the leisure) to start it yet.

Let me try a new name for my current (unpublished) novel on you: QUEST FOR THE PELICAN.[4] The only thing is that I can't find a proper quotation for [the] fly leaf to indicate the nature of the Pelican.

Hope you feel up to your Minnesota expedition—you couldn't come by on your way? 'Twould be fine.

F. joins me in the warmest.

Yrs.

1. 1960 Presidential campaign, in which Roman Catholic John F. Kennedy ran against and defeated Richard M. Nixon.

2. Samuel Alphonsus Stritch (1887–1958), Cardinal, Archbishop of Chicago.

3. See Letter 24, note 3.

4. As these letters show, Cheney had considerable difficulty arriving at this, his final title choice for the novel he was never to publish. There were at least seven working titles: "To the Victor," "Heart of Madness," "Nigger Lover," "The Pressure on Our Hearts," "Hard Road to Love," one O'Connor refers to (in Letter 117) as "the fish title," and finally "Quest for the Pelican."

119. *To Brainard Cheney from Flannery O'Connor. TLS 1p.*

15 September [19]60, Milledgeville

Dear Lon,

Tell Tom Stritch if he gets to Georgia not to fail to come to see us. We are still having a passel of company. After your visit I had a call from Mrs. Gordon Tate Herself from Princeton saying her aunt in Chatanooga had summoned her and she would like to come see us on her way back. She said she would come on the following Tuesday but arrived instead on Monday. She stayed until Wednesday and we haven't heard from her since she left. However, the people over at Wesleyan are having one of those Arts Festivals that no college can now do without and have invited her to be on the panel (me too) and she wrote the man she would come as she would be glad to continue her visit with us. So it appears we are to be honored again. She is deep in that novel[1] and much involved with it, but all one afternoon she sat and talked Allen [Tate].

I am sorry to hear about Mrs. [Andrew] Lytle. I don't know about their disasterous trip to Mexico. What happened?[2]

I like QUEST FOR THE PELICAN better than any yet and if I run up on any proper quotation I will let you know. Seems to me there is a poem I read once, but I can't think what it was. Might not have been any good. What has [David] McDowell done? Do you have a publisher?

I wish I could come by on my way to Minn. but I will be doing mighty well to get there. I always assume I ain't going to get where I'm going, but am the better pleased if I do arrive.

Love to you and Fannie,
Flannery

1. Presumably, "The Narrow Heart." See Letter 89, note 2.
2. Edna Lytle had an attack of pneumonia in Mexico during the summer of 1960. She was brought back to a hospital in Memphis, where she was diagnosed as having lung cancer.

120. *To Flannery O'Connor from Brainard Cheney. TLS(cc) 1p.*

Smyrna, Saturday, [October] 15th [1960]

Dear Flannery,

This letter has been put off in the hope that I might have some news for it. But I've given up on the news.

I was happy to have a note on Mrs. G. T. [Gordon Tate], Herself, God bless her! And I hope the Wesleyan affair went off pleasantly for you both. And there couldn't be better news about her than that you gave of her absorption in her new novel.

We hear that Edna Lytle [Mrs. Andrew Lytle] is much restored from her cobalt treatment (she is now in Gainesville). Just what that means, however, we don't know. She is due back in Memphis for examination and possibly an operation in about a week, I think.

Fannie is off conventioneering for the second time since school took in for the fall. She got back from Chicago, just long enough to touch base (literally, ½ day on campus) and take off for Asheville, N.C., where she has been since Tuesday and won't be back til Sunday.

I'm adjusted to single-footing it, all right; but I can't say that I like it!

Tom Stritch has been here (N.) [Nashville] for his Uncle Eugene S's funeral, but I only got in a phone talk with him—he was hurrying back to labor. He seems to feel quite optimistic (as a Democrat) about the Presidential election. I told him that is, perhaps, easier in the atmosphere of Notre Dame, Indiana, than this Baptist-Church of Christ belt. I think Tennessee is going Republican and for no other reason than the oldest prejudice of them all.

No news to report either from my would-be publisher, or my would-be producer—in New York. Cheerless.

Joe Wright at Vanderbilt is going ahead with the thing called, I CHOOSE TO DIE, with music and dancing.[1] But undergraduate talent is most uncertain—it remains a pig in a poke. By the way, the opening is set for November 2nd—won't you be traveling about that time—either to or from Minnesota? We would be most honored and delighted to have you stop by? Not that the play would be (at its best) any real reason—but we add it as inducement. I know it's a bad word to use, but I count it my *experimental* effort at Christian comedy, or rather tragi-comedy, in this case.

I haven't been able to run down a single allusion to Christ as Pelican, either in verse or prose. I'm still counting on you!

My argument for your stopping off here, is to break your journey—we will promise, not a single party, if you want it that way?

Love to you and Regina,
Lon

1. "I Choose to Die." Music, Phillip Slates; choreography, Joy Zibart; direction, Joseph E. Wright. Produced, Nashville, Vanderbilt University Theatre, November 2–5, 1960.

121. *To Brainard Cheney from Flannery O'Connor. TLS 1p.*

Milledgeville, 22 October [19]60

Dear Lon,

I have just got back to your kind invite but the sisters in Minnesota drained me of my anyway inconsiderable store of energy. I will have a few days to recuperate before the Wesleyan thing and Mrs. Gordon Tate Herself. They are also having Miss KA [Katherine Anne] Porter. According to Ashley [Brown] these two have not confronted each other for fifteen years, or maybe it is spoken to each other for fifteen years. Anyway, the occasion should be of interest.

I am weary of riding upon airyplanes and being The Honored Guest. I think the reason I like chickens is that they don't go to college.

Cheers to you & Fannie,
Flannery

122. *To Flannery O'Connor from Brainard Cheney. TL(cc) 2pp.*

Smyrna, Tenn., November 24th [1960]

Dear Flannery,

A letter from Ashley Brown to Fannie has given us a report on the Wesleyan festival. He found Caroline [Gordon Tate] embattled against the world, but that you and Katherine Ann [Porter] complemented each other in the seminars.

We would so much like to have your report on it, too.

The Vanderbilt production of my play, I CHOOSE TO DIE almost bore me out with the hero.

Joe Wright (VU director) who made of it a piece of practice work for his undergraduates, instead of drawing in more competent talent, turned up without a single man adequate to his role.

Then, when he mimeographed the manuscript (the one small material profit I had hoped to get from it was some copies of the play) for use by the cast and staff, he had only the dialog run off, dropping all of the stage instructions, etc. And, incidentally, dropping a good many lines, in the sloppy job done. And the play depended for its effects very importantly on staging business and what was done and how done.

I was scarcely able to work *in theater* with Joe at all, because his people were such amateurs I had to let him get what results he could with them by his own ideas and methods.

On top of that, of course, it was put on a stage and

with sets far different from those in my mind, with which I had worked the play out—to be sure this always happens to some extent.

Then on top of that I prescribed a couple of my own notions (for staging) that were too cinematic and wouldn't work out on the stage and with sets Joe and his stage manager had built. They had to be dropped. And I had no ready substitute for them—they were aimed at *weighting* some of the melodrama of situation and lines.

In the circumstances I was not able to work in theater with my collaborators, either—so that I really never knew what the dancing was going to look like nor the music sound like until I saw it on opening night! As, I suppose, might have been anticipated in the circumstances, the song and dance team went-to-town on this *carte blanc* opportunity. So that we had in the dance and music introduced to extend the effect and significance of the climax (a scene lasting 1½ minutes) a business that went on for five minutes and almost lost the climax!

But desite of these drawbacks, I may say Wright (and his stage, music and dance directors) put it across as a show—an effect of astonishing impact. If not the effect I had in mind, still enough of it for one reviewer to get it.

The composer, Philip Slates, has done some pretty exciting music for it, I think.

At one point, however, I made a scene between us—very unChristian, even childish. But right on top of finding the unusual liberties the director had taken with the script (which in effect placed interpretation of the lines wholly in his hands) and the fact that Wright had abandoned my most important stage business, and that I couldn't communicate with the actors at all and sitting there watching all of my lines being done the way I most hoped wouldn't be done, why it came about that—after trying for two weeks to get it over to the composer that I only wanted a couple of phrases from *Just Before The Battle, Mother* parodied in falsetto (trumpet accompaniment), he insists in putting on the whole song and a barbershop quartet, why, why I blew my top.

Ah me, the delights of the theater!

Anyhow, I got hung up on it and can't abandon it just yet. I should, of course, have already have dropped it and got back to my novel. But having readjusted it for obvious thinnesses and thicknesses that appeared in the production and having tried to find substitutes for the cinematic trick I had to abandon, I am now impressing Fannie into reading it critically to try to weed out the melodrama, if possible.

I've had a nibble on it for another amateur production. (The drama dept. at UT [University of Tennessee].)

Could you find the time and the fortitude and endurance to read it for me some time?

Fannie is calling me—we've got to go to town to eat turkey with Sister Lee [Jessup].

I really had some other things to talk about but they must go by the board for the nonce.

Luck!

F. joins me in love,

123. *To Flannery O'Connor from Brainard Cheney. TLS(cc) 1p.*

December Twenty-first [1960]

Dearest Flannery,

The state of your bones makes us appreciate you a little more this Christmas season! It may be that you have asked for seven league boots in a house of dwarfs. But we are going to stand on each others shoulders in this thing. And all together and, of course, mostly because it's Christmas, may be it will amount to something. But you can count on us trying.

And Atlanta is only our first stand.

We are going to make what wassail we make this Yuletide at Cold Chimneys.

There will be one Bhuddist and one Hindoo, Fannie's charges. But, in any event, they will be respectful.

And we have now a new chaplain (we've been a month without) over at Sewart Air Base, whose Latin is beautiful to hear!

I don't seem to make any literary advance. No news

on my publisher, if any—I've called him but couldn't get him to call me back—and I had already written him a month ago. Also, my off Broadway production deal is fast proving itself a dud.[1] I'm trying to carry on with the work in progress; but Christmas social activities are weighing me down.

Fannie has just finished her monthly book column for the *Wilson Library Bulletin*,[2] by the hardest—and we are going to town to mail it and take Xmas gifts to our departing sister and party, bound for Florida to spend the holiday.

It is that this is the season of Hope. And everybody, but everybody's got a share in it. Fannie joins me in love to you both and a great Christmas!

Lon

1. See Letter 115, note 1.

2. From November, 1942, until June, 1972, Mrs. Cheney edited "Current Reference Books," a monthly review column in the *Wilson Library Bulletin*. (When she retired, Mrs. Cheney was honored in an article entitled "Friends Salute the Profession's Number-One Reference Reviewer," *Wilson Library Bulletin*, 47 (September, 1972), 86–88.)

124. *To Brainard and Frances Neel Cheney from Flannery O'Connor. TLS 1p.*

Milledgeville, 7 January [19]61

Dear L&F,

We hope you all had a good Christmas. All the African contingent here celebrated long and furiously and are just now sobering up with the help of some words of warning of my mother's.

In the hospital they discovered that what is making my bones disintegrate are the steroids that they have been giving me for these ten years to control the lupus. So now they are trying to withdraw the steroid drugs and see if I work without them. This means that I am to stay at home and cultivate my garden for a while.

Did you know that Robert Fitzgerald is going to be in this country for four or so months? He is taking Roetheke's (sp?) place at the University of Washington for ten weeks;[1] after that I hope he will come to see us.

Cheers to you all for the new year. Let me know about the play ["I Choose to Die"] and the publisher.

Yours affectionately,
Flannery

1. Theodore Roethke, 1908–1963, was professor of English, 1948–62, and poet-in-residence, 1962–63, at the University of Washington, Seattle.

125. *To Flannery O'Connor from Brainard Cheney. TLS(cc) 1p.*

Smyrna, Sunday 22nd [January, 1961]

Dear Flannery,

We pray that the doctors effect a successful withdrawal of the steroid drugs! My chemistry is too weak to understand what this means, but my faith is stronger.

Cased on omnibus review by Arthur Mizener in the SEWANEE REVIEW[1] last night. Of course omnibus reviews are reprehensible in any circumstances, but it seemed to me that he failed to say anything relevant about THE VIOLENT BEAR IT AWAY at all, at all! And he didn't do much better with the other novel by a Southerner, Madison Jones' *Forest of the Night*,[2] if I recall the title right.

I had heard about Robert Fitzgerald's visit to this country and I am looking forward to being on a symposium with him in April at the University of Detroit. This is something that Andrew Lytle recommended me into (I'd never heard of U. of D. It's Catholic, I take it). We are to discuss: Christianity and the Tragic Vision. That's all I know about it, except that I accepted their invitation. The invitation was a hurried note just before Christmas with a promise of something more explicit on it later. However, I am planning to make the most of the occasion and head in that direction some days ahead of time to stop by Notre Dame to visit Tommie Stritch. He expects to have Robert with him then also!

This is confidential: but I've given up on [David] McDowell. When I finally got hold of him by phone a couple of days before Christmas, he was pretty vague about his plans and his outlook and [his] emotional tone was quite altered from what it was in the summer. Moreover, though nothing of the sort was said, I got the impression that he felt me to be a liability. I will do no formal breaking off: I think it won't be necessary. But I'm out prospecting for a new publisher.

I tried your old editor (Robert Giroux, whom I once met) just taking the initiative. But apparently he has given me the silent brushoff—three weeks gone and not so much as an acknowledgment.

It so happens that Morrow & Company (with a new young president) has been giving me some attention. I know their old editor (Francis Phillips: a regular New York liberal) and I have little hope that they will take me on. However, I've sent my last novel ["Quest for the Pelican"] to them.

Fannie joins me in love to you both.

Affectionately,
Lon

1. "Some Kinds of Modern Novels," 69 (Winter, 1961), 154–64.
2. New York: Harcourt Brace, 1960.

126. *To Brainard Cheney from Flannery O'Connor. TLS 1p.*

Milledgeville, 24 January [19]61

Dear Lon,

Don't give up on [Robert] Giroux yet. He is very slow and don't acknowledge manuscripts. I have been helping some Dominican Sisters with a book they wrote. I edited it, wrote an introduction, typed the whole thing and sent it to Giroux around the first part of December. No acknowledgement. Yesterday I got a letter saying they would take it. My introduction to the book is going to be printed in the April issue of JUBILEE,[1] and I'd like you [to] see it. The book is called A MEMOIRE [*sic*] OF MARY ANN.[2] It's very badly written but should be published and Giroux had the good sense to see it.

I appear to be doing all right so far.

Cheers to you & Fannie,
Flannery

1. "Mary Ann: An Excerpt from *A Memoir of Mary Ann*," *Jubilee*, 9 (May, 1961), 28–35.

2. *A Memoir of Mary Ann*, by the Dominican Nuns of Our Lady of Perpetual Help Home, Atlanta, Georgia (New York: Farrar, Straus and Cudahy, 1961). Mary Ann Long was a twelve year old girl who died of cancer after living nine years with the nuns at the cancer home in Atlanta. When she was approached by the nuns for help in publishing an account of Mary Ann's life, which they regarded as miraculous, O'Connor was quite dubious about the project but offered editorial assistance. She became increasingly interested in the project, however, convinced finally that there was something of the miraculous not only in Mary Ann's life but in the success of the publication as well. A full account of O'Connor's involvement can be read in the collected letters, especially those to Robert Giroux, in *The Habit of Being*.

127. *To Flannery O'Connor from Brainard Cheney. TLS(cc) 1p.*

Thursday, Smyrna [February? 1961]

Dear Flannery,

It was very reassuring to learn that you are making it under the new medical regimen.

And thanks for the word about [Robert] Giroux—I wish now I hadn't got my mss. ["Quest for the Pelican"] off to Morrow in such a hurry—though I had waited over three weeks. Morrow will probably turn it down.

I will be looking for your piece in JUBILEE—very interested to see it.

Andrew Lytle was in N. [Nashville], for a couple of days—up to a funeral—and I saw him off on his return flight last afternoon late. He reports that Edna [Lytle], still quite uncomfortable, and very short of breath and vitality, is nevertheless recuperating. She has to drive herself, but she does and gets household matters attended to and her children. She is gradually growing stronger, he says.

He is spending most of his time, outside of classes, nursing her—not so much waiting on her, he says, as nursing her emotionally and spiritually.

There will be no writing for him for a year, at least.

F. is still in Chicago, on her midwinter junket with her pals of the ALA [American Library Association] board—will be home Sunday morning.

No news with me, professionally.

Herewith, the play ["I Choose to Die"] I've been threatening you with—in its post-production rewritten form #1.

Best of luck!

Love,
Lon

128. *To Brainard Cheney from Flannery O'Connor. TLS 1p.*

Milledgeville, 13 February [19]61

Dear Lon,

I think the play ["I Choose to Die"] has real dramatic impact. I can't exactly visualize the dancing in there but I'm not so hot at visualizing plays anyhow. I certainly would like to see it put on.

I enclose an opus of mine.[1] I don't think too much of it.

You ought to enjoy the meet in Detroit. I saw the list of people that were invited and it reads like the Catholic Who's Who. I couldn't go because I figured there would still be ice and snow then and I am not asking for a fall. Also I didn't want to have to write a paper.

We have been celebrating Secession vigorously around here. Lance Phillips (the Englishman you met here a couple of times) wrote a pageant for them, which was very successful. Now they are trying to make this a second Williamsburg (or wherever that it [*sic*] they put on that Virginia pageant) and make the pageant a going thing. They smell money in it and are trying to make Brother Phillips give them the copyright, but he is only going to do it if they guarantee him a rising percentage of their net profits. He says Paul Green[2] makes a lot of money. I hope he can get it out of them, but they ain't going to pay for anything they don't have to.[3]

When are you all taking another trip to Georgia? Let us know and include us in on it.

Cheers,
Flannery

1. "The Partridge Festival," *Critic*, 19 (February–March, 1961), 20–23, 82–85.
2. North Carolina playwright (1894–) who wrote and fostered the writing of outdoor symphonic dramas.

3. January 19, 1961, was the anniversary of Georgia's secession from the Union. The Secession ordinance had been adopted in Milledgeville, which was the State capitol from 1807–1868, and the anniversary was celebrated with Confederate flags, Civil War decorations in store windows, visits by state dignitaries, a 50-unit parade with bands and color guard, a Nike missile display, a luncheon, a dinner, a period costume square dance, and a pageant, "Their Massive Pride," telling of events before, during, and after the Secession convention.

129. *To Flannery O'Connor from Brainard Cheney. TL(cc) 1p.*

Smyrna, April Tenth [1961]

Dear Flannery,

Fannie is down stairs with her nose glued to our new tv. She doesn't know how to change the *record* yet, so she just sits and watches whatever comes on. But that does about as well as any other method. My excuse for getting it was to be able to see JFK's press conferences—but he seems to have quit just as we got it. At least, none since!

This, it would seem, is to give you a delayed reaction on your story: The Partridge Festival. But it wasn't intentional. I aimed to write some time back. But anyhow I still have a warm and pleasant memory of it. Singleton is a persuasive character. A pregnant post modern social institution, I'd say. Perhaps the story is not one of your great ones, but I found it very amusing. In Singleton, I think you've got something like an explosive for comic carthesis [*sic*] for the green intellectual sickness.

I am just back from the Detroit junket. Fact is, I got back last Wednesday. It would be more accurate, I suppose, to say I've just got over it. Anyhow I first tried to look at my novel mss. today—I tasted it, too—the flavor seemed like cold mutton. Though, I hope to warm it up, or get warmed up as time goes on.

The Detroit do was interesting, since I'd never been on one such before. Still I felt somewhat like a yard child in a horsehair parlor.

But my Easter visit with Tommie Stritch was without stint or stricture—even the snow storm! Tommie was fine. He now has a quite comfortable and convenient and cozy, what I guess comes under the category of a shotgun house. But it is all he needs, to be sure. With quite enough lawn along with it.

I was impressed with the extent and picturesqueness of the Notre Dame campus. I think it has considerable atmosphere and charm. We attended Saturday night services at the Sacred Heart Church (there on the campus) and I thought the choir was very fine. When we got out we stepped into a whirling, blinding snow storm which seemed much more appropriate to Christmas than Easter.

So I guess I got my money's worth on my spring trip up North!

Ice or no ice, snow storm or no snow storm, you were wise, I think, to pass up the junket. I spent close to a month, what with the reading I did and all, getting together the piece of mine, which they called "Tragic Roots of the Utopian Dream," but I called, "Can the Common Man Be Converted to Christianity."[1] I don't think they liked it. All events they couldn't fit it into a Shakespearean pattern and didn't know what to make of it. So they didn't. They just let it lay.

And I have deep suspicion that they (CRS)[2] don't intend to publish it, regarding it as far too illegitimate for *Renascence.* Moreover, we didn't get no honorarium— they just said that if there were anything left after they paid all the bills they might split it among the crowd—I'd rather take my chances with a one-armed bandit!

[Final lines, closing and signature obliterated]

1. Subsequently published as "Christianity and the Tragic Vision—Utopianism USA," *Sewanee Review,* 69 (Autumn, 1961), 515–33.

2. The Catholic Renascence Society, Inc., publisher of *Renascence: A Critical Journal of Letters.*

130. *To Flannery O'Connor from Brainard Cheney. TLS(cc) 1p.*

May Tenth [1961]

Dear Flannery,

JUBILEE just reached us and I read your piece. I found

it engrossing and profound. I take it this is your preface for the nuns' story? Your pronouncements on art, morals and theology are brilliant and illuminating.

I am inspired now to read the nuns' account of Mary Ann!

You do something to humanize Hawthorne for me, too! I am presently rereading THE SCARLET LETTER. Though usually considered his greatest work, I believe, the change in sexual morals and manners in this day makes it difficult to accept. I read this MY KINSMAN, MAJOR MOLINEAUX with real relish, however. It is, really, an anecdote, but profound.

Your preface is quite a piece. I want to think about it before making specific comment. But I certainly like it.

I trust no news from you is good news? A letter (lst in some time) from Ashley [Brown] yesterday, intimated that he gathered you had not been very well of late. I hope he is wrong!

We are well enough. Fannie is quite busy running the library school now, but the longer days of spring make commuting easier.

Professional news with me is somber. [Robert] Giroux turned down my novel (QFTP) ["Quest for the Pelican"] without a backward glance. Verdict: "I do not think it is a book which we could successfully publish," which he described as a "publishing rather than an editorial judgement," whatever that means.

Perhaps, it is that I have the wrong "pitch" on desegregation? I have thought of writing [Chicago publisher] Henry Regnery (whom I know slightly) telling him that New York publishers won't tough it because of its viewpoint (I believe HR has conservative reservation on the race issue) and ask him if he's interested.

In response to [the] Giroux letter I wrote to ask him if he would mind telling me why he thinks it's unpublishable. I haven't heard from [him] or got my mss. back yet (as of April 13th) but I suppose I will in due time.

I'm about to get warmed up on the work in progress, after so much interruption. But I haven't got enough down on paper yet to have any feeling about how I'm doing.

Fannie joins me in love to you and Regina.

As ever,
Lon

131. *To Brainard Cheney from Flannery O'Connor. TLS 1p.*

Milledgeville, 14 May [19]61

Dear Lon,

Thanks for your word about the introduction to the Sisters' book. It was Hawthorne that gave the thing its possibility. I persuaded them to dedicate the book To the Memory of Nathaniel Hawthorne. The book is pretty bad as far as the writing goes but they get the child across and that is all that matters in this one.

Ashley [Brown] is wrong. I am doing fine. I am almost off of the steroid drugs and am better for it, not worse.

Regina is fixing to sell out the dairy and go into beef. The D. P. [displaced person, Mr. Matisiack] gets more impossible daily and it will be a real burden off her to get rid of him. Right now we are praying for a buyer.

I gave the Sisters I wrote the introduction for a pair of peafowls for the patients at the Cancer Home. They built a seventy five foot run behind the building and say the patients have never had anything they enjoyed more. The Sisters gave me a portable television. They don't have any money of their own but one of them had a brother who gave it to them to give to me. About all we watch is the news but we are enjoying that and have seen some of the Press Conferences.[1]

I hope Regnery will like the book. [Robert] Giroux will probably never get around to telling you what makes the book unsalable. I am going to have a story called "Everything That Rises Must Converge" in New World Writing in the fall.[2] It is my reflection on the race situation.

Cheers to you & Fannie,
Flannery

[P.S.] When are you'all coming this way?

1. Televised press conferences held by President John F. Kennedy.
2. *New World Writing*, 19 (1961), 74–90.

132. *To Flannery and Regina Cline O'Connor from Brainard Cheney. TLS(cc) 1p.*

June Thirteenth [1961]

Dear Flannery & Regina,

It may seem irresponsible of us to speak of delights of our visit with you all, since the near fatal and grim incident involving you.[1] But we just cannot deny that we had a wonderful time!

And, after all, if you had to have one of your hands caught in the hay baler, it could have been a lot worse!

But it was a great satisfaction to find you both so equal to eventualities and stout of heart. We sure did eat high of the hog and the sights of Andalusia Farm were never more spectacular in their beauty.

We did not get home finally until about 1 o'clock on Saturday afternoon. Conveniently our guests didn't arrive til 5 o'clock. We bade them godspeed this morning. They ([Fannie's] brother Collier and wife) are heading for Mexico in a few days.

Please give our thanks and warm regards to Miss Mary [O'Connor's aunt] and our sympathy to Shot!

With love to you both,
Lon

1. O'Connor gave a full account of this episode in her June 10, 1961, letter to "A": "We had an awful accident here Thursday. Shot [Regina O'Connor's Black tenant] was sucked into the hay baylor up to his elbows. It was some time before he could be got out and he is pretty badly damaged but lucky to be alive. It didn't break any of his bones, but tore out some big gaps of flesh and gave him several third-degree belt burns. Regina and Lon Cheney, who was here at the time, stayed with him until the mechanic could come to get him out of the machine and the doctor could come. Then they took him to the hospital in her car and the doctor says he will be in there for some time. Of course he was fooling with the motor on—something she has told him a thousand times not to do. We are used to minor crises but this was major . . ." (*The Habit of Being*, p. 442).

133. *To Brainard and Frances Neel Cheney from Flannery O'Connor. TLS 1p.*

17 June [19]61

Dear L&F,

We want you all to come again soon so we can give you a visit with less dramatic impact and more eating at home.

Shot is doing very well. He can use his right hand all right and he can move the left one a little. Regina takes Louise everyday and Louise brings in all the colored sick news. He is in the room with a man whose daughter stobbed him and a man who had a stroke on the street and another man with the high blood.

Regina closed the deal on the cow sale, got her price, and the cows have left.

I have just got a letter from the Ford Foundation wanting me to come to a conference in New York August 30 of the people they gave the money to, so I guess I won't get to Smyrna as New York is enough travelling for me in one month, too much, but since they gimme all that money, I feel I have to go. Sold to the Ford for $8,000.

Cheers to you all,
Flannery

134. *To Flannery O'Connor from Brainard Cheney. TLS(cc) 1p.*

July Fourteenth [1961]

Dear Flannery,

This is written in the hope that you may already be able to reply to it. It will become apparent if you are not.

Needless to say, we are eager to have news about you and the hospital.[1] Have you gone? If so, what luck? If not, when are you going? Etc.

It seems a great while since I (with [Roque] Fajardo)[2] sat on your front porch and learned of your plan to go to the hospital, you said then, I believe, early in July?

A letter from Robert Fitzgerald says he can't come down here, but is finishing up at Bloomington on the 29th, and is leaving this country to return to Italy on the 30th!

He suggested that I meet him and Tommie Stritch (and the Nimses)[3] in Chicago on the evening of the 29th. But, I'm afraid I can't make it.

Among other reasons, there is the matter of finances. We are having to have done some renovation that is costing us heavily—even though I got it down by $500 by switching contractor and this that and the other. But we couldn't put it off any longer—having put it off for ten years! The back end of the house (ceiling) was about to rot out.

So we are having that quaint arrangement of shower room, dark room, half-bathroom and whathaveyou upstairs, outside my bedroom, reshuffled. We are supposed to get two bathrooms, a dressingroom and a passage way from my quarters to the front of the house (the top of the stairway) without having to go through the bathroom, out of it.

The contractors wrecking crew came and tore out and down (Oh, I forget to say: just after we contracted for the renovation, the ceiling fell in the diningroom) the rear part of the house and, it seems, have left me to my quiet and speculations—as to when, if ever they will return. The back speculations—as to when, if ever they will return. The back of the house is a wreck and the front looks like a warehouse.

Fannie, with perfect timing, chose this week to attend a convention in Cleveland.

I am working as well as can be expected, holed up in the library, in last refuge.

Please let us hear from you—if convenient.

My trip to Georgia (which I may tell you about later) I'm afraid accomplished nothing, except that very pleasant visit [with] you and Regina.

My love to you both,
Lon

1. O'Connor expected to have a hip operation, but her doctors decided against it.

2. Roque Fajardo, a long-time friend of Cheney's, had been on his staff when Cheney was public relations advisor to Tennessee Governor Frank Clement.

3. John Frederick Nims (1913–), distinguished poet, translator, and editor, was educated and taught at Notre Dame, where Stritch taught.

135. *To Brainard and Frances Neel Cheney from Flannery O'Connor. TLS 1p.*

Milledgeville, 23 July [19]61

Dear L&F,

We went last week to find out about the operation but the doctor says it would be too dangerous for me to have it so that is out. I will have to go confer with the Fords, dragging my weary bones, more or less.

Last week end Ashley [Brown] and Caroline [Gordon Tate] spent with us. She has joined Alcoholics Anonymous and can't talk about anything else. She thinks they are working out St. John of the Cross's mystical ascent. She's got it all figured out. Didn't drink so much as a drap of sherry the whole time she was here. She looks a great deal better, don't talk about Allen [Tate] all the time and is less bitter about things in general.

The Sisters' book [*A Memoir of Mary Ann*] has hit the jackpot. Good Housekeeping is going to feature it in their Christmas issue and paid $4,500 for the privilege. It has also been bought by Burns & Oates in London.

Shot is still in the hospital and longing to get home. He says he had a close escape and when he gets out again he's going to start going to church. He can use his hands a little bit, but not much. It may come in time.

We went up to north Georgia and bought us a registered Shorthorn bull, so we feel pretty much in the beef bidnis.

I was visited yesterday by a soldier from Ft. Gordon (reservist) who is a reporter for the Nashville Tennesseean. He goes back to Nashville next week and said he was going to look you all up. His name is Rudy

Abramson, should he show up. He is a friend of the Zibarts.[1]

Cheers,
Flannery

1. Carl and Alan Zibart owned Zibart's, a Nashville bookstore, and were good friends of the Cheneys and the other Vanderbilt connected people and were very active in the Nashville literary community; Joy Zibart, Alan's wife, was choreographer for Cheney's two plays (see Letter 2, note 2, and Letter 120, note 1).

136. *To Frances Neel Cheney from Flannery O'Connor. ALS 2pp.*

Milledgeville, 5 August [19]61

Dear Fannie,

I enclose a po-lite letter for the files about Patty Almy.[1] She lives up the road from us and is a good friend of mine & I am sure you would enjoy having her around. She had to take an education course (workshop) at GSCW [Georgia State College for Women] this summer. She said they were graded on groupiness and that she flunked watermelon cutting and touring (they took them to the woolen mills & she didn't go) but that she made it up by going to a picnic they had and bringing her ukelale (sp?) and by doing a lot of bridge playing. When you all come again, I'll have her down.

Shot has had his skin grafts & ought to be home in a couple of weeks—at which time our troubles will begin.

Cheers to you & Lon,
Flannery

1. Mrs. Almy was applying for admission to the George Peabody College Library School, which she later attended.

137. *To Brainard Cheney from Flannery O'Connor. ALS 1p.*

6 Sept. [19]61

Dear Lon,

Enclosed is the latest item [newspaper clipping] from Lumber City.

Shot got out of the hospital yesterday & now the

devil is busy thinking up something for his idle hands to do. We had a peaceful summer.

I have bought myself a pair of swans.

Cheers to you & Fannie,
Flannery

138. *To Flannery O'Connor from Brainard Cheney. TLS(cc) 1p.*

Smyrna, Saturday, September Eight [1961]

Dear Flannery,

Thanks for the news of my native heath! And I am excited over the prospect of your adding Swans to your polyglot flock!

The Holiday Magazine article[1] on it was highly amusing. I was entertained, although some of the incident was familiar to me—maybe *because* it was familiar, even!

I've been having bits of news about the Lumber City difficulties with the Telfair county ring for some time. But I'd heard nothing of this latest incident. The sheriff is supposed to head the ring (and has for 25 yrs.) and be the chief bandit. Recently the rather simple son of an old friend of mine (now dead) was offered on altar [*sic*] of the ring's security. His name was Eli Willcox. The ring had picked him up several years ago and made him ordinary, then when they got into trouble with the FBI over padding the voting rolls, they made Willcox the goat.

My other friends in LC (of the Knox clan) were sorry for his misfortune, but not very sympathetic. They have been heading up the opposition (such as they've been able to maintain) for years. They had been notably unsuccessful, until the FBI got into the picture some months ago. The [Atlanta] Constitution seems to be taking an interest in it, too. I don't know who Murphy McRae is—wrong last name for LC—most of the Telfair County McRaes live in the countyseat by that name. But he has my moral support.[2]

Fannie is at home now, more or less, taking her

summer's rest at last—though she manages to get into Peabody [College] two to three days out of the week still! We've been up on the Mountain (Sewanee) once for a week-end. Spent a little time with the [Andrew] Lytles. Edna is looking well, but still frail and deeply insecure in her feeling about her health. Andrew (in characteristic fashion) has been trying to renovate the summer cottage so they may live in it during the year (while he is editing the SR [*Sewanee Review*]), trying to be his own architect and contractor, supervising the work of an eighty-three-year-old carpenter and his sixty-year-old helper and an eccentric plumber who won't speak to the carpenter. The results show it! But as Edna testily remarks, "Of course we can't do it the normal, easy way—we've got to make some sort of expensive botch!"

He, A., has scheduled a re-write of my piece on the common man I did for the Renasance Society for [the] fall issue of SR.[3] And, incidentally, he is letting me review THE MOVIEGOER [by Walker Percy][4]—a rough draft of which I've got done. My admiration of the work has gone up—I think it makes a really important comment on, as I see it, heresy, modern and post modern. I'm only a convert and a rather freewheeling theologizer—I rather wish you could look it over before I turn it in.[5]

I hope Shot eludes the devil this time! F. joins me in love to you and Regina.

As ever,
Lon

1. "Living with a Peacock," September, 1961. See Letter 11, note 1.
2. D. Murphy McRae was editor of *The Lumber City Log*, a weekly newspaper published in Lumber City, Georgia.
3. See Letter 129, note 1.
4. New York: Alfred A Knopf, 1961.
5. Subsequently published as "To Restore a Fragmented Vision," *Sewanee Review*, 69 (Autumn, 1961), 691–700.

139. *To Flannery O'Connor from Brainard Cheney. TLS(cc) 1p.*

Smyrna, Tenn., Jan. 25, 1962

Dear Flannery,

This letter has been in my intentions now for many a day. But for this reason or that I couldn't get down to the typewriter. Til now.

The NOW is relaxed through my midwinter spell of kidney pains and given poignance through my failure to get to see Tommie Stritch (who has been here to speak to the Catholic Women's Literary Club & is leaving tonight) and some sense of melancholy through the prospect of my wife's departure tonight for her ten days in Chicago at this season.

My wife's absence from the scene is relieved, if grimly, by the knowledge that I will get in uninterrupted work on my novel ["The Tiger Returns"]—I hope.

So how is it with you?

We have been reestablished here now since New Year's Day.[1] And at last have all the furniture at the refinisher's back. Indeed, we are in good shape, except for paying for it. I've already plunked out 400 bucks that the insurance companies wouldn't pay on the house (this, they said, was for the improvement over its former state). And I'm waiting to hear from the adjuster to confer for adjustment on contents, when we expect to have to put out more. This, however, has been somewhat minimized by the results of an impulse that took Fannie, under the influence of all of the fresh paint and paper on the walls. She decided to replace the curtains in the livingroom and diningroom (made by her now deceased aunt out of ozeneberg; ruined by fire) with the handiwork of an interior decorator. She just got the bill yesterday: fourteen hundred bucks plus—we don't yet quite know how much plus.

You must come to see us while these fancy interior-decorating curtains still have their pristine gloss and help us enjoy 'em—of which we've got a right smart to do to come out even on the deal.

With interruptions, I've been rereading my novel mss., for ten days. So far so good, it seems to me on first blush (I'm about ⅔ the way through). My reaction, when I'm through it, however, may be very different.

Will you be too tied up to read it? I am eager to have you do so. I'm trying for something pretty difficult. I should be through with it (that is, this reading) early in February.

It seems too so long since we've had any word of or from you—please do write and give us the score!

F. joins me in love to you both,
Lon

1. Cheney had spent October and November at Yaddo, in Saratoga Springs, New York, working on "The Tiger Returns." Two weeks after he left Smyrna, a fire broke out in the basement at Idler's Retreat, causing considerable damage.

140. *To Brainard Cheney from Flannery O'Connor. ALS 2pp.*

Milledgeville, 27 Jan. [19]62

Dear Lon,

I was cheered to hear from you and I'll look forward to seeing the novel. Send it anytime. You all ought to come down and see us and my swans. Those swans do a heap for the place.

We are expecting Ashley [Brown] to roll in shortly for the weekend so I expect to hear much literary gossip from the world outside.

Somebody who has read Katherine Anne's [Porter's] book[1] writes me that it is a skillfully concocted *Grand Hotel,* very old fashioned. I hope she makes a pile.

Those curtains must be made of gold.

Cheers,
Flannery

1. *Ship of Fools* (Boston: Little, Brown and Co., 1962.)

141. *To Flannery O'Connor from Brainard Cheney. TLS(cc) 1p.*

February Thirteenth [1962]

Dear Flannery,

Here it ["The Tiger Returns"] is.

But before you wade into it, let me tell you that it is only a harbinger of things more terrible to come. We are coming down to look at your swans!

About the middle of March, I think it is—if that suits. Between terms in the academic calendar, by which all of our movements are now guided.

I do wish Katherine Ann [Porter] luck. But have seen no recent mention of her novel.

Only Fannie has read TTR—and she was reserved in her comment. I wish you would cut loose. F. did raise one questions: my use of the four-letter Saxon word for fundament. My use of it was calculated, to be sure: (1) the reverie are a man's meditations; (2) there is the taint of Late Victorianism to be counteracted.

Let us know if that time will be convenient with you all for a visit from us—and we'll negotiate further with you, later—if it is.

Things here seem to be running along normally, thank you.

Naturally I'm eager to have your reaction—it's been almost four years since I've published any fiction.

What are you working on at the moment?

Best of luck!

F. joins me in love to you both.

Lon

142. *To Brainard Cheney from Flannery O'Connor. TLS 1p.*

Milledgeville, 18 February [19]62

Dear Lon,

We're cheered to hear you're coming to see us. March will be fine. Patty Almy wants to meet Fanny. Why don't you all bring Lee [Jessup]? We'd love to have her too. We'll try not to stage another calamity.

I've read somewhat into the novel ["The Tiger Returns"] but not far enough to render an opinion. I'm glad you're fictionally back in south Georgia howsomever.

A gentleman called me up this week named Martin and said Dr. Cheney had told him he ought to bring a set of books, Our Wonderful World, over here to show me. I couldn't decide who Dr. Cheney was and then it dawned on me—Fanny. Over the telephone this gentleman sounded rather like a Negro but I don't suppose he is. We're not quite up to integrated society yet; he is going to bring the set of books over though. I told him I didn't want to buy a set but he allowed he just wanted my opinion on it.

Let us know when to expect you and we'll put out the flags.

Yours,
Flannery

143. *To Flannery O'Connor from Brainard Cheney. TLS(cc) 1p.*

February Twentysecond [1962]

Dear Flannery,

Just run upon EVERYTHING THAT RISES MUST CONVERGE, in NEW WORLD WRITING. It's beautiful! As beautiful as a steel-jacketed bullet. And the most wholesome comment I've seen on the [race] Issue.

Thanks for the note of yesterday—and thanks for including Lee [Jessup]. I haven't seen her yet, but I will transmit your invitation. More about this later.

I'm just back from the Mountain [Sewanee, Tennessee], a visit with Andrew Lytle: who says your novella ["The Lame Shall Enter First"] is powerful. But at the moment he seems to be having trouble with Peter Taylor—or perhaps it's Peter who is having trouble with the New Yorker Magazine, getting a release for the piece of his SR is to run.[1]

I was given the assignment to do a piece on Peter's dramatic work. But I've got pretty mixed up over it. And I have a hunch it isn't going to get done.[2]

This, to be sure, doesn't involve you and Your Issue.

In the language of the hour, we are all *go*. But don't ask me where!

Love,
Lon

1. "At the Drugstore," *Sewanee Review*, 70 (Autumn, 1962), 528–58.

2. Subsequently published as "Peter Taylor's Plays," *Sewanee Review*, 70 (Autumn, 1962), 579–87.

144. *To Brainard Cheney from Flannery O'Connor. TLS 2pp.*

Milledgeville, 22 February [19]62

Dear Lon,

Cut loose I shall. I think the over-all pattern of the book ["The Tiger Returns"] is good, having it all flashback from the funeral and all, but I have strictures on several other things.

1. A great deal, particularly in the last half of the book, depends on Marcellus' relationship with David Ransom. Now this relationship is never really dramatized. David makes a very impressive corpse, but his existence is only reported. If there were some scene, even if it were set when they were children, to show (not report) this friendship between these two boys, then later when Marcellus realizes that David's death has meaning in his awakening, the reader will be able to believe it. I've got to be shown Marcellus' and David's friendship. Before David becomes a corpse he has to be a person. It strikes me that you have left out the corner stone, the thing that will hold the book up in the later chapters.

2. The whole book is shown through Marcellus' eyes. Now I think you need to be able to stand back and get some distance on Marcellus from time to time. You need to establish the narration objectively, see Marcellus from the outside sometime as well as seeing the events from his eyes. You say it's a meditation, but in my opinion that does not give you the right to all the liberties you take in the form of colloquialisms, etc. You are always dropping the tone when you ought to raise it. Fannie is exactly

right about the four letter Anglo Saxon word and that just points up the problem here—you need a higher toned use of language. This would not give the book a Victorian look but would simply give you an instrument that you haven't got now for raising the level of the story when you need to raise it. The Blossom (I don't know whether the book can take a name like that or not) business with the abortions is important to the theme, but I don't think you need to invite the reader into that hotel room at all. Most of the sex I would say is overdone, beginning with the rent in Julia's drawers. You ought to avoid grotesque descriptions—"lips like purple grapefruit" etc. You may know what you see there, but the reader don't.

3. There ought to be a lot less reported and more dramatized through out. For instance, when they cut Dunk down from the tree, you then report what he says. I think we ought to hear him say it. You could at least break up long stretches of reporting with some scenes. Caroline would blow a fuse over this.

4. If this were mine, I would not let the title Roman Catholic enter it at any point. You begin that with the woman in Washington. You don't need the woman in Washington. You don't need to make any reference to the Irish one's religion as that will be understood as soon as she says "mortal sin" and she should not refer to her "church" and what it teaches. It will be understood well enough that she gets it from her church. You don't have to have her say it. Then the worst thing you do is to say that they both discovered their *preference* was for the Catholic Church. This kills me. The word *preference* just will not do. For those who come into it, the Catholic Church is not a preference but a necessity; but you still don't have to say Catholic Church. You need just say the Church. Then when they get remarried at the cathedral by the monsigneur and their friends don't understand why *that* church, etc, it will be plain what The Church is. In other words, when you say the Church, you can mean only one, and the reader will get the point without thinking that what he's been reading is a piece of Catholic

propaganda. Whenever you deal with the Catholic Church, you have to cover your tracks, iffen you are a member.

5. I think you ought to go through this book sentence by sentence and be sure that it's clear what pronouns refer to what and whom, take out such words as *chilily, intoxicatedly,* such colloquialisms and slang as *on their pins, dried up* (for stopped talking), *'em* when you mean *them, 'im* when you mean *him* (except in direct discourse), eliminate some of the "dry grins" and such things that lower the tone as on pp 234 at the funeral the "marsh mellow in boiled custard" image. Here you want to raise the tone, not lower it.

The best parts are the funeral and the negroes and in the woods and the autopsy and everywhere Adam comes in and Melanie. You've got it all down. I'd just go over it again now and take my time and iron out the rough edges. I'm absolutely certain about point 1 and point 4, but about the latter, you could consult Tom Stritch if you want to check the born-Catholic instinct.

I've about wrote myself out. I'll send the manuscript back under separate cover. The swans are looking forward to their guests. Let us know when to expect you.

Cheers,
Flannery

145. *To Flannery O'Connor from Brainard Cheney. TLS(cc) 1p.*

March, Ash Wednesday [1962]

Dear Flannery,

Thanks for your sound criticism of THE TIGER RETURNS! In Tommy Stritch's words, "You couldn't be more right!"

I read your letter over, but I haven't really sat with it yet. I was and still am in the throes of the article (plus during last week the throes of flu) on P. [Peter] Taylor. I'm trying to get through with it, even though it will not (it seems now) be used until summer or later.

I'm not yet sure about one point that you make, but

as for the rest, I would only repeat You couldn't be more right.

This, too, is to ask whether it would be convenient for us (Fannie & I: Lee's [Jessup's] not going to be able to make it, on account of she's getting ready to go to the hospital April first for an appendectomy, but she thanks you very much) to come by on Thursday the 15th and stop over night, departing the next day?

Fannie has an appointment Wednesday evening in Atlanta. We thought we might drive over to Milledgeville the next morning? Then we've got to go on to South Carolina to see her brother & sister and back to Smyrna by Saturday. If the time doesn't suit you, just drop us a line.

A letter from Ashley [Brown] yesterday reports his recent visit with you, and his plans to [go to] Africa? this summer.

Looking forward to seeing you!

Fannie joins me in love to you both.

Lon

146. *To Brainard Cheney from Flannery O'Connor. ALS 1p.*

Milledgeville, 8 March [19]62

Dear Lon,

We'll be looking for you in time for lunch on the 15*th* and wish you could stay more than one night. By the 15*th* I may be more articulate on the subject of pint-of-view in your novel. It admits of debate.

Cheers,
Flannery

147. *To Flannery O'Connor from Brainard Cheney. TLS(cc) 1p.*

March Twenty-first [1962]

Dear Flannery,

Thanks for a wonderful time!

It was, to be sure, an imposition: we should not have

come visiting during lent. And I'm to blame, rather than Fannie. But she told me that she would not be able to get away any other time. And we did want very badly to see you. She was so in need of a break, too. Maybe you can offer it up.

It was fine to get in some talk with you. And we have decided that the swans are your most admirable pets: they do not bark and they know the secrets of the pond—not to mention their attainment as Easter egg hiders!

Have you found their nest yet?

It was a leisurely trip; that is, we took our driving in broken doses. After a night with F.'s brother, Collier, we started back a bit before noon and spent the night at a motel in Gainesville [Georgia], paused again at Monteagle [Tennessee] in the early afternoon to see Edna and Andrew's [Lytle's] sister Polly Lytle Darwin, though A. had not returned from his junket to New York. Got home Sunday night.

It's not to my credit, either that I have been piddling around with another piece until today, not having felt up to tackling revision on my novel ["The Tiger Returns"]. But I am over my *relaxation* finally.

We've just had word that Ralph McGill's wife, Mary Elizabeth, died this morning. It probably was a relief to her, since her case was reckoned as uncurable and she had been in the hospital since the day after Christmas. But she mustn't have been more than fifty—she was sort of a child bride when Mac married her. And I still think of her a juvenile. Sad! Ah me.

The trouble I've seen! But I won't go into that now.

Thanks again. And I do hope that you are still on the mend. Perhaps, by now you are entirely over your flu?

F. joins me in love,

Lon

148. *To Brainard and Frances Neel Cheney from Flannery O'Connor. TLS 1p.*

Milledgeville, Georgia, 8 April [19]62

Dear Lon and Fannie,

We really enjoyed your visit, lent or no lent, and I have toted things in my tote bag in oriental fashion. We hope you all will make another visit this summer.

The gent from Our Wonderful World finally showed up with two huge boxes of books which he lugged into the house and proceeded to open all over the living room. He was white and pure Georgia. Said Dr. Cheney he just insisted that I get your opinion on these books. Dr. Cheney is a lady, I says. Well maybe so, says he, and keeps right on explaining to me how these books are valuable in the curriculum and librarians can't do without them. It has gradually dawned on me that this man thinks I'm some big-time librarian. So I am going to write him a letter that will let the air out of him gently.

I am fixing to take off to Raleigh this week. When I go to Chicago the 1st of May, I am also going down to Notre Dame and talk there. Then I will have to go back there again the 1st of June as the Sisters at St. Marys have elected to give me an honorary degree. Sort of a bird house with a chimney, entirely non-negotiable I understand, but you can't exactly say thanks but I don't want nare honorary degree.

Love,
Flannery

149. *To Flannery O'Connor from Brainard Cheney. TLS(cc) 1p.*

May Twentyninth [1962]

Dear Flannery,

Thanks for the post card from Notre Dame!

I have changed my profession since then.

Politics has raised its ugly head. And waved filthy lucre at me and touched my gambling bone. The thing is that I thought I about had my novel worked over. So I told them, all right I would write speeches, etc., for the underest dog in a four man race. Give me a week.

But when I read the mss. over, I decided that I was farther away from finished with it than I was when I started. I think I know in the main what I need to do: reorganize the whole, cut-back on Marse-Melanie and put it in dramatic form—which at last I saw it almost wholly lacked—and wasn't properly organized either.

But I couldn't do it in a week.

I decided I wasn't even ready to begin to do it at the moment. So I just put the mss. on the shelf til after the election campaign, which won't be over until August 2nd.

My candidate (for Governor) is a man named Olgiati—the mayor of Chattanooga. He is a Swiss Italian, born in the Cumberland mountains. I do not think that he ever got further than the fifth grade (judging from his English) and he began life as bricklayer. But he has made Chattanooga the best mayor they ever had.

But the ironic touch is that his father, a linguist, came to this country as an interpreter, a trade he followed in New York for a time, but later came down to the Swiss colony at Tracy City, Tenn., where he married, had four children and died. Rudy (the candidate) was the oldest, six years old. They moved to Chattanooga and he soon thereafter began supporting his family—the story goes on in the traditional pattern.

But his English is such that, I write the speeches, and then Roque Fajardo (whom you will remember)[1] who has been understudying him for two months, then translates them into his lingo, then we try (at least Roque does) to coach him to say them.

The image we are trying to *project* is THE QUIET MAN. We are thinking of teaching him a sign language, too.

He has a mysterious way of getting things done right. And we think he has integrity.

He is running against Frank Clement[2] and one other.

Do hope all is well with you. Please write, though I probably won't get around to answering til this is over! F. joins me in love to you both.

Lon

1. See Letter 134, note 2.

2. Three-term governor of Tennessee for whom Cheney was public relations staff man, 1952–58.

150. *To Flannery O'Connor from Brainard Cheney. TLS(cc) 1p.*

August Sixth [1962]

Dear Flannery,

Here it is August and I don't seem ever to have heard from you—not since I wrote in May!

I do hope nothing is wrong?

You may have figured that I wouldn't—campaigning as I was—have time to read a letter. But that's not even a joke! Or a very poor one if any.

We are, and long have been, eager for news of you.

As you may have guessed: my campaigning is over. I hope for a long time. I'm afraid I'm too old for it!

The underdog I was backing never did come out from under. It was about the worst managed campaign I ever heard of.

I don't want to talk about it now—it would be unfortunate to get me started on it!

I say that I (inadvertantly) got Andrew Lytle into it—and I made a speech up at Sewanee that he presided over!

CONGRATULATIONS on the REVIEW on O'CONNOR![1] And forgive me in being so slow to mention it—I suspect secretly it is that I am disappointed that I didn't get called on to contribute. I haven't read anything except political propaganda, etc., for two months. But now I will read the Review. And tell you more about what I think of it later.

I did hear your story read ["The Lame Shall Enter First"] (by Leigh Connell)[2] and think it wonderful—I will read it again for myself. And say more then.

At the moment (to recuperate) I am reading the *Purgatorio* (Ciardi's translation).

Fannie is holding on by the hardest, but still has a grip of the Peabody Library Summer School helm. She has eleven days more to go.

At the moment, the Millers (German friends of Nashville) are with us. They pulled up stakes in N., and took off for Europe last April (I believe) to be gone for a couple of years. But after 4 mos. they decided that N. was home and they wanted quick to be back there.

Couldn't you manage a trip to see us? By the end of the month the weather here ought to be quite pleasant. We would so love to see you!

F. joins me in love to you both.

Lon

1. *Sewanee Review,* 70 (Summer, 1962), contained O'Connor's story, "The Lame Shall Enter First," 337–79; and two essays on O'Connor: Robert Fitzgerald, "The Countryside and the True Country," 380–94, and John Hawkes, "Flannery O'Connor's Devil" 395–407.

2. Longtime friend of the Cheneys, who were his godparents when he joined the Catholic Church; he admired Flannery O'Connor greatly.

151. *To Brainard Cheney from Flannery O'Connor. TLS 2pp.*

Milledgeville, 9 August [19]62

Dear Lon,

I have been thinking of you and was about to write & ask whether since Clements [*sic*] has been returned to the governor's chair, you were going to return yourself to literature?[1] We have had the usual rat-racey summer; however, nobody has fallen under the tractor or been eaten up by the baler. Shot just got a letter from his insurance saying they would pay him $13.80 for 100 more weeks. He has 15% damage in one arm and 35% in the other. But he is able to do what he wants to do.

We had our first attempt at a sit-in here—at [a drugstore]. . . . They were all outside ajittaters from Atlanta. A neighbor came in and told us about it, said a "carful of nigger sports in burmuda shorts and yachting caps" blew in and stopped at the negro cafe. From there they sent a woman around . . . to case the joint. [The store] had been tipped off by two local negros—a school teacher and another who gives out the sheriff's bootlegging rights—so [they] sent the word out to the backwoods. This neighbor said the drug store began to fill up with the toughest folks the county could produce and these sat all day in the drug store with their switch blade knives honed and read newspapers and comic books—some who had never been known to read before. Anyway the colored woman sent to get the lay of the land came in and ordered three coffees to go, looked around, got her coffees and went back with the word. The sit-in folded. But that night the klan met right across the road from us. . . . Our colored man has been gone from here ever since. I hate to see it all get started.

I'll be glad to hear more of what you think of the review. I wish my contribution had been better. I find that story sort of thin.

I'd like to get up to see you but I suspect the weather will be against it for some time to come. Let us know if there's any chance of you all getting down here. I got news of Fanny from Mrs. [Patty] Almy[2] who had a great time at Peabody and came home full of it.

The Wests and Talmadges spent an afternoon with us recently and Bob asked about you.[3]

Miss White and Mary Jo have just took off for Europe for two months—they are getting three of their cities paid for with green stamps.[4]

My one-eyed swan keeled over and died. I don't think now I had a mated pair. I think she was her supposed consort's mother. They are said to live to be 100 and she must have been 99 when I got her.

Regina is building herself a pond, that is she and the govermint are building it. If any body asks you, there's no money in beef.

Love to you both,
Flannery

1. Frank Clement was reelected governor of Tennessee in 1962; he served one final term, until 1968.
2. See Letter 136.
3. See Letter 94, note 2.
4. See Letter 90, note 3.

152. *To Flannery O'Connor from Brainard Cheney. TLS(cc) 3pp.*

Smyrna, Sunday, October 7th [1962]

Dear Flannery,

Suddenly it's quite a time since your August letter!

First we thought we would drop by to say hello (Fannie and me) on our little tour of August-end. But F. was so exhausted after our ride to Newberry [South Carolina] (to see her brother there) that we just turned tail and went back through the Smokies, in a dawdling fashion, to home. And here we have been since.

I am a bit disturbed about F. She takes the responsibility of the library school so hard—and does it all in the most expensive way. This fall they've had a 25 per cent increase in student body. And the new man she had added to the faculty is turning out to be about as much an invalid as the other man she has! And no more man, perhaps, if a better teacher. That has been a problem, too: Peabody students (including library school students) have been picked up by police during a two months round-up of homosexuals hereabouts.

And being director, of course, wasn't enough for little Fannie, but that she had to be president of the Southeastern Library Assn., meeting this week in Memphis, all week—she is now in the library writing her speech!

I was interested to have your local desegregation news. I believe your man didn't get elected Lieutenant-Governor, did he? Did the Negro vote play an important part in the election? A news story out of Atlanta, reporting that Negroes there had in the main voted for a South Georgia (I believe it was) man that was distasteful, because he seemed to be less so than somebody else—from Atlanta, I believe. I couldn't be more vague! But, despite that handicap, I am really interested.

I get most of my Georgia news now from "The Lumber City Log," which seems to have a continuing voting scandal in one way or another in the county to keep up interest.

I suppose you have been exercised over the Mississippi debacle?[1] I have been strangely so. And I confess that my sympathies have been deeply divided. The performance of our federal government somehow reminds me of a backwoodsman in frontier Georgia (I think I made use of him in LIGHTWOOD)[2] who walked twenty miles to the settlement and back one night to get medicine for his croopy baby and after putting a spoonful of the precious stuff down the infant's goozle—when the baby tried to heave it up, choked him to death trying to keep it down.

And I can't but believe that after the dust of battle has settled (say fifty years hence) we will find ourselves about as much segregated as ever, though more precariously united—I take it something after the pattern of denied-but-defacto segregation they have in the East.

Incidentally, this is, too, a forewarning of my intention to come by to see you, I don't know yet just when, but I would like to make it convenient for you all. I hope to get out of here by next Wednesday—and I could spend Thursday night with you all, if that suited—if not I could come by on my way back from Florida a week later—or, of course, we could postpone it [until] some more convenient time?

I have spent a good bit of last month getting acquainted with de Chardin's THE PHENOMENON OF MAN and his THE DIVINE MILIEU. Pierre Teilhard has been quite an experience for me![3]

Perhaps, I get over excited about any book that reforms or extends my viewpoint. But TPOM is the book I have been waiting for, looking for, for fifteen years! Coming to it tardily, as I have, I realize that my exhibition of enthusiasm may seem naive to you, if not wearying.

Yet, I suspect that your being a cradle Catholic and, so to speak, well adjusted to the idea of mysticism from birth, you may not sense altogether what an iconoclast de Chardin is for the idolatry of Modernism.

His work is, I think, the most important philosophical statement for Christianity since the *Summa* [*theologica*] and, I predict he will eventually rank along side St. Thomas and St. Augustine in the history of The Church.[4]

I am the more taken with de Chardin because I found my way to the Church out of the inadequacy of the scientific milieu. To be sure the history of Protestantism had some effect in pushing me toward Catholicism. But it was the report on the state of things in physics and biochemistry that reached me in the Thirties that first shook my faith in the godhead of Science. And the Confession that Erwin Schroedinger made in his *What Is Life* lectures in the Forties confirmed my then advanced suspicions.[5] It became plain to me then that the scientific one-way descent into the doodle hole to explain life was headed in the wrong direction. And at the same time WIL disclosed for me the *invincible* prejudice existing in materialistic opinion dominant among scientists.

Of course many have called for a restitution of Religion (Christianity) in the world presented by modern science—as diverse as [Arnold J.] Toynbee, Northrup (MEETING OF EAST AND WEST)[6] and Schroedinger, himself. But it is one thing to sense that the comprehensive view must be there, and quite another to see it.

The biochemists and paleontologists will probably be slower to give de Chardin their *imprimatur* than the Church. But then their sort of ignorance (and prejudice) is far more nearly invincible.

Speaking personally, reading THE DIVINE MILIEU, after TPOM, has been the most illuminating Christian experience for me since I read Jacques Maritain on the creative intuition[7] and Guardini's THE LORD.[8] With my limited education, the traditional language of Church liturgy and the legalistic language of papal pronouncements and even the familiar imagery and metaphor of Scripture—I have to confess—have much less meaning for me than scientific statement. It's just a fact of life, or rather a condition of my limitations that a scientific presentation of the world has more reality for me than the other. This, I am afraid, is true for nonCatholic moderns generally. And, hence, as I see it, the extraordinary importance of de Chardin's work at this juncture.

The contingency in my plans for travel, by the way, is the circumstances of work on my novel-in-the-works, THE TIGER RETURNS. Beginning with you, I have been passing it around and revising after each suggestion about it—Alan Zibart—then Allen Tate—now Walter Sullivan. I am optimistic enough to hope that Walter's criticism won't precipitate any very drastic revision. If not, I will hasten it off to Elizabeth McKee.[9]

I will reserve further comment on [the] Sewanee Review issue on you, until I see you—though I still think it a pretty good job. And your story, too!

Fannie joins me in love to you both—

As ever,
Lon

1. Reference is to U.S. Justice Department enforced desegregation of the University of Mississippi. U.S. marshalls and thousands of federal troops escorted James Meredith, a Black graduate student, to classes, and rioting ensued.
2. See Letter 2, note 1.
3. Pierre Teilhard de Chardin, *The Phenomenon of Man* (New York: Harper, 1959) and *The Divine Milieu: An Essay on the Interior Life* (New York: Harper, 1960).
4. Cheney wrote in a marginal comment: "No one so brash as a convert!"
5. Erwin Schrodinger, *What Is Life? The Physical Aspect of the Living Cell* (Cambridge, England: The University Press, 1944).
6. Filmer Stuart Cuckow Northrop, *The Meeting of East and West: An Inquiry Concerning World Understanding* (New York: The Macmillan Co., 1946).
7. *Creative Intuition in Art and Poetry* (New York: Pantheon Books, 1953).
8. Romano Guardini. *The Lord* (Chicago: Regnery, 1954).
9. O'Connor's agent, through whom Cheney was trying to find a publisher. Cheney's relationship with McKee proved unsatisfactory to him.

153. *To Brainard Cheney from Flannery O'Connor. ALS 2pp.*

Milledgeville, 9 Oct. [19]62

Dear Lon,

We are much cheered you are imminent. Come on your way *to* Florida as you might miss us on your way back. I have to be in Atlanta on the 26*th* and my French translator, M. Coindreau,[1] is coming on the 23rd & staying until the 25*th*, so we wouldn't get to do any talking if you came then. This is his 3rd visit to us. He's in the middle of doing the Violent Bear.[2]

I'm glad you have discovered Teilhard. I think he's great. The science is over my head but he's also a great visionary.

Our telephone no. is 452-4335 but it's hard to get us on it as there are 8 parties on it representing about 150 head, ⅔ of them idiots.

Cheers,
Flannery

1. Maurice-Edgar Coindreau had translated *Wise Blood* into French and written an introduction for the edition: *Le Sagesse dans le sang* (Paris: Gallimard, 1959).

2. *Et ce sont les violents l'emportent.* Translation by Maurice-Edgar Coindreau of *The Violent Bear It Away,* with a preface by J. M. G. LeClézio. Paris: Gallimard, 1965.

154. *To Brainard Cheney from Flannery O'Connor. ALS 2pp.*

Milledgeville, 24 Nov. [19]62

Dear Lon,

I'm still distressed we missed a visit but I hope you all will plan another—maybe during the holidays? I took enough antibiotics to get me on the road and have got back from my trip.[1] The first thing they showed me in Dallas was Gen. Walker's house—a battleship grey two-story monstrosity with a huge picture window in front in which you see a ceramic Uncle Sam with a lamp over him. Texas & U.S. flags flying on the lawn. I also heard a typical Texas joke. Texan calls up the White House and says, "Is Pres. Kennedy there?" Voice says "Nawsuh, he ain't here." "Well, is Miss Jackie there?" "She aint here neither." "Well, where is Mr. Lyndon?" "He done gone too." "Well, who's running things up there?" "We is."

Travel is very broadening.

Caroline [Gordon Tate] seems to have taken a new lease on life in California.[2] She's painting up a storm and having a grand time.

Love to you both,
Flannery

1. On October 27, 1962, O'Connor wrote her friend Maryat Lee: "I do highly hope you will get down before Nov. 15 or after Nov. 21 as between those dates I will be on the road, war permitting. I am going to East Texas State College,

University of Southwest La., Loyola at New Orleans, & Southeast La. College, 4 talks in 6 days and too much too much. My bones are not up to it" (*The Habit of Being*, p. 496).

2. Caroline Gordon Tate was writer-in-residence at the University of California at Davis, 1962–63.

155. *To Flannery O'Connor from Brainard Cheney. TLS(cc) 1p.*

Monday, December Third [1962]

Dear Flannery,

Just killed a wasp, crawling under the sheets to my bed. We've had wasp weather all fall. I don't know how they get in, but they are with me every day.

Thanks for the invite to come by during the holidays—I'll try. But the chances are not good. Sue Jenkins is supposed to arrive on the 21st to spend Christmas week with us. There is a contingent of Japanese [librarians] booked for here and there during the Yuletide. And others.

But I will write you again later.

At the moment I am trying to get started on a piece on Caroline (G) [Gordon Tate] I've been aiming at for a couple of years now. I think I've about made up my mind what I want to say. But somehow I can't get down to it.[1]

We are all currently sound, head to hoof.

Just up with Andrew L. [Lytle] yesterday. Things are a bit grim with him: Edna [Lytle] had had a massive hemorrhage the night before. Though she was about and chipper enough to the eye when we got there.

We hope you all have a gay and not too burdensome Christmas!

F. joins me in love to you both.

Lon

1. Subsequently published as "Caroline Gordon's Ontological Quest," *Renascence*, 16 (Fall, 1963), 3–12.

156. *To Flannery O'Connor from Brainard Cheney. TLS(cc) 1p.*

Saturday, January 12th [1963]

Dear Flannery,

This may sound like the camel with his nose in the tent. But, I would inspire you to look at it on the other hand—that is, to as lief be hung for a hog as a shoat.

Which is by way of leading up to an added request. JUL[1] has neither of the magazines (Kansas Magazine nor Xavier University Studies) with reviews of TVBIA [*The Violent Bear It Away*] that I am after.[2]

Since I already have one review (the one from Renascence)[3] to return, may I not borrow the other two, too? You remember that I am the well-trained and scrupulous product of a professional librarian who thinks murder and mayhem are trifles compared with book-lifting or book-not-returning.

And I'll stake her reputation on their being returned and in a reasonable length of time, too.

I have finished a draft of the piece on Caroline.[4] But don't feel good about it. Fannie is reading it now. If you don't resist it, I may send it on to you? I would very much like your criticism. And opinion generally.

I certainly did enjoy my visit! And was pleased to have a look at your essay on the religious *concern*.[5] It is fine. Have you seen an anthology titled: CHRISTIAN FAITH & THE CONTEMPORARY ARTS?[6] I am just now taking a look at it—it is the thing with Red [Robert Penn] Warren doing the introduction—with a piece in it by Walter Sullivan. Would send it on to you, should like to see it?

Had a pleasant stop-over with Andrew Lytle. He reports that if the cobalt treatments go well with his wife, he may be able to bring her home by the middle of the month. She will be able, perhaps, to carry on at home for a time. He was leaving the following day for Memphis.

All is well with us here.

Trust you all had a pleasant trip to A. [Atlanta], to see your aunt and that she is recuperating nicely.

Fannie joins me in love to you both.

Lon

1. Joint University Libraries. See Letter 90, note 2.

2. Robert M. McCown, S.J., "The Education of a Prophet: A Study of Flannery O'Connor's *The Violent Bear It Away*," *Kansas Magazine*, [no volume number] (1962), 73–78; and Sister Simon M. Nolde, O.S.B., "*The Violent Bear It Away*: A Study in Imagery," *Xavier University Studies*, 1 (1962), 180–94.

3. Robert O. Bowen, "Hope vs. Despair in the New Gothic Novel." *Renascence*, 13 (Spring, 1961), 147–52.

4. See Letter 155, note 1.

5. Presumably "The Novelist and Free Will," *Fresco* [University of Detroit, Detroit, Michigan], N.S. 1 (Winter, 1963), 100–01.

6. Finney Eversole, ed. (New York: Abington Press, 1962).

157. *To Frances Neel Cheney from Flannery O'Connor. ALS 1p.*

13 January [19]63, Milledgeville

Dear Fannie,

My heart was lifted up by that prayerful card as I hope yours will be by the enclosed clipping.[1] I am up now and my mamma is down. When we both get down at the same time we go to the hospital but we didn't manage to make it this time. The wind is howling and moaning and the slush is piling up. Grim. Happy New Year to you & Lon.

Love,
Flannery

1. Reference obscure.

158. *To Brainard Cheney from Flannery O'Connor. ALS 1p.*

Milledgeville, 14 Jan. [19]63

Dear Lon,

Herewith the essays.[1] We did enjoy the visit and it's a good thing you picked last week instead of this one, because we're now froze up.

I'd like to see the piece on Caroline. But I think that is good advice not to show it to her.

I haven't seen that anthology and I think I can pass it by for the time being.

Cheers to you & Fannie
Flannery

P.S. There is a good essay on Teilhard & [Maurice] Blondel in the current issue of THOUGHT.[2]

1. The reviews Cheney had asked to borrow in Letter 156.

2. Christopher F. Mooney, "Blondel and Teilhard de Chardin: An Exchange of Letters," *Thought*, 37 (Winter, 1962), 543–62.

159. *To Flannery O'Connor from Brainard Cheney. TLS(cc) 1p.*

Jan. 23, 1963

Dear Flannery,

Just read this piece on Caroline over and it sounded heavy-handed to me. But I'm too dull now to do anything about it!

I suppose I should ask myself why I am burdening you with reading it: I've already sent it on to RENASCENCE!

I didn't intend to go off half-cocked. The truth is that [*Renascence* editor] John Pick's letter (I had written him to ask whether, after so long a time, he wanted to see it) saying send it on, hit me at a moment when I was feeling frustrated over all and sundry that I couldn't button up or bring to a head, or even get under way. So I just hauled off and sent it to him to get it off my work table.

His acknowledgment note sounds foreboding: ". . . just as soon as I've had a chance to consult with some of our editorial advisers I'll try to give you a final decision."

Moreover, I think now that it is too brief. I'd been afraid of getting it too long. And, among other things, I cut out my notes on her developing strategy and tactics in technique and style, which I believe now was pretty important to my theme.

I've been wrassling over a start on my piece on your stuff,[1] with the poorest sort of results. In my general pitch, I'm trying (or going to) to explain your humor as based of the religious point of view—but I'm short of theology!

But I think I may have had an intuition here. Quoting from THE RIVER, Mrs. C. [Connin] stood staring, "with a skeleton's appearance of seeing everything." We have the feeling that the skeleton, with nowhere to hide anything, itself, must be able to see through us with his own inner visibility. That is the source of religious realism and the premise for Miss O'Connor's humor.

How about it?

Sorry to hear about your water pipes! We've had a freeze up, too, since the last time we had ours wrapped.

F. joins me in love to you all.

Lon

1. "Miss O'Connor Creates Unusual Humor Out of Ordinary Sin," *Sewanee Review,* 71 (Autumn, 1963), 644–52. See Appendix D.

160. *To Brainard Cheney from Flannery O'Connor. TLS 1p.*

Milledgeville, 1 February [19]63

Dear Lon,

If I had read those early novels of hers [Caroline Gordon Tate's] I could say something maybe that made sense about this, but I've never read a one of them. Your thesis sounds good so I'll have to take it on faith. Two things about the paper have occurred to me though and you can see what you thing about them. The first page and a half, the introduction I reckon it is, is very abstract and eliptical. I would make it shorter or more concrete or something, i. e., I'd get into the thing quicker.

The other thing that worries me is this phrase "the odor of sanctity." I just find it hard to take this phrase that is used for the incorrupt bodies of a few saints and apply it to a society. It seems to me you ought to talk about the phrase and tell the reader how you're using it before you just spring it on him.

That about the skeleton's appearance of seeing everything sounds good to me. I couldn't analyze the image myself, I just know it's right for the spot.

I read about how it was 13 below in Nashville. That is mighty sorry weather to have to endure. It was 5 above here and all our pipes froze and broke again. Not all, that is, but the main one from the tank. This time R. [Regina] is having it encased in rubber.

I am betting on the ground hog tomorrow. Cheers to you and Fannie.

Love,
Flannery

161. *To Brainard Cheney from Flannery O'Connor. TLS 1p.*

Milledgeville, 13 February [19]63

Dear Lon,

I really like this[1] and I can't find anything wrong with your theology. I got some ideas from it myself that I may work into that paper for Sweet Briar to kind of pull it together.[2] My only objection is on page 9, the passage marked. Here it seems to me you handle him kind of roughly. I don't think he has any squeamishness over adjusting to the realism of it, he just don't realize that this realism is nowhere at odds with the religious spirit. He likes the passage: anything he likes he attributes to the devil. He says the cat-faced baby, the old woman the size and shape of a cedar fence post, the woman with the two children whose faces were like pans on either side to catch the grins that overflowed from her—all this kind of thing he must attribute to the devil. For no other reason than that he thinks it's good. His devil is an impeccable literary spirit who makes the creative process go, and so far as I can tell this devil is his God.[3]

Anyway I think this is real good and I'll be glad if they [*Sewanee Review*] print it. I'm not sure you ought to call it his "joke" because the poor boy is serious about it, dead serious.[4] He thinks he's made a big discovery and I wouldn't be surprised if he didn't write a book about [Nathanael] West and drag me in as part of the supporting cast.[5] There is a new book out called NEW AMERICAN GOTHIC by somebody name Irving Malick (sp) that drags me over the coals.[6] I haven't read it but Hawkes did & told me about it.

Love to you and Fannie,

Flannery

1. A typed draft of Cheney's essay on O'Connor.
2. Her paper was never published.
3. O'Connor is referring John Hawkes' essay, "Flannery O'Connor's Devil," *Sewanee Review,* 70 (Summer, 1962), 395–407.
4. Cheney's working title for his essay was "Miss O'Connor's Humor Is Funnier Than Mr. Hawkes' Joke, And Better Grounded."
5. Reference is to John Hawkes' comparison of O'Connor to Nathaniel West. See Appendix D.
6. Irving Malin (Carbondale: Southern Illinois University Press, 1962).

162. *To Brainard Cheney from Flannery O'Connor. ALS 2pp.*
8 April [19]63

Dear Lon,

I got this[1] back from the lady what borrowed it. You can send your right arm by return mail. There's a book out on him [Teilhard] by an Episcopalian named Ravel (I think) published by Harper & Row.[2] Conn West[3] tells me it's very good. Also enclose the first litry supplement of our diocesan paper.[4]

I certainly enjoyed meeting your sister [5] and wish you all could have stayed a while.

Cheers to you & Fannie
Flannery

1. Claude Tresmontant, *Pierre Teilhard de Chardin: His Thought* [English translation] (Baltimore: Helicon Press, 1959).

2. Actually, Charles E. Raven, *Teilhard de Chardin: Scientist and Seer* (New York: Harper and Row, 1962).

3. See Letter 94, note 2.

4. *Georgia Bulletin*, March 21, 1963, contained O'Connor's "Fiction Is a Subject with a History—It Should Be Taught That Way," Book Supplement, p. 1.

5. Presumably Martha Cheney Brandon, who lived in Valdosta, Georgia, since O'Connor already knew Lee Jessup, Cheney's Nashville sister.

163. *To Flannery O'Connor from Brainard Cheney. TLS 1 p.*

April 17th [1963]

Dear Flannery,

Thanks so much for the loan of Tresmontant! And for the copy of your diocesan *rag* with your fine piece and picture! I thought your piece sound and to the point, and beautifully free of educationist gobbledegook.

[Andrew] Lytle tells me he will run my piece on your humor next fall—I'm supposed to make a few changes and/or corrections, but I haven't got it back yet.

Edna [Lytle] visibly draws nearer her end—it is difficult to make a guess in such, but I do not expect her to survive the summer.

I was doing fairly well on work up (for some weeks) until Easter. We've been out every night since it seems and my head is but a weary bone!

Vanderbilt is having its annual literary flingding next

week—so I guess I'll be in for another round of socializing, what with [Andrew] Lytle, [Eudora] Welty and somebody named Carlos Baker [Hemingway biographer] from Princeton as visiting firemen.

Best of luck!

And love to you both,
Lon

164. *To Flannery O'Connor, Andrew Lytle, Tom Stritch, and Allen Tate from Brainard Cheney.*[1] *TLS(cc) 3pp.*

Thursday, August 15th [1963], Smyrna, Tenn.

To: Flannery, Andrew, Tommy and Allen—

After a spring and summer with Teilhard, I am convinced that he presents the challenge of our time. His science-based vision of evolution calls a confused world to coherence. It is not, however, a new religion or philosophy, but a new *science* that he proposes. If his Complexity-consciousness *Law* is accepted, he will turn our universe more topsy turvy than Copernicus did for the Middle Ages.

And I really believe the question is not whether, but when.

As I see it, he climaxes and completes the revolution (only prefigured by [Charles] Darwin) initiated by [Albert] Einstein and [Ernest] Rutherford to make the view of modern science synonymous with evolution.

It may well be that his new science will call for a new methodology.

And this may be why he wrote his Phenomenon Of Man in simple allusive language rather than in scientific. Though I can think of several other good reasons. To be sure there was no single science dedicated to all of the ground he covered. Then he may have thought of the treatment [Gregory Johann] Mendel and other revolutionaries got when they proposed that the pack reverse its course when it was in hot pursuit of the Great Stability, headed in the other direction.

For example—and this, as a journalist, is my litmus

on whether to take Teilhard seriously—there are a number of reputable biologists who have pointed out the inadequacy of natural selection to explain biological evolution. (Chancellor McCrady makes a convincing case showing that while natural selection may be a limiting circumstance, it cannot be an efficient cause, in his essay in *Religious Perspectives in College Teaching*.)[2] Erwin Schroedinger, as far back as 1942 (in his *What Is Life*) using orthodox methodology, demonstrated that a living organism (molecule of the wing of a dropsila fly) was characterized by a resistance to entropy increase that statistics could not explain.

But does any of this impress the materialist scientist? If he can be cornered into answering you at all he will say that, if it can't be measured statistically it is out of the field of science.

Well, there are some of us old enough to remember that there were sciences before statistics came along. And Einstein has been quoted as saying, "I do not believe God shoots dice with man."

In connection with Schroedinger let me recall this. He based his work importantly on recent discoveries in biochemistry made by Max Delbruck, at that time at Vanderbilt. I asked Max, then thirty-odd years old and a marxist materialist, what he thought of Schroedinger's conclusions. He replied, indulgently, "I am grateful for the mention, but Erwin has got to be an *old* man now!"

Aye, in my opinion, Teilhard didn't intend to let the materialists laugh him out of court, or give him the silent treatment, either. And to be sure, his new scientific outlook is based, not on what the littlest piece will prove, but also on what can be learned from the biggest whole. But obviously he sought friends in court who were not materialists, or even scientists.

And that's where *we* come in, I think; and gives my excuse for writing this letter. I will be more specific. There is first a lot of question asking that can be done by laymen. But there is more.

Because of the language in which he wrote any man who understands the king's English (or French) can help assay what Teilhard meant by what he said. And at this stage of the game a lot of this still needs to be done, I believe.

I have given the reviews on P.O.M. (that I could lay hand on) a close reading and I have been shocked at the obvious misreading men like Michael Polanyi have given it. And even Oliver Rabut, in his book[3] (incidentally, Tommy, who is Rabut?) who is supposed to be sympathetic, but sounds like an old-fashioned positivist, is guilty of misreading him.

Fellows, we may not know anything about biology, but we are pretty experienced about prejudice and what it can do to the mental processes.

I have been trying to run down a report appearing in *Time* Magazine that there was a gathering of some forty "scholars" in Venice last June a year ago to discuss Teilhard.[4] There must have been something in print to come out of it. Do any of you know anything about it?

And this brings me nearer to what's been running through my mind. Could a useful gathering of mixed character be assembled in our neighborhood? Andrew, how do you think McCrady would view such a thing at Sewanee?

Incidentally, for you who are RCs or may be curious about Teilhard's Christian orthodoxy, I am not unaware of the monitum issued against him. But have you read the late Pope John's *Pacem In Terris?*It reads like a preface to *The Phenomenon of Man!*

Yrs. in [illegible],
Lon

1. It was not uncommon for Cheney to write joint letters—or to send carbons—to friends he thought might be interested in an idea or a project.
2. Edward McCrady (Vice-Chancellor and President, and Professor of Biology, The University of the South), "Biology," in *Religious Perspectives in College Teaching*, Hoxie N. Fairchild, *et al.* (New York: The Ronald Press Co., 1952), pp. 235–261.
3. *Teilhard de Chardin: A Critical Study* (New York: Sheed and Ward, 1961).
4. "Pilgrim of the Future," *Time*, 80 (July 27, 1962), 60.

165. *To Brainard Cheney from Flannery O'Connor. ALS 2pp.*

19 Aug. [19]63, M'ville

Dear Lon,

I was cheered to hear you are on with the Teilhard business. There is a right interesting book called "T. de C., Scientist & Seer" by Charles Raven, an Anglican Canon.[1] I think you'd like to read it. He throws some light here & there that I haven't got out of anything else on T. I had the book but lent it to a lady in the Bronx who is a slow reader but if you have trouble finding it, let me know and I'll hurry her along.

The enclosed on the monitum is cheering also. It's this thing about grace you've got to watch out with. Comes down from the top it does. Not up from the bottom.

I hear via Mrs. Almy that Fannie is working her head off.

Cheers to you both,
Flannery

1. See Letter 162, note 2.

166. *To Frances Neel Cheney from Flannery O'Connor. ALS 2pp.*

Sept. 3 [19]63. M'ville

Dear Fannie,

I don't know whether your proposed anthology is a job for Ashley [Brown] or Louie Rubin but I think somebody should look into it.[1]

Under separate cover you should be getting an envelope of peafowl feathers plus a few mites for authentic flavor. I killed three as I did them up & have been itching since but they (mites) may not survive the trip to Connecticut. Did you all pause on the way up to march on Washington?

Tell Sue Jenkens Brown hello for me.

Cheers,
Flannery

1. "Probably a piece of foolishness," according to Mrs. Cheney, who has no recollection of proposing an anthology seriously. (Letter to the editor, February 20, 1985.)

167. *To Flannery O'Connor from Brainard Cheney. TLS(cc) 3pp.*

Smyrna, September Twentyfifth, Wednesday [1963]

Dear Flannery,

The summer fades, the fall brightens. *Allons!*

The Cheneys are in residence again at Cold Chimneys, after a feverish five weeks tour of granite New England that almost wound up in the unpunished American Sodom-and-Gomorrah. And, after three days of it, I won't deny that I am shaken and depressed.

I suppose it is that I am an old fool. One is, to be sure, most reluctant to admit his folly and even more, his age. But only on this excursion to the cities of the plain have I come to see what I am up against.

You told me, some years ago. But I couldn't comprehend you. I suffered the misapprehension of the convert, unacquainted with invincible ignorance as such—not to mention hostility.

But let me hasten to congratulate you on your—it would be inaccurate to say recognition—achievement of central position in *Esquire's* literary *Establishment!*[1] Indeed, the measure of your achievement is that you are not recognized! For I am convinced that not a single one of all of Today's spawn of Nihilism understands you. Yet it is the mark of your genius that they are engaged by your incomprehensibility. Even more, I suspect. For God moves in mysterious ways.

I think I am not going to get my last novel ["Quest for the Pelican"] published—though I am still committed to trying. I am preparing now to go over it again to see if I can turn it at least a little toward nihilistic *reality.* I don't think I can—and would there be any point in trying?—reach the conventionally Christian-hearted. Yet it is perhaps the moral order out of which it is written that is insupportable, in this Day's extremity. But *spes spero,* with requisite resignation. I am then going to send it to David McDowell. If he likes it well enough he will informally take on the task of trying to find a publisher—since, as of the present, he has nothing better to do with his time.

He hasn't seen it. It was with Doubleday while I was in NYC—or more accurately, on its way back to Smyrna. David thought my sending it to Doubleday very unknowing. But where? He was, nevertheless, incredulous about a *worthy* (assuming it to be so) book's not finding a publisher. Anyhow he volunteered. It may be merely that misery likes company.

I am deeply disturbed over David—not so much his state (though the failure of two tries at establishing his own publishing business and two years without a job have taken their toll on him) as I am at his circumstances. It would appear that he has been rejected by the "Establishment." Not that he hasn't been at fault. He was awhile, I am told, drinking too much and was arrogant about the book peddling world. But he has been drinking beer and eating crow now for a long spell. Yet the doors of the publishers remain closed to him.

An underlying cause, I am persuaded to believe, is their liberal prejudice against his conservatism—they haven't forgiven him for publishing Buckley's *Up From Liberalism.*[2]

Recently he has been trying to get on with Farrar, Straus and Cudahy, through Bob Giroux.

Supposedly (or so he told me) his old friend Cal [Robert] Lowell is trying to help him.

But I had this experience. In my talking to Red [Robert Penn] Warren a couple of days before, I brought David's name up as a possibility for promoting a literary enterprise (I append a copy of a letter to explain it). Red was interested in the enterprise, but he would have put the hatchet to McDowell (I don't say out of malice) though he recanted when he saw I was close to him. Red submitted the *mystery* of David's long unemployment, but his prejudices were plainly showing. Then Fannie and I had dinner with the Lowells and I brought up the matter of David with Cal. It was casual and I didn't, of course, ask him what, if anything he had done with Giroux.

But Cal spoke deprecatingly, saying that David ought to try to find employment outside New York. And he quoted Warren on David's state and disabilities.

This a bit shocked me, since he was supposed to be so much nearer David. Cal was sympathetic, but seemed uncommitted. And I can't but recall that he has recanted so much! And I am told that now he is the darling of the *J.I.'s* (If, like me, you don't know: Jewish Intellectuals).

All of which labored detail is by way of leading up to a request—as perhaps you may already suspect. If you feel that you want to, could you or would you try to do something in David's behalf with Bob Giroux? Moreover, if you feel disposed to act in David's behalf, would you spark old Caroline [Gordon Tate] to act, too?

Why?

You may know David better than I do. But here's my thinking on it. Although I make no case for his piety, he is an orthodox (at least he is an Anglican Catholic) Christian and believes in the Christian viewpoint. Moreover, he is remarkably well educated and intelligent for a New York editor and has a rare editorial gift. It is the gift of being able to submerge his own preconceptions in an effort to understand what you are trying to do, with a talent for helping, not hindering you in doing it. In fact he is the best editor I ever encountered in the publishing business. And he is not committed to the mass market.

Do you ask what you can do? Maybe nothing. I can't say. But I think washing him down the drain would be a distinct loss to the publishing world.

The enterprise tentatively outlined in the carbon attached here is one I would like to interest you in, too.[3] Besides Red, I discussed it with Leonie Adams[4] and Cal. All professed to be for it. And Red offered some practical suggestions. But I will go into these another time. This letter has run on too long already!

Fannie was able to put in a few hours work up at Robbers Rocks. But I did nothing more than try to pursue my criticism of Rabut's criticism of Teilhard, and but little of that.

Eva[5] sends her regards.

I did get the lower pasture "mowed" as Eva calls it, but I say scythed—the weeds stood head high.

Fannie joins me in love to you all,

Lon

1. The July, 1963, issue of *Esquire* was devoted to the current state of the American literary establishment. O'Connor was listed in L. Rust Hills' "The Structure of the American Literary Establishment: Who Makes or Breaks a Writer's Reputation? A Chart of Power," pp. 41–43. An excerpt from O'Connor's planned third novel, "Why Do the Heathen Rage," was also included, pp. 60–61.

2. William F. Buckley, (New York: McDowell-Obolensky, 1959).

3. Concerned about the survival of the novel as a serious art form, Cheney, Allen Tate, and Andrew Lytle had approached David McDowell with a plan to draw together "individuals of intelligence, taste, and even [moral] direction" into a "Jacobean Community" which would "provide a consensus to preserve the art of the novel and enhance our literature and assert moral leadership." One practical function of this "community" would be to sponsor publication for novelists of merit who could not find a commercial publisher. A letter from Cheney to David McDowell on July 3, 1963, in the Vanderbilt University Special Collections, outlines the project in detail.

4. Léonie Adams (1899–), distinguished American poet, lived in New Milford, Conn.; she and her husband, critic William Troy, were friends of Caroline Gordon Tate.

5. According to Mrs. Cheney, Eva was an "eccentric past middle age woman" who lived near Sue Jenkins Brown in Tory Valley and helped her at times.

168. *To Brainard Cheney from Flannery O'Connor. TLS 1p.*

Milledgeville, 27 September [19]63

Dear Lon,

I've never met David McDowell, but I wrote Giroux and told him you had asked me to recommend him and that while I had not met him I respected your opinion and I quoted you as saying "he is remarkably well educated (I left out 'for a New York editor') and has a rare editorial gift. It is the gift of being able to submerge his own preconceptions in an effort to understand what you are trying to do, with a talent for helping, not hindering you in doing it." Then I said that your opinion came from experience as he had been your editor. I doubt if that does any good, but not knowing him myself that's about all I could do. The best way for you to get Caroline in on it would be through Ashley [Brown]. He can do more with her than anybody right now. She probably knows I don't know McDowell and if she thought you were behind it, that would squash it with her I'm afraid.[1]

Did you ever get hold of that Charles Raven book on Teilhard? If not, I can lend it to you as the person who had it sent it back.

I'm taking off for one of my bread-winning expeditions October 14–19—Hollins, Notre Dame of Maryland, and Georgetown. I'll be cheered when it's over, and I can get back to obfuscating the J.I.'s When they find out what I'm doing, they'll drop me off the reading list. They think I'm writing about incest.

Me and Regina are going to a luncheon today at the college [Georgia State College for Women] for the Governor [Carl E. Sanders] and get the official smile shined upon us. It is rubbery and appears 100% humorless, at least on television. I want to see if television conveys the truth.

Cheers to you and Fannie.
Flannery

1. Cheney had fallen into disfavor with Caroline Gordon Tate when he tried to preserve his friendship with both of the Tates during and following their divorce. This was a source of great pain to Cheney, who had a very high regard for Caroline Tate.

169. *To Flannery O'Connor from Brainard Cheney. TLS(cc) 1p.*

September 30th [1963]

Dear Flannery,

Pardon my haste, but I am trying to make the next mail.

I was about to write you not to bother to extend yourself in David's [McDowell's] behalf, when I got your letter. But it is all right anyhow—no harm done.

Saturday afternoon he called me from NYC to say that he had accepted a place with the Curtis Publishing Company as fiction editor for six magazines—despite the Post's questionable activities and the dire results therefrom, the job seems to offer advantages. They told him they want to publish serious fiction of quality—and also, that they might have money to promote our Jacobean Community idea.

In all events, any port in a storm!

I would so much like to see the Raven book on Teilhard!

I preat [*sic*] in haste—hope you have [a] great time on your tour—By the way A. [Andrew] Lytle will be there with you at Hollins, he tells me.

In haste.
Lon

170. *To Flannery O'Connor from Brainard Cheney. TLS(cc) 1p.*

October 12, 1963

Dear Flannery,

This is largely to call your attention to the "Father Teilhard" article in the October 12th issue of *Post* (Curtis Pub. Co.).[1]

This is enterprising of them and it is about as good a simplification as you could expect to find in a popular magazine. Furthermore it gives a current round-up on the news on the Teilhard Movement, both here and abroad.

Here, too, is my piece on Caroline.[2]

I'm not happy about it—it seems quite cramped—now that I see it in print—although I cut it. I didn't ever see proof on it, and there are bulls in it, as you will see.

Incidentally I have just had the following wire from David McDowell:

"Hope you are hard at work. Our fiction inventory is low. Please pass the word to Flannery, Donald [Davidson] and Walter [Sullivan]."

In haste.
Lon

1. J. Kobler, "Priest Who Haunts the Catholic World," *Saturday Evening Post*, 236 (October 12, 1963), 42–51.
2. See Letter 155, note 1.

171. *To Brainard Cheney from Flannery O'Connor. TLS 1p.*

Milledgeville, 21 October [19]63

Dear Lon,

Thanks for the copies of the piece on Caroline. I haven't got to read it yet because I've just got back from this week of traveling around. At Georgetown I met your friend Mildred Horn [*sic*][1] after the lecture and would have liked to talk to her longer but there was a push. I had breakfast with Ward Dorrence [*sic*].[2]

A lot of people told me about the piece in the Sewanee[3] and one teacher at Hollins said it had helped her considerably in understanding what I was doing. Do you by any chance have an extra copy of it? I don't take the Sewanee so I haven't seen it. Several people remarked they liked it.

Somebody sent me the piece out of the Sat. Eve. Post but I haven't got to it yet either.

T. [Tommie] Stritch reports that Caroline was to lecture at ND [Notre Dame] on last Thursday and then he apparently had a full weekend to entertain her in. I'll hope to hear more.

When are you all coming thisaway? I heard about some library meeting on Jeckyl Island and I thought you might be taking that in, but I guess not.

Cheers,
Flannery

1. Mildred Haun (1911–66) was a Vanderbilt educated Tennessee short story writer.

2. Ward Allison Dorrance (1904–), a short story writer, was a friend of Allen Tate.

3. See Letter 159, note 2.

172. *To Flannery O'Connor from Brainard Cheney. TLS(cc)*

Oct. 23, 1963

Dear Flannery,

Thanks again for lending me Raven's book! A rounded assessment of T's contribution, appreciative, and discriminating and sympathetically understanding, even if this sympathy tries to pull T a little his way. A finely turned dish of liberal English sweetbreads, if a bit too bland for me!

I think Raven's final chapter on T's critics is to the point, precise, effective broadside and sharp in detail. I find I can agree with most of what he says against T's conservative theological critics. It is what he implies for his own position that I can't go along with.

To wit: ". . . T came to reject the God who works from outside and independently in favour of One who works in the totality of things and by convergence and claims (justly) that this is St. Paul's meaning. Tresmontant adds a footnote indicating that this seems a forced interpretation of the Apostle."

I can't speak for St. Paul. But Raven's implications don't quite square with T's statements in POM: p. 270: "Omega . . . while being the last term in the series, it is also *outside all series*" (italics T's)—Or, p. 294: "Christ . . . put himself in position to subdue under himself . . . the general ascent of consciousness *into which he inserted himself.*" (my italics).

I can't recall exactly what Tresmontant said about T's interpretation of St. Paul. But what he did point out as unorthodox was T's implication that God was dependent on creation for His own completion.

Of course there is the question of T's view of evil, also. It is obvious that Raven doesn't believe in a devil at all. And he is probably socio-psychiatric in his view of man's pride and perversity and of original sin. And he would claim for T his slant on things, yet and however inadequate T's sketchy statement in POM on the nature of evil, he holds the door open to The Fall. But this question I think is incidental to the positive issue: the nature of God.

Definition of God's Infinity is surely the issue with T—as it is the issue with the liberals. I see it, too, as the issue at the ecumenical council between the Vatican and the modern world. The liberals of the Raven stripe obviously want to *limit* Him to human comprehension. While, it seems to me however presumptuous, the conservatives (some of them in our Church) lean a little backward in the matter of keeping Him uncommitted to His creation.

What do you think?

Of course even in our Church some have talked recklessly about man's *freedom of choice.* That quite misrepresents man's predicament. What his humanity put on him was the responsibility of choice. He can only gain freedom by making the right choices.

Anyhow, I want to applaud Raven's marksmanship on Dr. P. B. Medawar, especially, ". . . for his knowledge of men—under the skin—is, I fear, definitely subhuman"!

Thanks again for the loan!

We are hard at work and Fannie, at least, is writing. And there is no news with us.

F. joins me in love to you both.

As ever,
Lon

P.S. My piece on you is out in the fall issue of SR [*Sewanee Review*], I see—in the book review section.[1] I don't know why, but maybe he [Andrew Lytle, editor] didn't know where else to put it.

L

Returning Raven under separate cover. [handwritten]

1. See Letter 159, note 1.

173. *To Brainard Cheney from Flannery O'Connor. ALS 2pp.*

Milledgeville, 31 October [19]63

Dear Lon,

Thanks a lot for the copy of the Sewanee. I think that piece[1] is going to do a lot of good as far as giving people a second thought about my stuff. I haven't heard from [John] Hawkes—whether he's seen it or not. I'm going to his place—Brown [University]—this coming Spring to read.

I agree with what you say about the Raven book. Raven is too given to *natural* religion and I distrust folks who have ugly things to say about Karl Barth.[2] I like old Barth. He throws the furniture around. But there are good things in the Raven book. We may see Teilhard canonized yet. I don't know about his theories but I don't doubt his sanctity.

Cheers,
Flannery

1. Swiss Protestant theologian (1886–1968); rejecting prevailing liberal theology, Barth developed a radically Christocentric theology.

174. *To Flannery O'Connor from Brainard Cheney. TLS(cc) 1p.*

December 2, 1963

Dear Flannery,

Have you seen *The World of Teilhard de C* [Chardin]?[1] A collection of pieces on him by Americans I believe—most of them are anyhow. I've covered about two-thirds of them: they are mixed. If you haven't seen it and want to, would be most happy to pass this on to you?

This warns of a call for help. I'm about to put the bee on you to take a look at something I've done I call a short story (Only the 2nd I ever finished, that is brought to the stage of thinking of finishing it). It's not so short; however, being 25 pp. as it now stands. But that's short for me—and I hope I can compress it some more.[2] Mildred Haun was with us over the T. week-end and read it and suggested some compression.

If it won't be too inconvenient, I'll send it to you, but if you are covered up, just say so.

A letter from [Tommie] Stritch gave me a report on the C.G. [Caroline Gordon] visit & speech. It seems to have been strenuous for Tom. And he thought her performance very unbuttoned—too bad!

Suppose you've heard of Tom Carter's death?[3] Sad, indeed. Poor lad had suffered a lot and had been on pain-relievers of one sort or another for at least a third of his short life. Ashley B. [Brown] writes me he is his literary exec.[4] TC had a rare collection of Windham [*sic*] Lewis.[5]

Trust all is well with you. Fannie joins me in love to you both.

Lon

1. Robert T. Francoeur, ed. (Baltimore: Helicon Press, 1961).
2. This story, "Is It a Joke," was never published.
3. Carter, while still an undergraduate at Washington and Lee University, edited *Shenandoah*, in which Cheney published his review of *Wise Blood*. See Letter 1, note 1.
4. Ashley Brown, long-time friend of the Cheneys and Caroline Gordon, and instructor of English at Washington and Lee University from 1946–53, had sponsored *Shenandoah* and suggested to Carter that Cheney be asked to review *Wise Blood*.
5. Wyndham Lewis (1882–1957), English writer (who exposed the weaknesses of modern technological civilizations) and painter (who founded vorticism, first English abstract movement in art).

175. *To Brainard Cheney from Flannery O'Connor. ALS 1p.*

Milledgeville, 4 Dec. [19]63

Dear Lon,

I'll be cheered to see the story. 25 pages is not long for a story. I've just writ one myself about that length that I would send if I had a copy of it.[1]

Saw *The World of Teilhard* briefly. It was sent me to review but I decided I wasn't a taker.

I hadn't heard about Tom Carter. What a pity.

Love to you & Fanny.

Flannery

1. "Revelation," published in the *Sewanee Review*, 72 (Spring, 1964), 178–202.

176. *To Flannery O'Connor from Brainard Cheney. TLS(cc) 1p.*

12-6-[19]63

Dear Flannery,

This return mail response to your kind consent is prompted in part by the thought of marketing (eventually) the story in question. Though it may a bit take your breath away!

Glad to hear you say that the length should not prove prohibitory necessarily.

TWOT [*The World of Teilhard*] (the book of which we

have been speaking) and in which I have four more essays to read, I haven't found too important. The essay I have just today finished reading I think (to me) the most relevant and deeply supporting: [James L.] Foy's "Man and the Behavioral Sciences."[1] He supports Teilhard node and neuron so to speak.

That was a fine piece on you in *The Commonweal* by Rupp![2] And good play, too, as we say in the news profession.

We (F&I) are getting set to go out and rake leaves this fine sunny December [day] and must be about it at once, or 4:30 sundown will catch us—so my haste.

Thanks in advance!

Luck (& patience)

Lon

1. Pp. 115–130.
2. Richard H. Rupp, "Fact and Mystery: Flannery O'Connor," 79 (December 6, 1963), 304–07.

177. *To Flannery O'Connor from Brainard Cheney. TLS(cc) 1p.*

Friday, March Sixth [1964]

Dear Flannery,

Greetings! And *solicitations.*

Hope this finds you, sap rising and set for spring.

First, let me report that recently in phone conversation with David McDowell, he wanted to know if I had let you know that they (Curtis [Publishing Co.]) wanted you to submit something for them. I told him that I had so reported, but that since he seemed eager, I would repeat it. Maybe they pay well? in a pinch they don't mind paying off football coaches—though only in a pinch.

To the other part of this: Will you send me [Charles] Raven's (the one who wrote on Teilhard) initials—and is (or was) he not vice-chancellor emeritus of Cambridge U? I returned that book without setting down a note!

I'm about half way through a first draft of my piece for SR [*Sewanee Review*]—after so long a time.[1] I thought

I would never [be] getting down to writing—especially after I got started on *background* reading.

I ran into something exciting on the research frontier on the insides of the cell. I couldn't find any up-to-the-minute books, so I visited Vanderbilt's biochemistry department. The head gave me a simplified account of their *breaking down the code* of the DNA in the nucleus. Also, and this was the most exciting thing for me, told me that *gene* is about to disappear on the geneticists. That is, they (in cytology research) have found that, although the messenger molecule (RNA) may bring the translate information from the nucleus (DNA) to the ribosome (the stamping machine in the cell factor) a temperer (they don't really know what the hell it is) may decide they (at the stamping machine) won't use it, or will just use part of it, as the circumstances of the cell at the moment seem to warrant! Oh boy, doesn't that blow the random mutationists all to Kingdom Come! Listen, those cytologists are going to make out Teilhard's case for him.

We wish you would come up to see us?

Our love to you both.

Lon

1. Subsequently published as "Has Teilhard De Chardin *Really* Joined the Within and the Without of Things?" *Sewanee Review,* 73 (Spring, 1965), 217–36.

178. *To Brainard Cheney from Flannery O'Connor. ALS 1p.*

8 March [19]64, M'ville

Dear Lon,

That's Charles Raven and I'm not sure about the Cambridge business as the book has got misplaced. I just came back from the hospital Thurs—after major surgery and I'm not creeping even yet. It turned out okay but I feel pretty sorry and can't do anything.

One person or another at the *Post* keeps asking for something but I don't know what I could do that *they* would want. They ought to leave us Georgians alone. They got scalded once.

Cheers,
F

179. *To Flannery O'Connor from Brainard Cheney. TLS(cc) 1p.*

Wednesday, March Eleventh [1964]

Dear Flannery,

Your news was as grim as it was brief! And the glib ignorance of my letter to you, cheaping of spring and running on with other trivia, adds to the impact. We had gone too long without word of you and assumed too much!

May I infer that you are recuperating, since you could write a letter? And your returning home from the hospital should support some optimism, I hope?

Fannie and I are chagrined that we shouldn't have suspected something wrong, or have inquired of our mutual friends to find out. Anyhow we are distressed. And we hope and pray you are well on your way to strength and health again.

This does not require an answer or any other exertion on your part, but is only to let you know of our sympathy and solicitude.

Love.
Lon

180. *To Brainard and Frances Neel Cheney from Flannery O'Connor. ALS 2pp.*

26 March [19]64, Milledgeville

Dear Lon & Fannie,

I do appreciate being remembered in all those masses and it looks like I need to be. The operation was a success but it started up some complications that we haven't got in hand yet. But I hope we will before long as this sitting around doing nothing is about to kill me. The Mabrys[1] came through here last week and I sure would have liked to see them but I was in bed with fever and they didn't stop.

A happy Easter to you all from us.

Love,
Flannery

1. Mr. and Mrs. Thomas D. Mabry, of Allensville, Kentucky. Mabry was, with Ward A. Dorrance, author of a book of short stories, *The White Hound* (Columbia: The University of Missouri Press, 1959). He was another author who admired and was helped in his work by Caroline Gordon; he also greatly admired Flannery O'Connor.

181. *To Flannery O'Connor from Brainard Cheney. TLS(cc) 1p.*

April 22nd [1964]

Dear Flannery,

As you may have already concluded, I did not get away from Lumber City in time to come by Milledgeville on my return. And to be sure, you have enough on your hands now without having to entertain visitors!

But it was great to have a sight of you and to discover, for all the operations and infections, there was a solid residue of your charming person and personality remaining. I'm not on terms to make this important, but you can know that you're in my appeals for all I can make them worth.

Had quite a fine visit in LC. Among others the only daughter of my venerated dead friend, Robin Bess called on me. She (named Mamie) looks more like her father than any of the other children and is the stout mother of twelve living children—I suppose I should add, parent, along with her pretty weasly looking husband, Tobe.[1]

I haven't got down to reading the essay on Teilhard you let me have, but I will in a day or two. I was very much interested in what you reported on Andrew Lytle's thought for a Teilhard issue. He hasn't yet mentioned it to me. Do you think it would be all right for me to bring it up with him?

Lon

[handwritten P.S.] It would be wonderful if you felt like doing a piece on [Teilhard's] *The Divine Milieu.*

1. Robin Bess was a mulatto sharecropper whom Cheney's father had once defended in a trial; thereafter, he was Cheney's foreman, overseeing other tenant farmers for the Cheneys. When the elder Cheney died, Bess stayed on, helping Cheney's mother to run the farm. Bess was a man of unusual intelligence and high integrity, much admired by Cheney. When he was young, Cheney spent

considerable time in the company of Bess, who became something of a surrogate father to him. Cheney's novel, *This Is Adam,* is based on his experiences with Robin Bess, who died in 1953, and is dedicated to his memory.

182. *To Brainard Cheney from Flannery O'Connor. ALS 2pp.*

22 April [19]64, Baldwin County Hospital, Milledgeville

Dear Lon,

We were sorry you didn't get by Sunday. I was much taken with the paper on Teilhard,[1] not that I understand any of the scientific stuff but the work you've done on it is sure impressive & what I do understand makes sense. I was going to mail it back to you Monday but Monday I woke up covered from head to foot with the lupus rash. A sign that things are as screwy inside as out so I headed for the hospital and here I am for an indefinite stay, the guest of myself, as my insurance don't cover lupus. So I hope only a week or two. They've loaded me up with ACTH.

When you see Frances Nelson will you tell her how much I appreciated her letter about the story? She didn't put a return address on it. I remember them well. I thought he was Andrew's brother but I reckon it is a cousin.[2]

As soon as I get out of here I'll mail your essay back. If you want it sooner let me know and I'll get R. [Regina] to fix it as I know exactly where I left it.

A little boy in the hospital here flushed all his clothes down the toilet and has upset the plumbing completely on the 2nd & 3rd floor. The Lord blessed me by putting me on the 4th. Cheers to you & Fannie.

Flannery

1. See Letter 177, note 1.
2. Frances Nelson, a long time friend of the Cheneys, lived in Murfreesboro, Tennessee, and had relatives in Thomasville, Georgia; her husband, John, was a first cousin of Andrew Lytle.

183. *To Flannery O'Connor from Brainard Cheney. TLS(cc) 1p.*

April 25th [1964]

Dear Flannery,

Now I'm sorrier than you, than you can possibly be that I didn't at least pause for a minute, on my way back here. Truth is that I took the wrong route to get by Milledgeville!

But as well as I do know, I somehow can't realize the degree of hazard in which you live!

I suppose it is your redoubtable *hardihood* and humor that delude me.

Would so appreciate any word on how things go for you, medicalwise, as we say in the trade.

It comes to me that the little boy's clothes into the toilet is a token. I am pleased that you are above mechanical inconvenience there on the 4th floor, but maybe his *spell* will drain away your lupus rash, anyhow.

Herewith, I return Roslyn Barnes' piece.[1] I read it only casually. It's a scholarly thing and not my meat. It was evident to me that she knows her Teilhard and, perhaps, her [Gerard Manley] Hopkins, too. Her comments were discriminating and her quotations were apt. However, I felt a bit weighed down, rather than illuminated by them.

It seems to me that the piece (even for scholarly work) needs organization and analytical summation. There is thirty pages of it (and it begins quotation chopping in the 1st pgh and keeps it up to the end) whereas, with better organization and summation, it could be done in about half the space, or so it seems to me.

I had a brief conversation (over phone) with Andrew Lytle about it—I didn't go into my criticisms, but said I thought it would call for some editing. He seemed prepared to consider the piece, in any event—didn't seem let in the least by my comment.

I am heartened that you like my piece on T. I did put

out on it—though I feel greatly rewarded for my effort. Andrew told me that he was reading it.

I will pass your message on to Frances Nelson. We will probably see them in a day or two, or talk over phone, anyhow.

Fannie has been working too hard, but is home today relaxing a bit (though still working, to be sure).

She joins me in love to you both.

Lon

1. Roslyn Barnes was a friend and correspondent of O'Connor's; among other things, she shared O'Connor's enthusiasm for Teilhard. There are numerous references and letters to her in *The Habit of Being*.

184. *To Brainard Cheney from Flannery O'Connor. ALS 1p.*

11 May [19]64, Milledgeville

Dear Lon,

I'm out of the hospital but still in bed and not supposed to do anything. Miss Mary[1] & I got out the same day. She's with us now and seems satisfied for the time being.

Here is your piece on Teilhard. I sure do like it. When I get to feeling like it, I'm going to send Roslyn's piece back to her with your comments and some others and suggest she do something about it if she wants to sell it.

Cheers to you all,
Flannery

1. Mary Cline, 82, O'Connor's aunt, who had suffered a heart attack in March.

185. *To Flannery O'Connor from Brainard Cheney. TLS(cc) 1p.*

June Seventh [1964]

Dear Flannery,

Tommie Stritch (with whom Fannie and I were having drinks) came away from a long distance talk with Robert West Wednesday afternoon to report your being back in the hospital—this time an Atlanta place. We are most distressed!

It does seem that you are having more than your share!

Of course you've had more of it a long time now. And I don't know what I mean, anyhow. But over the past year or so, it has looked like my more talented friends have more ill health—even the greater the talent the greater the misfortune!

This observation may have a subjective smell about it. But it has made me right self-conscious of late about my own healthiness. There seems to be nothing reasonable about it—certainly no warranty for it: except a lack of talent.

I was thinking on it especially that Wednesday (it being my 64th birthday). Unless the Lord has [a] hole card He's getting ready to turn over that will knock my eyeballs out—the only sense I can make of it is He knows I can't stand much! Moreover, He knows, I take it that I couldn't survive much of a cross current and nothing but long forbearance can get the little in me out.

Having just reread the cat story I sent to Andrew Lytle some time ago and he has returned, to see some of its now more apparent errors, I'm sure His tolerance is not paying off—unmixed mercy.

Fannie is getting the library school summer session underway—I may say without vacation. But she seems somehow to be bearing up under it. It is, I think, the expectation of being able to lay her burden down in September: Peabody has finally got a director for the school and one she deeply approves of: her old friend and former boss (in Tokyo) Bob Gitler.[1]

We are expecting Tommie [Stritch] and Andrew [Lytle] for dinner this evening and you may be sure you will be in our thoughts and intentions.

I suppose it isn't so much the issue (as Andrew Lytle's Presbyterian deacon phrased it) that taking God up one side and down the other, He does about as much harm as He does good—as in knowing when you are well off—or rather, in knowing that if you come up with your little that counts, you are always well off!

Love,
Lon

[handwritten marginal note] According to Teilhard, but it ain't easy to see!

1. See Letter 110, note 2.

186. *To Brainard and Frances Neel Cheney from Flannery O'Connor. ALS 2pp.*

Piedmont Hospital, Atlanta, 19 June [19]64

Dear Lon & Fannie,

I'm getting out of this institution tomorrow after *one month* in here. I'm for medicare; otherwise I got few convictions and almost no blood. I'll have to stay in bed for a while. When you call up this hospital & inquire for a patient, a record says, "The patient is resting comfortably. She has peaceful days and nights." "Plumb funerary," my cousin says. I would call it embalmed.

Anyway, I just wanted to thank you for your prayers & urge you to continue to keep me in them.

Affectionately
Flannery

187. *To Flannery O'Connor from Brainard Cheney. TLS(cc) 1p.*

July Eleventh [1964]

Dear Flannery,

Do hope there are breezes stirring about Andalusia Farm to keep you cool. Summer is a poor season in bed!

Here the day is insufferably muggy!

Since our last, we have had a visit from Ashley B. [Brown], and gossip fore and aft. Though for the life of me I can't recall any of it now.

My only bit is a salesman's joke: LBJ won't allow orange juice to be served at the White House: it looks too much like gold water, or suppose I should have written it Goldwater.

But Ashley was full of his plans for a year in Brazil—which, although it had not come previously into his plans for travel, or fellowships, or cultural attacheships, seems to be a pretty exciting place to spend a year just now—right under the Volcano, so to speak.[1]

We (Tommy Stritch, and Fannie and I) are supposed to have a rendezvous with Robert Fitzgerald in Bloomington this month—that is, or was: today or next Saturday—and it begins to look like a fizzle—I've not heard from Tommy, since his first letter to Robert. But I hold to a thin strand of hope.

Fannie took her vacation last week at St. Louis at an ALA [American Library Association] convention: it's curious how one man's meat is another man's poison!

I've been a bit under the weather, with a kidney infection, but am about straight again—haven't been able to do much work, however.

Your sense of humor may not be broad enough to include this type. But I am enclosing an anecdote which I hope may amuse you. It's experimental for me. If you feel inclined, I would, of course, be grateful for your assessment of it. But it will surely be enough for me if you are enough amused by it to read it.

We hope that the summer has brought you zip and that you are now able to wander from your bed a bit!

Fannie joins me in love to you both.

Lon

1. Ashley Brown was Fullbright professor, Federal University of Rio de Janeiro, 1964–65.

188. *To Brainard Cheney from Flannery O'Connor. ALS 1p.*

16 July [19]64, M'ville

Dear Lon,

I always did think your best writing was about Riverton and that boy. But I reckon the NAACP would get you for this. To me it sounds like part of a novel or a book of reminiscences (sp?). I like the writing anyway.

Since I got home from the hospital I've written two stories and if I ever get copies of them, I'll send them along.[1] I work 2 hours a day and rest 22.

I hope you all get to see Robt. [Fitzgerald]. If I were on foot I'd just come up there and join you.

Cheers,
Flannery

1. "Parker's Back," *Esquire*, 63 (April, 1965), 76–78, 151–55; and "Judgement Day," in *Everything That Rises Must Converge*, ed. and intro. by Robert Fitzgerald (New York: Farrar, Straus & Giroux, 1965), pp. 245–69.

Flannery O'Connor died on 3 August 1964, in Milledgeville, Georgia.

Appendix A

Brainard Cheney's Review of Flannery O'Connor's *Wise Blood,* in *Shenandoah,* 3 (Autumn, 1952), 55–60.

Complaint about our Patent Electric Blanket has been common enough. In varied note it has make [*sic*] up the bulk of our literature and art for half a century, to be sure—not to mention the more oblique use of it in political oratory.

The day when the outcry arose over who could or should come under the blanket, or how far it could or should be stretched, now dims in memory (except for Politics' ghostly official ritual). And for a long time now complaint has been directed at the blanket itself.

Political short-circuits having produced two devastating general electrocutions in the past forty years and brought about a chronic state of localized slaughter, no one even among its manufacturers regards the old blanket with complacence any more. Inspecting it and proposing fumigation, renovation, etc., are the preoccupations of our age. In this country, where the blanket was warmest and most of the people slept next to it, in the raw, there was paradoxically in the distant South a ravelling edge.

The edge of man's social covering has always interested the artist, and the existence of these loose antique strands in the South has not gone without notice. It has received literary treatment over more than two decades. The significance of our unravelling even has been suspected.

No more dramatic representation of it, however, has come to my attention than that made in *Wise Blood* by Miss Flannery O'Connor. And let me add, no wiser blood had brooded and beat over the meaning of the grim rupture in our social fabric than that of this twenty-six year old Georgia girl in this, her first novel.

Two earlier novels dealing substantially with the same material—Erskine Caldwell's *Tobacco Road* and William Faulkner's *As I Lay Dying*—can, I believe, be drawn upon to illuminate and give us perspective for Miss O'Connor's dramatic revelation. These three stories present the same sort of people in the same passage of history, although a quarter of a century separates the Lesters and the Bundrens from Hazel Motes. To be sure a little more has transpired historically for "Haze," than had for Jeeter or Anse. There has been a political revolution in this country and another world war. But this is of no great importance in their predicament.

The significant difference comes in their creators' definition of this predicament.

Caldwell—no artist and only a dull pornographer and entitled to mention in this company only because of the accident of his comment on the material in question and public reaction to it—saw only the physical poverty and hunger of his Lesters in *Tobacco Road.* In the Marxist *morality* which he reflected, this was mortal sin, and, with the anger of the sentimental and confused, he heaped every conceivable indignity that could be heaped on the human animal, upon them.

Perhaps the only reason why he did not do them deeper degradation was because he knew of no other dimension in which to degrade them. His references to religion were purely nominal. He had too little imagination to use his woman preacher, Bessie, for anything more than a labelled effigy on which to smear sexual imbecilities. He granted Jeeter and Ada Lester a tragic death only because death for him was merely phenomenal—and literary.

In *As I Lay Dying,* Faulkner knows that death is not merely phenomenal and he remembers that there is a more persistent hunger than physical hunger. The Bundrens are not absorbed in their precarious economy. At the story's opening, however, Addie, the religious one, is dying and their drama concerns itself with the ritual burial of her remains. Their religious rite gives them significance while it engages them, yet they do not seek salvation and when it is ended they slip back into naturalistic anonymity. Faulkner, one of the great visionaries of our time, showed religious perspective here, but he had not then been granted the grace of vision.

To be sure time has passed, events have transpired and we all understand more about the limitations of materialism than we did twenty years ago. This is true even for artists and their Lesters, Bundrens and Moteses, too. *Tobacco Road* received serious critical as well as popular acceptance and praise, while Faulkner was being rebuked for *As I Lay Dying* by those who slept warmly, in the raw, next to The Blanket. But to make my point, the suspicion I wish to give voice to here is that Lesters, Bundrens and Moteses alike, were gnawed by the same secret hunger.

It has remained for Miss O'Connor, twenty years after their earlier appearance, to see what these people's destitution signifies and to fully appreciate their motivation.

Wise Blood is not about belly hunger, nor religious nostalgia, but about the persistent craving of the soul. It is not about a man whose religious allegiance is name for a shiftlessness and fatalism that make him degenerate in poverty and bestial before hunger, nor about a family of rustics who sink in naturalistic anonymity when the religious elevation of their burial rite is over. It is about man's inescapable need of his fearful, if blind, search for salvation. Miss O'Connor has not been confused by the symptoms.

And she centers her story frankly and directly on the religious activity and experience of her simple and squalid folk. Didactically stated her story seems over-simple: Hazel Motes, an hysterical fringe preacher, tries to found a church "Without Christ" and, progressively preaching nihilism, negates his way back to the cross.

The point is, however, that there is nothing didactic about her statement of it. Her statement is completely dramatic and dramatically profound.

I would agree, however, that Miss O'Connor could not have done what she has done twenty years ago. We have here essentially the same people and the same essential motivation, but the Lesters and Bundrens could not have been made to force the issue of the Church Without Christ. The technique Miss O'Connor employs had not ripened then and, if it had been so employed perhaps could not have been generally understood.

In contrast to Caldwell's reportorial naturalism and Faulkner's poetic expressionism, she uses, under the face of naturalism a theologically weighted symbolism.

When the story opens, Hazel Motes, from Eastrod, Tennessee, and just released from the Army after four years' service, is on his way to preach "the church without Jesus Christ Crucified." He doesn't believe in Jesus and he doesn't believe in sin, he confides to passengers on the train taking him to Taulkinham, the city.

His first act to disprove his belief in sin on his arrival is to share the bed of Mrs. Leora Watts, said to be the "friendliest bed in town." His mission complicates his life with that of a phony, blind, street-corner beggar-preacher and his young daughter, whom Haze plans to seduce to prove to the blind preacher that he is serious in his repudiation of Christianity.

Haze is impressed with the preacher's story that he blinded himself with quick lime to justify his belief that Christ had redeemed him. Still Haze suspects its validity. In the course of events he succeeds in finding out what the reader already knows, that the preacher had funked his demonstration with the quick lime and not put it in his eyes, and is not blind. Moreover, the preacher's fifteen-year old nymphomaniac daughter turns the tables on Haze in his plans to seduce her and forces him to take her into his bed.

To the theater crowds, he preaches nightly from the hood of his rat-colored, high-back automobile, which he bought for $40.00—preaches at the outset that "Jesus Christ is just a nigger trick," and he talks about a "new Jesus." Later he contends that he cannot commit blasphemy, because there is nothing to blaspheme.

His talk about a new jesus attracts a street mountebank who wants to join him, capitalize on his *idea* and make money out of it. When Haze refuses, the mountebank, Onnie Jay Holy, finds a double for Haze and tries to carry on without him.

Haze, who feels that he is trying to bring Truth to the world—the truth that there is no truth—will have no counterfeit of himself preaching a new jesus to take people's money. When warning does not stop his deceitful imitator, he runs him down with his car and kills him.

In his treasured automobile, he plans to drive to another city to found his church, leaving behind his crime, the people who did not appreciate his message of truth, and the preacher's feckless daughter who has proved too much for him. On the journey, he is overtaken by a traffic cop, who, when he finds Haze has no driver's license, has him drive his jalopy up on the next hill-top, to see the "puttiest view you ever did see." Here the cop pushes Haze's car over the embankment to its destruction, with the words, "Them that don't have a car, don't need a license."

For a long time Haze stares at the desolate view "that extended from his eyes to the blank gray sky that went on, depth after depth, into space." When the now solicitous patrolman offers to give Haze a lift, he says he wasn't going anywhere.

Up to this point the surface action has simulated naturalistic motivation, but evidently Miss O'Connor felt that, to a world which does not yet accept the idea of the devil, she had better emphasize his allegorical appearance. It is the first apparent clue to Haze's reemboidment [*sic*] of the Christ myth, this ironic *temptation* from the mountain-top.

He returns to blind himself with quick lime and spends his remaining days in mortifying the flesh. The anti-Christ messiah's lone disciple is his hard-bitten landlady, a shrew who had always felt cheated. And her curiosity to know what that "crazy fool," sitting on her porch, staring off into space with his sightless eyes *sees,* finally gets her. "Why had he destroyed his eyes and saved himself unless he had some plan, unless he saw something that he couldn't get without being blind to everything else?" And his other silent penance—rocks and broken glass in his shoes, barbed wire around his chest—when she nosily discovers it, fascinates her by its very illogic: she suspects that she is being cheated somehow, because of something he sees that she can't see. She pursues him, finally falls in love with him, and with mixed motives tries to force him to marry her.

He will not "treat" with her, flees her house into a storm, dies of exposure and a policeman's billy. His death only fixes his fascination for her.

Miss O'Connor employs symbolic motivation, allusion, parallel, irony and understatement, among other things, to suggest her indirect and deeper meanings. The surface story as a whole makes its allegorical emphasis by being beside any logical point, except the allegorical point. These are all known devices, but she employs them with fine skill and tact and dramatic insight.

There is the obvious suggestion in *Wise Blood* that that terrible heretical misconception of religious freedom which regards every man as potentially his own priest, has come to the end of its row. But the dramatic impact for me lay in my share of the landlady's chill (and fascination) over the undescribed vision that filled Haze Motes' sightless eyes—Haze Motes, who had never got far enough under the Patent Electric Blanket to be lulled to sleep in its security.

Appendix B

Frances Neel Cheney, "Universal Themes in Southern Scene" [review of *A Good Man Is Hard to Find*], *Nashville Banner,* 1 July 1955, p. 23.

When Flannery O'Connor's short novel, "Wise Blood," appeared several summers ago, it was recognized as the work of a promising young writer. Before that she had published some short stories, and since then, she has appeared in the Kenyon Review, the Sewanee Review, Harper's Bazaar and the anthology "Modern Writing."

Now in her first collection of short stories, we have some examples of her best work, work that reflects her clear view of the world. Readers who choose to read these ten stories as pure naturalism, as grim humor, or as allegory alone, are missing their full import, for they must be read with all of these in mind.

Most of the characters are country people, though the city and country are both scenes of action. Their setting in the South is due to Miss O'Connor's knowledge of the Southern scene, but their themes are universal. One of the most moving is "The River" in which a four-year-old boy, neglected by his alcoholic parents, seeks salvation in the River of Life. This is much more than a macabre tale of a little boy's drowning himself because he was unloved by his parents, though the extent of their neglect is strikingly brought home by such details as his rising in the morning while his parents were still asleep, to eat two crackers with anchovy paste, some raisin bread heels and peanut butter.

The title story takes a family by car on the way to Florida, the father driving fast, while his eight-year-old boy, John Wesley, reading comic books on the back seat, urges, "Let's go through Georgia fast so we won't have to look at it much." The grandmother didn't want to go to Florida, and it was of her that the escaped convict who "did in" the family said, "She would of been a good woman, if it had been somebody there to shoot her every minute of her life."

Perhaps the most humorous story is "A Late Encounter with the Enemy," in which Miss Sally Poker Sash, 62-year-old school teacher, received an answer to her prayer that her 102-year-old grandfather, General Tennessee Flintrock Sash, would like to sit on the platform at her graduation exercises. The description of an earlier occasion, during which he was dressed up in a general's uniform and introduced at the "Preemy they had in Atlanta" is a view of the premier showing of "Gone With the Wind" which we have not had before in fiction.

Miss O'Connor's eye for the setting is very evident in "The Artificial Nigger," when Mr. Head and his ten-year-old grandson make an excursion to Atlanta, getting lost in the city, and after a day, mostly filled with a child's terror and an old man's shame, returning to the country. The feel of the countryside they rode through on the train, the Atlanta streets they wandered lost in, all are very real to the reader.

Also impressive is her ear for the spoken word and the conversation of her characters has a naturalness which we expect from a real artist.

But it is finally the total meaning of these commentaries on the modern world which established the author as a distinguished writer. These are no impressionistic sketches, small, incompletely understood slices of life. The meaning is there for each reader to grasp.

Appendix C

Brainard Cheney, "Bold, Violent, Yet Terribly Funny Tale" [review of *The Violent Bear It Away*], *Nashville Banner,* 4 March 1960, p. 23.

This story was conceived of violence and violently carried out and, in the tenor of the title and the Scripture from which it is taken, only the violent will bear it away, it is my guess—only those who are willing and able to do imaginative violence to their habitual mode of feeling and thinking about the values of Life.

It is the boldest and most brilliant achievement of a young writer whose work includes already some of the most original and important American fiction of this century. This novel, also, sets a new high mark for Miss O'Connor's achievement in her use of humor. It is only through the strategy of her humor, indeed that she is able to present so violent a tale.

For Mason Tarwater, the inspiration for the action of this

piece, had conceived himself an Elijah, bent on bringing up his young grandnephew to wear his mantle as prophet and soul saver, after his death. Most of the rest of the world concerned regards the old man as mad. For who can do the modern view more violence than a brimstone prophet?

The boy, Francis Marion Tarwater, in a state of doubt, rebels against the commitment his great uncle has put upon him almost immediately after the old man dies, which has just occurred when the story opens. The boy's apostasy takes him from the Tarwater wilderness farm, Powderhead, to the city to see his school teacher uncle, George Rayber, himself once the old man's choice for successor but who eluded him to become an apostle of Scientism and the self-proclaimed prophet's most hostile critic.

A fourth character, Bishop, Rayber's idiot son, serves as a center of action, since old Tarwater had commissioned Francis Marion to baptize Bishop. The boy has no intention of carrying out his uncle's command, but compulsive impulse stirs in him. The school teacher uncle proposes to cure Francis Marion of his traumatic experience and his complex and of his religion, too, by approved psychological methods. The action of the story surrounds this effort and its conflicts, which eventually turn Bishop into an idiot-evil symbol of the old man for Rayber and Francis Marion, still threatening them with his madness.

Perhaps the reader can sense here that this is pretty strong meat, but there is no gothic taint to it. For it is the genius of Miss O'Connor's humor that she nowhere appears the partisan of human fallibility. This is, to be sure, something we have learned to expect of her writing, but I would like to try to define her viewpoint a little further.

Her first novel, "Wise Blood," produced contempt, confusion, or incredulity on the reading public of a world in a morbid state of mind from taking itself too seriously. Through some of her short stories appearing in the volume following "A Good Man Is Hard to Find," in which she put her humor to more recognizable uses, the incredulous part of her reading public began to be illuminated and even amused, if at some cost to self-regard.

What the word-debasing-and-debased Western World has needed for more than a century is a real humorist. And I hail Miss O'Connor in that role.

From religion to politics to Science to manners, sentimentality has been rife in the land for a long, long time. Sentimentality, as we know, has to do with inflation of the ego. It is what is known as the human complaint. It is not new.

But when scientists, after Galileo, established their Archimedean or universal point from which to view the physical world, it was, I suppose, inevitable that man would discover a new Reality, confusing himself again with God. Under this error, of course, the world has grown more awful to contemplate the longer man has looked at it—for the viewpoint was still human and human only, wherever, it might be located in space or time, or however many eyes were at the knot hole. Whatever he did to refine or lengthen his measuring stick, he could only measure distance—not God. So erring modern man has been for a long time now trying to deny the existence of Infinity. In the literary world this sentimental view has taken the name of Existentialism.

And to keep this within bounds of a book review, let me return at once to Miss O'Connor's use of humor. Her original achievement, her genius is that she has restored to humor the religious point of view. That is, man looking at himself, not in the presence of time and space, however great, and certainly not this humanly-conceived time and space looking at man. But man, looking at himself in the Presence of Infinity—Infinity for Whom there is no unknown, nor unknowable, from Whom there are no secrets. But an Infinity of Love and Compassion as well as Awfulness.

In "The Violent Bear It Away," Miss O'Connor has turned her humor—though not for the first time—on religion, itself. That is to say, on the contemporary state of religious practice. In "Wise Blood" she confronted the logical conclusion of a post Christian world's denial of Christ. In this work, coming eight years later, she may be regarded as creatively probing the Christian commitment under Existentialism.

It is, to put it with exactitude, a terribly funny tale. And a profound comment on the human condition in this post modern day.

Appendix D

Brainard Cheney, "Miss O'Connor Creates Unusual Humor Out of Ordinary Sin," *Sewanee Review,* 71 (Autumn, 1963), 644–52.

(Cheney's response to an article by John Hawkes, "Flannery O'Connor's Devil," *Sewanee Review,* 70 [Summer, 1962], 395–407.)

Man has always claimed the rights of a free will, the while he was trying to evade the responsibilities. But the consequences have been catching up with him uncommonly of late, after a prolonged and immoderate time of free wheeling.

These rights have proliferated during their long detachment. We isolated not merely the historical categories of liberty, such as religious, moral, political, and social, but later on those better described as irreligious, immoral, pressure-political, other-directed social. Indeed, of more recent times our rights have been limited only by mental hygiene and available police protection.

But now we have come to talk about responsibilities. Talk deep. And not only about responsibilities, but the reason for responsibilities, the ontological reason. This has become a talking point and even a viewpoint. And this is the case, not only in homiletics and moral philosophy, but in the arts as well.

Humanism has been under accelerating attack since the end of the last World War. The search for religious faith has recently become a literary land run. And there have been a half dozen notable attempts among novelists to dramatize Christian conversion. In these efforts, writers have resorted to the strategies of satire, irony, symbolism, allegory, fable, and even anecdote. And, to be sure, humor, too. It has remained to Flannery O'Connor (insofar as I have been able to discover) to create a brand of humor based on the religious point of view.

In a world as secular as ours the phrase "the religious point of view" requires definition. In this country in particular, the Protestant movement has added uncertainty to such a viewpoint. To address this issue to a more specific context, there appeared in *The Sewanee Review* (Summer, 1962) an article on Flannery

O'Connor's work by John Hawkes, who apparently does not understand the religious viewpoint and, hence, the diabolism he would attribute to Miss O'Connor.

Perhaps the first element in the religious perspective to consider here is that of man's free will. In some idiom or other, as we know, all of the world religions have recognized man's deficiencies, for life both in the here and the hereafter. They have offered personal salvation at a price. The religious man must choose the costly way. This has had especial emphasis in the Judeo-Christian tradition. In the religious mythology which underlies our Western culture and civilization, the one restraint that an omnipotent God places on Himself is the freedom allowed man in the matter of following God's will. But there is no freeloading. Responsibilities represented in the Ten Commandments, the Beatitudes, and, among the orthodox, in the communion of a Christian church come along with Christ's redemption of us. It is from this orthodox view that Miss O'Connor sees the humor of man's predicament. And more.

Without recalling all of the reforms since the Reformation by which the unorthodox have watered down their Christian responsibilities, we haven't forgotten that the pabulum eventually became fare for an infant agnosticism. And this infant under modern force-feeding methods has grown into a gargantuan adolescent secularism. And the force-fed secularist has outstripped his begetters only to find that bone and flesh and blood (he is unsound and suffers strange ills) suffer consequences. From the Christian viewpoint these are the ills of the will—the free will.

It has been roughly a century since modern man, even in his churches, has thought of himself as cursed with a fallen nature. He has thought increasingly well of himself, in his new scientific independence. When the consequences of his irresponsibility began to catch up with him, he blamed first the narrow-minded in his church. Then he blamed society and machinery and practically everything in sight, except himself. The top sentimentalists blamed God. They blamed Him at first for being mean. More recently they blame Him for *not* being—in other words, for not being as they think He ought to be. In the literary world they are called Existentialists, and/or Beatniks.

The genius of Miss O'Connor's humor is that she nowhere appears the partisan of human fallibility. This is the initial requirement of the orthodox outlook: the Christian must realize that he is as liable to human weaknesses as any sinner or the unbeliever. She gives us an apt simile for this viewpoint in her story, "The River": where Mrs. Cronin stood, staring into the room, "with a skeleton's appearance of seeing everything." We have the feeling that the skeleton itself, with nowhere to hide anything, must be able to see through us with its own inner visibility. That sense of conscience, that nakedness before God, is the source of religious realism and the premise for Miss O'Connor's humor.

She has given this nakedness an even sharper irony in her story "A Temple of the Holy Ghost." Although, for the fourteen-year-old girl with whom the viewpoint lies, the thought of the circus hermaphrodite as temple for the Holy Ghost is mysterious and awful, she has no sentimental complaint against the ways of God. It is Miss O'Connor's position that irony is only a human emotion.

Apparently this quite escapes Mr. Hawkes in his *Review* piece titled "Flannery O'Connor's Devil." In a *tour de force* remarkable only for foolhardiness, in which he brackets her with Nathaniel West, Mr. Hawkes speaks of her "inverted attraction for the reality of our absurd condition."

Miss O'Connor has a genius for the grotesque, and she makes effective dramatic use of misfortunes in a God-given world. This is her *metier.* But I would challenge Mr. Hawkes to support with evidence the view he attributes to her. Nowhere in any of her work with which I am acquainted has she as author viewed our condition as being *absurd.*

From religion to politics to science to manners, sentimentality has been rife in this land for a long time. It is, to be sure, the human complaint. When scientists, after Galileo, established their Archimedean Point from which to view the physical world, it was, I suppose, inevitable that man would discover a new Reality, confusing himself again with God.

Under this error the world has grown more awful to contemplate, the longer man has looked at it—for the viewpoint was still human and human only, wherever it might be located in space or time, or however many eyes were at the knothole. Whatever he did to refine or lengthen his measuring stick, man could only measure the human limitation called distance. So erring modern man for a long time has now been trying to deny the existence of Infinity.

This is *not* the religious point of view. The religious view is not man looking at himself in the presence of time and space, however great, and certainly not this humanly-conceived time and space looking at man. It is man looking at himself in the presence of Infinity—Infinity for Whom there is no unknown nor unknowable, from Whom there are no secrets. Yet there is something very essential to be added to establish the religious view, and I add it here: an Infinity of Love and Compassion, as well as Awfulness.

Perhaps Miss O'Connor has introduced God's charity nowhere more subtly, or more dramatically, than in her disarming story "A Good Man Is Hard to Find." Recall the "secular" picture of the vulgar couple and the barbarous children and the quaint grandmother on a boring excursion that she first presents. Her satire here seems secular and that is what she intends.

The reader may not suspect what is going on until the Misfit dispatches "Bailey Boy" and the two children. Perhaps even then he will but reluctantly and tardily perceive that God has made the misfit of a secular world His agent, too; and that the grandmother is engaged in a religious ordeal, that the issue is not her mortal life, nor the lives of the invincibly ignorant members of the family, but her immortal soul.

Indeed, though she has a growing suspicion, the grandmother herself doesn't know until her moment of truth that God, Who can "write straight with crooked lines," is revealing Himself to her, is offering her the charity of salvation that a responding charity can win for her. Despite all of her ignoble efforts to save her own skin at all costs, despite her denying Him, He compassionately gives her a last chance.

Recall the dramatic paradox in which the Misfit, responsive to the grandmother's inferential denial, "Maybe He didn't raise the dead"—says, " 'I wasn't there so I can't say He didn't. . . . I wisht I had of been there,' he said, hitting the ground with his fist. 'It ain't right I wasn't there because if I had of been there I would of known. Listen lady,' he said in a high voice, 'if I had of been there I would of known and I wouldn't be like I am now.' [In modern error, but under conviction.] His voice seemed about to crack and the grandmother's head cleared for an instant. She saw the man's face twisted close to her own as if he were going to cry and she murmured [in charity], 'Why you're one of my babies. You're one of my own children!' "

Mr. Hawkes sets out to show that Miss O'Connor and the late Nathaniel West, for all their obvious differences, are joined in a "remarkably similar" diabolism. This would make a very pretty paradox if it could be supported. Mr. Hawkes's effort, it seems to me, fails in the case of both parties to his parallel.

I am not well acquainted with the work of Nathaniel West and perhaps come to it too late to read it with any deep sympathy. Mr. Hawkes says, "West's preoccupation with the 'Christ business' begins as joke in *The Dream Life of Balso Snell,* reaches a partly confused and sentimental climax in *Miss Lonelyhearts,* and in *The Day of the Locust* finally dwindles to sporadic and surface satires on the freak Hollywood church as bad answer."

I have not been able to lay hand on *The Dream Life of Balso Snell,* but my conclusion on reading *Miss Lonelyhearts* (on which he largely bases his case) is that the "Christ business" is no more than a joke in it, too. True, Miss Lonelyhearts was the son of a Baptist preacher and retains sentimentally some garbled pulpit language, but he is not committed to it, nor does he really believe in it. Even as he sees it, it is a sentimentally fraudulent incarnation, palmed off through an utterly fraudulent newspaper enterprise—and, I might add, on people in sentimentally fraudulent trouble. No religion operates in the story; there is no work for the devil to do, and the devil doesn't waste his time on anything so pointless. Mr. Hawkes' anointed devil, Shrike, for all his sacrilegiousness and profanity, does not function as a devil. As Mr. Hawkes' comment on *The Day of the Locust* might suggest, religion operates to a far less degree in that novel, which is to say not at all.

Mr. Hawkes declares his inability to recognize the devil early in his essay, when he says, "their [Miss O'Connor's and Mr. West's] employment of the devil's voice as vehicle for their . . . true (or accurate) vision of our godless actuality . . . ." Throughout, Mr. Hawkes seems to be unable or unwilling to distinguish between his own sense of values and that of Miss O'Connor, the only one of the three who believes in the devil.

The whole essay is shot through with this. I quote: "Surely if the elements of Flannery O'Connor's fiction could be referred point for point to the established principles of a known orthodoxy . . . ."! My response is that they very well can. If they were referred to this "known orthodoxy," he might conceivably see that "the characters of Flannery O'Connor are not *judged,* victimized, made to appear only as absurd entities of the flesh"—as he erroneously concludes.

In the face of Miss O'Connor's own declaration of her belief in "the devil" (Lucifer, a fallen angel), Mr. Hawkes still persists: "My own feeling is that just as the creative process threatens the Holy throughout Flannery O'Connor's fiction by generating a paradoxical fusion of improbability and passion out of the Protestant 'do-it-yourself' evangelism of the South, and thereby raises the pitch of apocalyptic experience when it finally appears; so too throughout this fiction, the creative process transforms the writer's objective Catholic knowledge of the devil into an authorial attitude in itself in some measure diabolical.

Mr. Hawkes could only make such a wrong-headed conclusion from his substantially accurate analysis (though not "the creative process" threatening "the Holy," but the human fallibility of her characters) because of his invincible ignorance (it seems) of the Christian view of things. He concludes: "This is to say that in Flannery O'Connor's most familiar stories and novels the 'disbelief . . . that we breathe in with the air of the times' [quoting her] emerges fully as two-sided or complex as 'attraction for the Holy.' " To be sure and why not? This *disbelief* is party to our central religious conflict of the day. And I might add that it constitutes a strategic circumstance of Miss O'Connor's drama and satire.

May we allow Mr. Hawkes to pinpoint further his contention about Miss O'Connor's viewpoint? He quotes two passages from *The Violent Bear It Away,* giving dialogue between young Tarwater and the devil, as illustrating "the shifting substance" of Miss O'Connor's "authorial attitude." About the first, he says: "*The Violent Bear It Away* actualizes the truth of the Devil's sentiments—Tarwater does not, in fact, 'mean a thing to a soul'. . . ." This would belie the whole action of the book, the obvious intention of the story, and amounts to blind perversity on Mr. Hawkes' part, if he does not, indeed, have tongue in cheek. For he continues in this vein, saying: "But surely in giving voice to his dry country-cadenced nihilism and in laying out the pure deflated truth of mere existence . . . the devil is speaking not only for himself but for the author." This smacks of the thumb screws and rubber hose and prepared confession of burlesque police work! And Mr. Hawkes' pietistic squeamishness over adjusting to the realism of Miss O'Connor's descriptive phrase "four strapping angels" might have come straight out of *Miss Lonelyhearts.*

I decline to believe that Mr. Hawkes is really serious in his contention about Miss O'Connor's diabolism. It is at variance with his appreciative acknowledgment: ". . . this comic writer is a serious writer—say, in her moral provocative use of paradox and her most original use of humor."

This brings us to the final element in Miss O'Connor's humor growing out of a religious viewpoint. I have referred to her *strategic circumstance* in today's issue of religious faith, and, while she has brilliantly made it hers in the context of our times, it is also timeless. As counterpart of faith, disbelief is always a circumstance of religious perspective, always an element in religious drama. However, the pervasiveness of the secular viewpoint today and the depth to which it has corrupted our sense of values, even among those of us who call ourselves orthodox Christians, constitutes so unparalleled a circumstance that it has provided for Miss O'Connor's genius a situation of humor that is, so far as I know, without precedent in our literature. Her humor bears a kinship to *Don Quixote*, but only collaterally.

The situation of humor is presented in "A Good Man Is Hard to Find." It is characteristic dramatic strategy of her short stories and it abounds in her novels too. She begins with familiar surfaces, in an action that seems secular at the outset, and in a secular tone of satire or humor. Before you know it, the naturalistic situation has become metaphysical, and the action appropriate to it comes with a surprise, an unaccountability that is humorous, grimly humorous, however shocking. It is paradox, to be sure, but it rests on a theology and a Christian perception more penetrating than most people in this world are blessed with.

Let us take, for example, her story "The Artificial Nigger." We begin here with nothing more uncommon than a rustic old man taking his rustic grandson for his first trip to the city. While their backwoodness is a bit grotesque and the old man's vanity provides touching humor, metaphysical drama doesn't overturn secular seeming until the man publicly denies his relationship to the boy to escape retribution and to give the humor a new dimension. Those familiar with her fiction may already have suspected a Tiger Christ in the "nigger" image, but who expected her brilliant *tour de force* with its compassionate irony in her "artificial nigger" as crucifix?

Mr. Hawkes concludes: ". . . if Bishop, the little idiot child, is intended to establish an innocence that points toward the apocalyptic, old Singleton, an insane comic figure in 'The Partridge Festival,' is intended to be exactly the opposite—crazy and lecherous and pointing toward the demonic."

But all of this is in accord with the religious view of the world's dichotomy. It is the genius of Miss O'Connor's Christian realism that her characters who are touched with Holiness reveal their human frailties and foibles too. The old prophet Mason Tarwater was a moonshiner and given to drunkenness at times.

Tactically this has an obvious satiric aim. But there is in it a deeper justification than dramatic tactics to get her prophets and saints by the censor; that is, make them credible to a secular world. The Christian knows that to life's very end the forces of God and of the devil carry on an unremitting and uncertain struggle for the possession of man's soul. What Miss O'Connor's humor so upsets is the smug, comfortable self-satisfaction, and/or, equally, the sentimental self-pity of the get of our secular day, who, in their invincible ignorance, have no notion of man's corruption—and even less of God's mercy!—a mercy that Miss O'Connor, consistent with her religion, reflects in her own compassion for her villains along with her heroes.

In *The Violent Bear It Away,* Mason Tarwater left a note for Rayber on Francis Marion's crib when he "delivered" him from it: "The prophet I raise up out of this boy will burn your eyes clean." The Rev. Robert M. McCowan in the *Kansas Magazine* perceives in the author's final words about Rayber, who is the object of her sharpest satire, this meaning:

"In her treatment of Rayber Miss O'Connor shows both a strength and a compassion which are rarely found together in the same artist. As he hears the cry of his child and he realizes that the prophecy of old Tarwater at last has its fulfillment, he stares with horror for the first time into the empty depths of his own soul. From this scene on we hear no more of him, but the logic of events easily suggests the sequel. With Rayber's life emptied of its one unifying force, and this at the hands of the boy whose confusion he had goaded into action, we are left to imagine for ourselves the remorse and hatred of self which, his eyes now 'burned clean,' will be the first step of a complete spiritual conversion, or, this grace rejected, the last step of his hell on earth."

If we wish to go beyond the covers of this book for evidence to support Father McCowan's surmise that Rayber's eyes may have been *burned clean* to his conversion, we may recall a similar extreme unction that came to Haze Moates [*sic*] in *Wise Blood.*

Romano Guardini has described the Beatitudes as ". . . no mere formulas of superior ethics, but tidings of sacred and supreme reality's entry into the world." I do not bring in Guardini for rhetorical effect; his words have actual relevance for us. But we should realize here that this entrance is always a revolution. Miss O'Connor's art is committed to religious revolution against a secular world. Perhaps one can only grasp the overtones of her humor finally by holding firmly to an unsentimentalized appreciation of the Sermon on the Mount.

Appendix E

Brainard Cheney, "Flannery O'Connor's Campaign for Her Country," *Sewanee Review,* 72 (Autumn, 1964), 555–58.

The shock of Flannery O'Connor's death came not in its unexpectedness but in the startling realization that her work is done. It was known that, suffering an unusual and incurable malady, she lived precariously throughout most of her writing career. Her last years were subject to increasing infirmity. Yet the news of her death left me, at least, almost nonplussed.

There must be recognition that the two novels, less than twenty short stories, and fewer essays are the work complete of the fiction writer, in my opinion, most significant in our time. But is her work done, indeed? Twelve years span the appearance of her first novel, *Wise Blood,* and her last story, "Revelation," published in this magazine, in the spring issue of this year. There is, I am told, a volume of her short stories in the hands of her publisher, and at least two of them have not been previously published. They will be important undoubtedly, for none of her stories is slight. And they will add to her work. Yet, perhaps, even here and now we may echo the question *complete?* and make a tentative assessment.

Flannery O'Connor staked out her true country and denoted her vocation in 1957, in an essay entitled "The Fiction Writer and His Country." The word, she said, "suggests everything from the actual countryside that the novelist describes, on, to, and through the peculiar characteristics of his region and his nation, and on, through, and under all of these to his true country, which the writer with Christian convictions will consider to be what is eternal and absolute." She added, "It is the peculiar burden of the fiction writer that he has to make one country do for all and that he has to evoke that one country through the concrete particulars of a life that he can make believable."

Vocation she saw as a limiting factor "which extends even to the kind of material that the writer is able to apprehend imaginatively," and, with the Christian writer, is felt to come from God: "and no matter how minor a gift it is, he will not be willing to destroy it by trying to use it outside its proper limits."

She began with the Woe, *Woe to you who are filled, for you shall hunger,* as theme, given embodiment in her novel *Wise Blood,* in

1952. It was satire; it was bitter parody on the atheistic Existentialism then pervading the literary and philosophical scene. But it was more. Haze Motes, with his self-mutilated sightless eyes and other penitential mortifications, and his landlady and fascinated pursuer, at the *denouement,* foretold a hunger now apparent.

Her first novel found a few vocal appreciators, but for the most part it met with incomprehension and open hostility. Her short story collection, *A Good Man is Hard to Find,* appearing three years later—though the stories offered more variety in material and treatment—was scarcely more sympathetically reviewed. This went for some of the literary periodicals of her own church. Catholic reviewers as well as others cried out against her unorthodox treatment of her characters and her "brutal laughter." But after they got over their initial shock and dismay, many of her readers began wrily to give voice to their more deliberate apprehension and perceptions.

Miss O'Connor, in the essay from which I have already quoted, set forth specifically what she was about and why. "The novelist with Christian concerns will find in modern life distortions which are repugnant to him," she said, "and his problem will be to make these appear as distortions to an audience which is used to seeing them as natural; and he may be forced to take ever more violent means to get his vision across to this hostile audience." With such a public "you have to make your vision apparent by shock—to the hard of hearing you shout, and for the almost blind you draw large and startling figures."

This explanation may in time have come to the aid of some of her critics. At all events, with many of "the hard of hearing" and "the almost blind" her enlargement got her point across. For, in addition to being a brilliant satirist, she was a true humorist and possessed an unusual gift for the grotesque. But she resorted to something far more remarkable to reflect her Christian vision to a secular world. She invented a new form of humor. At least I have encountered it nowhere else in literature. This invention consists in her introducing her story with familiar surfaces in an action that seems secular, and in a secular tone of satire or humor. Before you know it, the naturalistic situation has become metaphysical and the action appropriate to it comes with a surprise, an unaccountability that is humorous, however, shocking. The *means* is *violent,* but the end is Christian. And obviously, it works.

It occurs to me here that she accomplished what she set out to do to an astonishing degree. She got attention. She got reaction. And I believe that she got across her Christian vision to a significant public. This last is evident in the sympathetic critical emphasis her work now receives in the Catholic and in much of the Protestant press. As a measure of hostile attention and reaction, I would cite her front-rank appearance in "the structure of the American Literary Establishment," as this putative *entente* was presented in *Esquire* magazine, in July, 1963. Her prominence in this company is the more notable, since the prevailing vision of the Establishment is secular and atheistic.

But, *complete?*

Miss O'Connor said in her revealing essay that the writer's country "is inside as well as outside him" and that "to know oneself, is above all, to know what one lacks." Is this not a clue?

I have said that her theme changed but little, yet I think there was a progress. Without trying to step it off we may note that, in her short masterpiece, "The Displaced Person," its successive protagonists, Mrs. Shortley and Mrs. McIntyre, come to a tragic realization of the secular delusion; and, in her second novel, *The Violent Bear it Away,* little Bishop, as he is being drowned, is baptized. In her last story yet published, "Revelation," the world is no less secular, nor is the Christian revelation any less devastating to one corrupted by the world. Yet her heroine, Mrs. Turpin, finds the need and the humility (quoting again the essay) to measure herself "against Truth."

Do we not have here the *blessed* corollary of the Woe with which we began?

It is much too early to attempt any ultimate assessment of Flannery O'Connor's work. There is as yet but limited understanding of this original, powerful, and prophetic writer. But the prophet is not expected to wait on the fulfilment of his prophecy. In her own words, "The creative action of the Christian's life is to prepare his death in Christ." And this, I feel sure, she did.

Index